Georgia

A Bicentennial History

Harold H. Martin

W. W. Norton & Company, Inc.
New York

American Association for State and Local History
Nashville

To my wife, Boyce,

and my daughter, Nancy,

and a new generation of Georgians

Copyright © 1977
American Association for State and Local History
Nashville, Tennessee

Published and distributed by
W. W. Norton & Company, Inc.
500 Fifth Avenue
New York, New York 10036

Library of Congress Cataloguing-in-Publication Data

Martin, Harold H
  Georgia: a bicentennial history.

  (The States and the Nation series)
  Bibliography: p.
  Includes index.
  1. Georgia—History. I. Title. II. Series.
  F286.M42   975.8   77–5736
  ISBN 0–393–05606–6

Printed in the United States of America
1 2 3 4 5 6 7 8 9 0

Contents

Invitation to the Reader   vii

Acknowledgments   x

Preface   xi

1 The First Georgians   3

2 From Royal Rule to Revolution   33

3 War by Bayonet, Noose, and Knife   49

4 From Revolution to Rebellion   59

5 Georgia at War   94

6 Reconstruction—and Its Aftermath   112

7 Grady's Dream, Watson's Vision   133

8 Prelude to the Present   156

9 And Finally, It Was Monday   184

Suggestions for Further Reading   204

Index   208

Illustrations

A Photographer's Essay by Bruce Roberts   116

Original Maps by Harold Faye

    Georgia, Contemporary Map Keyed to Text   Facing Page vii

    Georgia: Transportation Routes 1840–1860   Facing Page 82

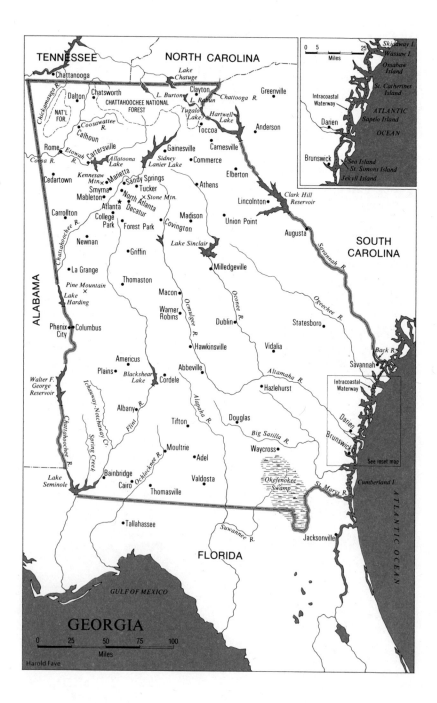

TENNESSEE

NORTH CAROLINA

Chattanooga

Lake
Chatuge

Clayton

Greenville

Dalton
Chatsworth
CHATTAHOOCHEE NATIONAL
FOREST

L. Burton
L. Rabun
Chattooga R.

NAT'L
FOR.

*Coosawattee
R.*

Tugalo
Lake

Hartwell
Lake

Anderson

Calhoun

Toccoa

Rome
Etowah Cartersville
R.

Gainesville

Carnesville

Coosa R.

Allatoona
Lake

Sidney
Lanier Lake

Commerce

Elberton

Cedartown

Kennesaw
Mtn.×

Marietta

Sandy Springs

Athens

Lincolnton

Clark Hill
Reservoir

Smyrna
Mableton

Tucker
North Atlanta
×Stone Mtn.

ALABAMA

Carrollton

Atlanta
Decatur

College
Park

Forest Park

Madison
Covington

Union Point

Augusta

Savannah R.

SOUTH
CAROLINA

Newnan

Lake Sinclair

Milledgeville

Griffin

La Grange

Thomaston

Pine Mountain
×
Lake
Harding

Macon

Warner
Robins

Oconee R.

Ocmulgee R.

Dublin

Ogeechee R.

Statesboro

Phenix
City

Columbus

Hawkinsville

Vidalia

Back R.

Savannah

Americus

Chattahoochee R.

Plains

Blackshear
Lake

Cordele

Abbeville

Altamaha R.

Intracoastal
Waterway

Walter F.
George
Reservoir

Tchawny-Nochaway Cr.

Spring Creek

Albany
Flint R.

Tifton

Alapaha R.

Douglas

Hazlehurst

Big Satilla R.

Darien

Brunswick

Chattahoochee R.

Moultrie

Adel

Waycross

See inset map

Lake
Seminole

Bainbridge
Cairo

Ochlockonee R.

Thomasville

Valdosta

Okefenokee
Swamp

St. Marys R.

Cumberland I.

ATLANTIC
OCEAN

Tallahassee

Suwannee R.

Jacksonville

FLORIDA

GULF OF MEXICO

GEORGIA

0   25   50   75   100
Miles

Harold Faye

Inset map

0   5   25
Miles

Skidaway I.
Wassaw I.
Ossabaw
Island

Intracoastal
Waterway

St. Catherines
Island

ATLANTIC

Darien

Sapelo Island

OCEAN

Brunswick

Sea Island
St. Simons Island
Jekyll Island

Invitation to the Reader

IN 1807, former President John Adams argued that a complete history of the American Revolution could not be written until the history of change in each state was known, because the principles of the Revolution were as various as the states that went through it. Two hundred years after the Declaration of Independence, the American nation has spread over a continent and beyond. The states have grown in number from thirteen to fifty. And democratic principles have been interpreted differently in every one of them.

We therefore invite you to consider that the history of your state may have more to do with the bicentennial review of the American Revolution than does the story of Bunker Hill or Valley Forge. The Revolution has continued as Americans extended liberty and democracy over a vast territory. John Adams was right: the states are part of that story, and the story is incomplete without an account of their diversity.

The Declaration of Independence stressed life, liberty, and the pursuit of happiness; accordingly, it shattered the notion of holding new territories in the subordinate status of colonies. The Northwest Ordinance of 1787 set forth a procedure for new states to enter the Union on an equal footing with the old. The Federal Constitution shortly confirmed this novel means of building a nation out of equal states. The step-by-step process through which territories have achieved self-government and national representation is among the most important of the Founding Fathers' legacies.

The method of state-making reconciled the ancient conflict between liberty and empire, resulting in what Thomas Jefferson called an empire for liberty. The system has worked and remains unaltered, despite enormous changes that have taken place in the nation. The country's extent and variety now surpass anything the patriots of '76 could likely have imagined. The United States has changed from an agrarian republic into a highly industrial and urban democracy, from a fledgling nation into a major world power. As Oliver Wendell Holmes remarked in 1920, the creators of the nation could not have seen completely how it and its constitution and its states would develop. Any meaningful review in the bicentennial era must consider what the country has become, as well as what it was.

The new nation of equal states took as its motto *E Pluribus Unum*—"out of many, one." But just as many peoples have become Americans without complete loss of ethnic and cultural identities, so have the states retained differences of character. Some have been superficial, expressed in stereotyped images— big, boastful Texas, "sophisticated" New York, "hillbilly" Arkansas. Other differences have been more real, sometimes instructively, sometimes amusingly; democracy has embraced Huey Long's Louisiana, bilingual New Mexico, unicameral Nebraska, and a Texas that once taxed fortunetellers and spawned politicians called "Woodpecker Republicans" and "Skunk Democrats." Some differences have been profound, as when South Carolina secessionists led other states out of the Union in opposition to abolitionists in Massachusetts and Ohio. The result was a bitter Civil War.

The Revolution's first shots may have sounded in Lexington and Concord; but fights over what democracy should mean and who should have independence have erupted from Pennsylvania's Gettysburg to the "Bleeding Kansas" of John Brown, from the Alamo in Texas to the Indian battles at Montana's Little Bighorn. Utah Mormons have known the strain of isolation; Hawaiians at Pearl Harbor, the terror of attack; Georgians during Sherman's march, the sadness of defeat and devastation. Each state's experience differs instructively; each adds understanding to the whole.

The purpose of this series of books is to make that kind of understanding accessible, in a way that will last in value far beyond the bicentennial fireworks. The series offers a volume on every state, plus the District of Columbia—fifty-one, in all. Each book contains, besides the text, a view of the state through eyes other than the author's—a "photographer's essay," in

which a skilled photographer presents his own personal percep-
tions of the state's contemporary flavor.

We have asked authors not for comprehensive chronicles, nor
for research monographs or new data for scholars. Bibliogra-
phies and footnotes are minimal. We have asked each author for
a summing up—interpretive, sensitive, thoughtful, individual,
even personal—of what seems significant about his or her
state's history. What distinguishes it? What has mattered about
it, to its own people and to the rest of the nation? What has it
come to now?

To interpret the states in all their variety, we have sought a
variety of backgrounds in authors themselves and have encouraged variety in the approaches they take. They have in
common only these things: historical knowledge, writing skill,
and strong personal feelings about a particular state. Each has
wide latitude for the use of the short space. And if each suc-
ceeds, it will be by offering you, in your capacity as a *citizen* of
a state *and* of a nation, stimulating insights to test against your
own.

James Morton Smith
General Editor

ACKNOWLEDGMENTS

For forty years as a working journalist, I was concerned with recording and trying to interpret the events of the passing moment, with telling the story of the breaking news and the men who made it. To move into the broader and deeper field of historical research required a shifting of mental gears, a change of interest from the ephemeral to the enduring, a search for larger meanings and for patterns shaped by time.

In beginning my research into the story of Georgia's past, I turned for guidance first to those never-failing sources of help and friendly counsel, the archivists and librarians at Emory University's Woodruff Library, at the University of Georgia at Athens, at the Georgia Department of Archives and History and the Historical Society in Atlanta, and the Georgia Historical Society in Savannah. The individual names are too many to be listed here, but they know my gratitude.

They came up with a list of books, by scholars both living and dead who had devoted their lives to studying and evaluating the men and events which over nearly 250 years have shaped this once wild land into the Georgia of today. In the Suggestions for Further Reading at the end of this volume, the reader will find acknowledgment of many, though not all, of the works I drew upon in the making of this book. The list makes evident my gratitude to individual authors, past and present, whose writings have been so valuable to me.

Finally, too, I would like to say my heartfelt thanks to the three men responsible for my taking on this unfamiliar task—to Dr. Bell Wiley, famed chronicler of the common soldier of the Civil War, for his encouragement; to Franklin Garrett, Atlanta's official historian; and to my editor, Jerry George, who with a Job-like patience has counseled and advised, in an effort to save me from error as I strove to weave into a meaningful tapestry all the varied threads and colors that make up the history of this always fascinating state.

Atlanta, Georgia   HAROLD H. MARTIN
June 1976

Preface

Ages of Earth Are in Us . . . .

$\mathcal{W}$E Georgians are a new people as races of men are measured in time, but the land we call our home is an old land.

Much has happened here in eons past; massive mountain ranges were upthrust and worn down again before the Rockies and the Andes were ever born; the inflow of mighty oceans and their slow subsiding gave us the patterns and the contours of the land as we know it today.

It is a land of great beauty and variety in its geographic profile, its climate and its vegetation. Moving inland from the Sea Islands and the tidal salt marshes, there is a gentle lifting to the flat bed of the ancient ocean that once covered all the southern half of the state. It was a shallow sea, and the vast coastal plain that it left behind slopes gently down a half-dozen broad, flat terraces, dropping only five hundred feet in a journey of one hundred fifty miles.

The soil that lay beneath this old ocean was clay and sand, marked in its richest places with little pellets of minerals left behind by the retreating waters. It is good land for the growing of peanuts, peaches, cotton, and tobacco. But its submarine origins are not concealed. Even today in the earth of Middle Georgia the plow may turn up a sharp, black-shining triangle, the petrified tooth of the shark that swam there a million years ago.

The shorelines of that old ocean can be plainly traced today in central Georgia where its highest tides beat against the land. It is called the "fall line," for here the great rivers tumbled rapidly to a lower level as the seas withdrew, and it runs across the state from Columbus, by way of Macon to Milledgeville and Augusta, in a procession of low upthrusts called the Fall Line Hills.

North of the fall line the climate cools, the vegetation changes from the wire grass and the saw grass and the cypress and the slim longleaf pine of the coastal plain, to the stately white and yellow pine, the gum and poplar and the Bermuda grass and Johnson grass of the Piedmont. Here the animals are different, too. The alligator and the muskrat of the watery flat lands give way to the fox and 'possum, though in both areas the wildcat is ubiquitous and so is the rabbit and the raccoon. Here the granite ribs of an ancient mountain range show through the flanks of the earth in the great quarries at Elberton and the massive bulk of Stone Mountain near Atlanta.

Further on into the mountains, cold springs rise at the foot of beech and oak and hickory, forming the headwaters of the big rivers that flow through Georgia to the sea—the Chattahoochee, the Ocmulgee, and the Savannah. Here, in the high hills, the rocky soil is rich in minerals, and deep quarries offer marble pink as peach blossoms, white as bone. The fox still walks here on moonlight nights, and the bear snuffles at the tent flap of the hiker on the Appalachian Trail. Now and then in the dark can be heard the wail of a panther, like a baby crying, and bobcats stalk the beavers which fell the trees along the shores of the man-made lakes and build their dams and lodges across the little streams that feed them.

From the sea to the mountains the birds are here—the mockingbird, the cardinal, the blue jay, the towhee, the brown thrasher, which is the "official" state bird. All are here today, as they were long, long ago, when our story begins. . . .

Georgia

1

The First Georgians

$\mathcal{N}$OBODY knows what peoples first made Georgia their home, who they were nor where they came from. The Cherokees of the Georgia mountains had a tribal memory of a "moon-eyed" people, white of skin, whom their ancestors found here and vanquished when first they came to the Georgia hills. Whoever these people might have been—far-wandering Northmen or Welshmen, or an Albino tribe of prehistoric Indians—they left no trace. In other places, though, there are tantalizing clues to the existence of prehistoric peoples. In Putnam County, near the town of Madison, there is a huge effigy of an eagle, made of stones of many sizes and shapes, rising twice as high as a tall man's head above the level of the ground. At Fort Mountain near Chatsworth in north Georgia, there is a stone defense work two feet high and twelve feet thick at the base, extending for fifteen hundred feet around the mountain's crest. More noticeable even than these stone relics, and equally as challenging, are the earth mounds erected by the prodigious toil of some ancient folk whose names are lost to history. From Nacoochee Valley in the north, to the lower reaches of the Altamaha, these curious half-buried structures are found. They lie along the banks of the Savannah and the Etowah, and the headwaters of the Chattahoochee. The mounds in the old Ocmulgee Fields near Macon, the mounds at Cartersville and at Kolomoki in Early County, are among the more valuable archeological sites in the nation. These sites—were they council house or burial vault or temple

3

of worship or all these combined?—had been long abandoned when Hernando de Soto passed this way in 1540, and great trees were growing from them when Oglethorpe founded Savannah in 1733. The Indians of Georgia by that time had no memory of their builders and no knowledge of the meaning of the effigies found in them.

There were two great tribes in Georgia when the white man first came—the Cherokees and the Creeks. Both were strong and healthy, for food was abundant and varied, and the climate was conducive to the growth of people, game, and crops. The Cherokees were the more numerous and the more civilized. Latecomers, they had moved into the Georgia mountains from the old colonies to the north, trying to escape the white frontiersmen. The Creeks were the fiercer fighting men and were more widely scattered, Creek villages being found westward to the land of the Chickasaws, Choctaws, and Natchez in what is now Alabama, Mississippi, and Tennessee.

Though early explorers, being scientists and ethnologists, saw the Indian as Rousseau's "noble savage," it is the frontiersman's concept of the Indian as a brute, a varmint to be exterminated, that has left its imprint on the white man's mind. Actually, according to the historian Oliver Lafarge the red man was both noble and savage. Physically, his skin was not much redder than a sunburned Englishman, his body odor, despite the bear grease, was less redolent, and his daily life was little different from that of the poor European of the 1600s. Both were illiterate, both worked with hand tools, cooked over open fires, lived in cold and drafty shelters, ate simple food, and slept on a hard bed. Their attitudes toward life, though, were vastly different. The Indian was not concerned with profit and loss; he did no more work in the fields than was necessary to sustain life. He might live like a peasant, but he carried himself like an aristocrat. Except when he was drunk, when he became as fierce as a bear, his manners were gentle, and as an orator he made the white phrasemakers who came after him sound like a mumbling lot indeed. He was religious, believing in a Supreme Being, and he also held to one of the concepts which later became basic to our democracy—the idea of government by the consent of the governed. His tribal chiefs were kings by the will of the people, not by the grace of God, and his war chiefs were subject to the wisdom of the old men in council.

There was another side to him, too—the ruthless savage the frontiersmen knew, who loved war and fought, not in open combat as did the Europeans, but in sneaking raids in which he killed and scalped a woman or a child as gladly as he killed another warrior. It was, in fact, a greater honor to have taken these scalps, for they meant that he had gone into the very center of the enemy camp. War was his "beloved occupation," and when he was not at war, he felt that his life was wasted. Skills learned in combat with other tribes served him well when he confronted the first white men who came to Georgia. Hernando de Soto was obsessed with the search for gold when he crossed Georgia, but he was said also to be "much given to the sport of killing Indians" [1] and the tough, high-handed soldiery he brought through Georgia with him in 1539–1540 were of the same brutal strain. The result was to affect the white man's relationship with the Indian forever—for as the historian Stevens put it, "from every drop of Indian blood thus spilt, there sprang up armed warriors," [2] who for years thereafter visited the early English settlers with the torch, the tomahawk, and the scalping knife.

As an example of human endurance, de Soto's two-year journey is one of the great exploits in history. As an achievement of any good or lasting thing, it was a failure. For all the prayers said and crosses left behind, it converted no Indians; it acquired no new lands for the king of Spain, no new markets for Spain's merchants. And consummate failure of all, it found no gold. De Soto left behind no physical trace of his passing. He left instead a legacy of hatred and distrust between aborigine and European that was to endure forever.

The capacity of the Spaniards to commit cruelties in the name of religion was not confined to their harsh treatment of the pagan Indians. They could be equally brutal in their treatment of

1. The Hidalgo of Elvas, *True Relation of the Hardships Suffered by Hernando de Soto,* . . . translated by James Alexander Robertson, 2 vols. (DeLand, Fla.: Florida State Historical Society, 1933), 2:5–313.

2. William Bacon Stevens, *A History of Georgia* (1847; reprinted Savannah: The Beehive Press, 1972), pp. 8–26.

Christian Europeans who questioned their sovereignty in the New World. In 1562, twenty years after de Soto had gone to his grave in the Mississippi, a French expedition, led by Jean Ribault, sailed northward along the Georgia coast, giving French names to the coastal rivers and making a little settlement called Port Royal, now in South Carolina, near Beaufort. It did not last, and within a few months its starving garrison sailed for home. Two years later a French expedition, composed in the main of Huguenots under Rene de Laudonniere, landed on the east side of the St. Johns River, at a place near what is now Jacksonville, and here built a fort they called Fort Caroline. To be challenged by the hated Huguenots, who were looked upon as heretics and traitors to be killed on sight, was more than Philip of Spain could bear. He sent out a captain, Pedro Menendez de Aviles, to drive the French from their precarious toe-hold at Fort Caroline. Landing in 1565, Menendez established first a permanent base to the south, which he called St. Augustine. He paused there long enough to erect a log palisade, and then marched north to exterminate the Frenchmen on the St. Johns. This he did with zest, putting to the sword those who opposed him, hanging those who did not, and burning the town and fort. His task was made easier by the fact that the place was weakly defended. Not knowing that Menendez was marching overland, Jean Ribault had loaded most of the Fort Caroline garrison aboard ship and moved south to attack St. Augustine from the sea. A storm wrecked Ribault's ships in shoal water, and the Spaniards, pretending to rescue the crews, took them ashore in small groups. Once out of sight of those still aboard, the Spaniards asked the fatal question: Were they Catholic or heretic? Those who professed themselves Protestants were hacked to pieces. A few recanted, declaring themselves Papists, and were spared.

Though French corsairs would continue to harry the Spanish shipping along the Georgia coast, there was no further strong effort by France to gain a foothold on the southeast coast of the new world. Nor were the English a greatly active threat in the Georgia area, except for the forays of a few pirates. The Spaniards were left in relative peace, to press on with their work of bringing Christ to the Indians. On St. Catherines and Cum-

berland, St. Simons and Sapelo, on all the islands under the rule
of an Indian "mico" named Guale—who was to give his name
to these golden islands forever—they established their presidios
and missions, their palisaded forts and little churches where the
sword stood guard over the cross. Nor did they confine their
missions to the coast. Before 1700, they had carried cross and
sword far inland, to northwest Florida and southwest Georgia.

It was not an easy nor a rewarding task for the patient, stubborn friars. The Indians believed in a great spirit, just as the
white man did; they believed in a life after death, just as the
white man believed in the immortality of the soul. These ab-
stract ideas were not difficult for them to accept, and the ritual
of the church at first intrigued and delighted them. But they
soon grew bored by the ritual—or frightened and perplexed by
the discrepancy between the gentle religion the friars preached,
and the harsh cruelties which the soldiers and the administrators
performed.

The first Spanish outposts in Georgia existed briefly under the
stern and intellectual Jesuits who founded missions, then under
the more patient and compassionate Franciscans, who built
churches. It was a troubled time. Years of peace would be followed by long periods of bloody war that reduced the island
posts to rubble as the Indians from the mainland brought the
coastal missions under attack. Always, though, the patient
Spanish churchmen would rebuild and go on, so that in 1606,
the year before Jamestown was founded, the bishop of Cuba
came to Guale and confirmed a thousand Indians.

For nearly half a century after de Soto's march, the English
did little to contest the Spanish claims to all the southeastern
United States, being content to turn her sea dogs loose on the
Spanish gold ships beating home from Mexico and Peru. Then,
in 1585, Sir Walter Raleigh set up his ill-fated colony on Roa-
noke Island, which left as its only trace rusty armor and the Indian word "Croatan" carved in a tree. Jamestown, the first permanent English colony, was founded in 1607, but it was more
than a half-century later before the English pushed further
south, to Charleston. And now the Spaniards in Georgia would
come under the pressure of attack by raiding bands of Indians
put on the warpath not by Frenchmen, but by British traders out

of Charleston.

Seeking at last to establish a permanent presence below Carolina, the English built a fort called Fort King George on the coast near the mouth of the Altamaha—the first English settlement on what was to become Georgia soil. Its existence was brief and undistinguished. Manned by His Majesty's Independent Company, from Charleston, the garrison was often mutinous, and was soon called home when rumors of Spanish attack made the Charlestonians nervous. Though the Carolinians' first effort to establish an outpost against the Spanish was a failure, their attempts to harass the Spaniards met with greater success. English pirates from the sea and English traders from South Carolina, hieing on the Indians, raided the Spaniards without mercy, and in 1702 the last Spanish mission, on St. Simons Island, was closed.

Thus ended the presence of the Spanish missionaries in the Golden Isles. But for another hundred years the bloody struggle would continue with Georgia a no-man's-land where Spaniards and Englishmen and their changing Indian allies (the English, like the Spanish, liked to have the Indians do their fighting for them) battled repeatedly in small but savage conflicts. While sweating soldiers in heavy armor groped for each other through the swamps and pine barrens, back home in England great schemes were afoot. It was a period when men's minds were inclined to accept fabulous promotions based on exploration, and the proposition advanced by a Scottish laird named Sir Robert Montgomery was among the most fabulous of them all. His plan was to persuade the Lords Proprietors of Carolina to sell him all the land lying between the Savannah River and the Altamaha, for a penny an acre for all lands occupied, plus one-fourth of whatever gold and silver might be found.

Sir Robert's scheme came to nothing, and the name of his proposed margravate of Azilia is lost to history now except on time-stained and faded maps. But there are students of the period who feel that from Sir Robert's plans for his feudal dreamland James Edward Oglethorpe derived at least some of his ideas for Savannah. The ordered development, the provision for mutual defense, the opportunity for sociability, were much alike in both Oglethorpe's and Montgomery's plans. Their ideas as to what the land should produce differed but little. Oglethorpe pushed for silk and wine; Montgomery promised silk and potash.

The failure of Montgomery's margravate to materialize in the form of forts and armed men protecting a colony of artisans and tradesmen, herdsmen and farmers, and the withdrawal of a grumbling and mutinous garrison from Fort King George, left Carolinians naked to their enemies as they had always been. The border war smouldered on, with clashes between English traders, doggedly pushing south, and the Spanish soldiery and their Indian allies stubbornly resisting the advance, making the Southern frontier a place of never-ending danger. Not only the Spaniards, but the Indians were an ever-present threat. In 1715, the supposedly friendly Yamassees had risen against the Carolinians in a bloody massacre that took the lives of many white settlers before the Indians were driven south to protection under the Spanish guns at St. Augustine. This terrible conflict had arisen out of the Yamassee resistance to white traders who cheated them, white planters who encroached on their lands, and Carolina's plans to take a census, which they did not understand. To avoid a similar tragedy, in 1730 Sir Alexander Cumming, His Majesty's Indian Commissioner, worked out a treaty with the Cherokees, giving the English traders protection in Cherokee country. In return, Sir Alexander took the Cherokee chiefs to London to meet the king. There, as a pledge of their fealty, they presented His startled Majesty with a new crown made up of five eagle tails and four scalps.

For years South Carolina had petitioned the king for a chain of forts and settlements to the south that would provide them some protection. Thus it was that, with the Yamassee moved south, and the Cherokee Treaty giving promise of a peaceful crossing of the Savannah, George II in 1732 granted a charter creating the Separate Colony of Georgia. The bubble of Azilia had burst, but something more solid and enduring had been created.

And now, in the jails and mews and stews of London, men and women beaten down by misfortune and the savage depression gripping England began to hear a whisper of hope. In all the cities of Europe, too, where Protestant minorities lived under religious oppression, the same comforting word was heard. For Moravian and Salzburger and Huguenot, as well as for the bankrupt and debt-ridden Englishman, there was truly a new world coming to birth—a Land of Beginning Again. And the name of James Edward Oglethorpe was soon to be written upon the pages of history.

Oglethorpe was a gentleman, but not a *gentle* man, for there was no softness in him. He was a soldier and the son of a soldier. Educated at Eton and Oxford, which he left early to become an ensign in His Majesty's Life Guards, he worked his way up to lieutenant. At twenty-three, carrying his father's sword, he left England to serve as Aide to Prince Eugene of Savoy, and he saw hard fighting against the Turks. In his mid-twenties he came back home, and at twenty-six was elected to Parliament. It was in this time that he visited a friend in debtors' prison, a young architect and city planner named Robert Castell, who soon was to die in jail of smallpox. This experience so stirred Oglethorpe that he persuaded Parliament to make a thorough survey of English prisons, an investigation which he led. What he saw aroused in him a sense of horror and repugnance. Deep feelings of charity and humanity welled up in him, and in the summer of 1730 he and Viscount Percival, earl of Egmont, and nineteen other gentlemen of England, sent a petition to George II. They asked of him a charter for a province to be called Georgia, lying to the southwest of South Carolina, where selected men and women of England who were of good character but who had fallen on evil times finally could be given a chance to start their lives anew. George II was not one to make snap judgments, and it was two years before he granted the charter. Nor were his motives, and those of his chancellor, Sir Robert Walpole, entirely eleemosynary. The trustees' grant would run for twenty-one years. During that time they would raise the money for the founding of the new colony, run it subject to the king's approval, and then at the end of that time it would revert to the crown as a royal colony. Thus the boundaries of South Carolina would be protected at no expense to the crown, new land would come under imperial control, the cause of mercantilism would be served by the creation of new markets for British goods, and London itself would become a cleaner, safer place by the transfer of a scruffy assortment of indigents to the new frontier.

However crass the king's motives might have been, the trustees' goals were purely philanthropic. They would own no Georgia land nor would they profit, other than indirectly, by any trade in silk or wine or spices that might develop. They were lords and commoners, country gentlemen and clergymen, businessmen and politicians. But all were altruists, stirred by an almost religious zeal for their huge philanthropic and humanitarian project. Many, like Lord Percival, had been friends and followers of the late Dr. Thomas Bray, an eminent clergyman and humanitarian who had founded the Society for the Propagation of the Gospel in Foreign Parts. There were some among them, too, who understood the art of press agentry, for handbills flooded London singing the praises of the Georgia-to-be as once the broadside writers had praised Montgomery's margravate. From pulpits and from the halls of Parliament there sounded the praises of the new land.

The public response was amazing. Oglethorpe came up with fifteen thousand pounds from "a Charity." Parliament added ten thousand pounds more. Individuals gave money and goods (Lord Joseph Jekyl, for whom the island was named, and his lady, gave six hundred pounds). Merchants with special interest in one comestible or another gave rare roots and seeds and vines. Military men gave weapons and drums; various churchmen gave a boatload of Bibles and books of admonition against drink and other sins of the flesh.

For more than two hundred years, Georgians have amiably endured the friendly insults of aristocratic South Carolinians and Virginians, who have been fond of pointing out that Georgia's founders were deadbeats and jailbirds. Actually, as the records amply show, they went through a process of selection far more rigorous than anything the emigrants to the older colonies were called upon to endure. Those wanted in Georgia were what Oglethorpe once described as "gentlemen of decayed circumstances," men of good family, and some education, who had fallen on evil days; "some undone by guardians, some by lawsuits, some by accidents in commerce, some by stocks and bubbles, and some by suretyships.[3] Every applicant was thoroughly checked, preference being given to a person who had a letter from his pastor testifying to his being of sound mind and morals. Any person in debt also had to have a letter from his creditors giving him permission to take ship. No one was accepted solely because he had been in prison for debt. Actually, of the 5,000 persons who had come to Georgia by 1750, only 2,000 came on public charity, and of these only 646 were British males who might possibly have been imprisoned by their creditors. The percentage of Georgians who were originally debtors was obviously very small.

Though the point was not openly stressed, a stout allegiance to the crown was also prerequisite to selection. Already, forty years before the Revolution, some of the old colonies in the north were showing signs of becoming headstrong, and the king's counselors saw in the new colony not only a buffer against Spaniards and Indians, but a buffer against new and disturbing ideas. Those who were sent over would be given their passage and fifty acres of land, tools and seeds, food and clothing for the first year. They also would enjoy all the privileges, liberties, and immunities of Englishmen. But they were not expected to reach out for greater liberties and privileges.

By the end of October 1732 the first shipload had been chosen. At the dock at Gravesend lay the galley *Anne,* a stout little ship of 200 tons. Aboard her were thirty-five families, made up of about 125 sober, moral, and industrious people, but counted at 91 "head" for passage purposes, for babies under two were not counted and older children were charged one half or one third the full fare—four pounds. The accommodations were not luxurious. The passengers slept in wooden cradles with boarded bottoms, and there were no separate accommodations for the babies, who were supposed to sleep "in any cracks available."[4]

3. James Edward Oglethorpe, *A New and Accurate Account of the Provinces of South Carolina and Georgia,* quoted by Charles C. Jones, Jr., *History of Georgia,* 2 vols. (Boston: Houghton Mifflin, 1883), 1:100.

4. Sarah B. Gober-Temple and Kenneth Coleman, *Georgia Journeys* (Athens: University of Georgia Press, 1961), p. 5.

On Friday morning, November 17, 1732, the *Anne* went down the Thames on the outgoing tide. Three days later she was out of the channel, and on the open sea. It was a long and tiresome voyage, though it had its happy moments when Mr. Oglethorpe himself stood godfather to the christening of a child, or celebrated his own birthday—he was thirty-six—with a pint of punch for each family head. On Christmas Day there were prayers and sermons, and a special dinner of mutton, beef broth, and pudding, with a pint of flip per adult. When in the closeness of the living conditions several people fell out with each other, Oglethorpe ordered a pint of rum for each and ordered them to drink and be friends again. (Later he was to turn strongly against rum.) And each day when the weather was good he brought the adult males on deck—a motley assembly of merchants, wigmakers, carpenters, tailors, weavers, basket makers, gardeners, apothecaries, and sawyers—and drilled them in the manual of arms with muskets, for as Georgia settlers each man must serve as a part-time soldier, whatever his trade.

Early on the morning of January 13, 1733, after two months on a rough and seasick passage, in sight of land near Charleston on the South Carolina coast, the *Anne* dropped anchor. Fearing that if his passengers saw Charleston close up, they would lose their zest for going on to the wilderness of Georgia, Oglethorpe went ashore alone at Charleston while the *Anne* turned south toward Beaufort and Port Royal, where new barracks of the Independent Company were waiting the settlers' temporary occupancy. From Charleston, Oglethorpe, with Col. William Bull, had gone on to the Savannah River to pick out a town site. And there, on a high bluff on the west bank eighteen miles above the river's mouth he found a place for the city that would become the womb and seedbed of his colony of Georgia.

Pleased to have these armed citizens interposed between them and their Spanish and Indian foes, the Carolina legislature provided for the Georgians' happiness by giving them breeding cows and bulls, sows and boars, plus providing them with transport and protection by scout boats and rangers to their new home. Equally important, they made available the services of Colonel Bull to serve as surveyor, boss sawyer, and builder. On February 12, the colonists set foot at last on Georgia soil. They spent their first night on the riverbank at the foot of the bluff, crowded into four big tents.

Rising next morning and making their way to the top of the bluff, the colonists got their first good look at this land they had come so far to find. Below them lay the gently flowing river, one thousand feet wide, divided by a broad island that was natural pasture land. Beyond lay the dark line of forest on the Carolina shore. Behind them, on the right bank where the city was to stand, tall pines, great oaks with beards of moss, and magnolias, whose white blossoms would soon perfume the air, stretched away to the horizon. The settlers had hardly had time to look around them when neighbors arrived to make them welcome. Near their landing site, on the north end of the bluff, was a Yamacraw village under a friendly old chief named Tomochichi. There, also, lived a trader named John Musgrove, and his half-breed wife, Mary, daughter of a Scotsman, who spoke the language of the Creeks. On the day he had landed while his people were still at Beaufort, Oglethorpe and Col. Bull paid their respects to Tomochichi, with Mary Musgrove acting as interpreter. Tomochichi made Oglethorpe welcome and promised to extend his people a friendly greeting on their arrival.

The greeting was startling in its warmth. While the new settlers looked on, amazed and half afraid, down the riverbank from the Yamacraw village there came a procession of about a hundred Indians. The men were straight and strong and almost naked, the king and the chief wearing "Cloaks and Drawers and a piece of cloth tied around their legs like boots, the women in Calico Jackets and petticoats." [5] They were following a medicine man who was dancing with antic gestures and waving in each hand a fan of white feathers, fastened to a rod with jingling bells, with which he stroked the face and flanks of Oglethorpe in a sign of friendship—meanwhile declaiming the valiant deeds of his tribal ancestors. Oglethorpe shook hands solemnly with all the Indians and gave them gifts of cloth. Not to be outdone, Tomochichi gave his gift to Oglethorpe—a buffalo skin on which was painted the head of an eagle. This gift had a special

5. Temple, Coleman, *Georgia Journeys*, p. 17–18.

meaning in two ways, Tomochichi explained. The eagle is swift, the buffalo strong—like the English, who flew over the seas in their ships, and were so strong nothing could oppose them. But there was another meaning; the feathers of the eagle are soft, and signify love; the skin of the buffalo is warm, and signifies protection. Thus the Yamacraws were asking Oglethorpe and his people to love and protect their little families.

Having the friendship of Tomochichi was fine, but the colony could not breathe easily until the chiefs of the Lower Creeks also asserted their friendship. This soon came about. In late May, Oglethorpe was called on by the head men of eight Creek villages, one of whom told Oglethorpe that he had heard the Cherokees had murdered some Englishmen in Carolina, and if he wanted these Cherokees killed, the Creeks would be glad to do so. Oglethorpe thanked him, but told him that this would not be necessary. The rumor that Englishmen had been killed by the Cherokees was untrue. He then gave gifts to the Indians—laced hats, coats, and shirts, and other material for clothing. He also gave them guns, bullets, and cutlasses with gilt handles. There were tobacco and rum for all, and food for their journey home. Out of these meetings grew arrangements of mutual benefit to both Englishmen and Indians. With Mary Musgrove interpreting, Oglethorpe worked out an agreement by which the Yamacraws ceded the site of Savannah and the adjoining area to the Englishmen, as far up the river as the tide flowed, "for as long as the sun shines or the waters run." [6] The other Creeks confirmed the cession. A year after these arrangements were agreed to, Oglethorpe took his friend Tomochichi, his wife, his nephew, and five of his warriors home with him to London. There the old chief and his fighting men made a tremendous impression on the English, who stood in the streets and cheered them as their carriages passed. They had wanted to go before the king half-naked, as they dressed at home, but Oglethorpe persuaded Tomochichi and his wife to array themselves in scarlet robes trimmed with gold. The warriors, however, did appear

6. Hugh McCall, *The History of Georgia 1730–1784* (1811, 1816; reprint 1909 edition, Atlanta: Cherokee Publishing Co., 1969), Appendix 2, p. 250.

in tribal paint, and Tomochichi's small nephew made a great impression on the Archbishop of Canterbury by reciting the Lord's Prayer in both the Yamacraw dialect and English.

From the moment of their initial landing the settlers had been at work. First they had lugged their supplies from the boats in the river up the steep bluff, lifting what they could by a makeshift crane and backpacking the rest. Once this was done, Oglethorpe divided them into three groups, one to clear land for planting, another to begin the fort and palisade, the remainder to cut down the trees where the town would be. Before a month was up the first square had been marked off, forty house lots had been cleared of trees, and the first house begun, a log structure that was to be the model for those to follow. A frame of sawed timbers, twenty-four feet long, sixteen feet wide, and eight feet high, the ground floor was big enough for one large room and two small ones, with a cockloft above that would hold two beds. Sixty feet in front of the house and ninety feet behind it were cleared of timber.

At daylight on Saturday, July 7, 1733, the Englishmen in Georgia held their first formal meeting. They began with prayers of thanksgiving. They then went to Johnson Square, named for the South Carolina governor, gave names to the streets and wards—the first and main street was named for Colonel Bull—and each freeholder was given possession of his land. In the afternoon the chief bailiffs were named, with the power to appoint such lesser officers as constables and tythingmen, or ward bosses. Courts, both civil and criminal, were formed, and the first jury was empaneled by the newly appointed town clerk.

Not all those who had climbed the bluffs in February were still alive in July. As the fierce heat of their first summer came upon them, the people began to die in appalling numbers of a fever and a bloody flux, which Oglethorpe claimed was caused by their stubborn habit of drinking rum. It was hardly likely that the children who were dying were drinking much rum, nor was the young minister, Dr. Henry Herbert, who had come over at his own expense to serve the spiritual needs of the colony without pay, addicted to it. Falling dreadfully ill, he died at sea while trying to get home to England. William Cox, the colonists' doctor, had been the first to die, on April 6, leaving two children and a pregnant wife. At Oglethorpe's orders Dr. Cox had been buried with full military honors, the men marching with the corpse to the grave and firing small arms and cannon over it. This continued as others died, until a day when four were buried, one after the other, and the sound of the guns had a bad effect on many others who were sick. Oglethorpe then ordered that the practice be discontinued. As the summer wore on, the deaths increased. A man without a wife, a woman without a husband, were almost helpless in this primitive society, and as one died, the surviving spouse would take another mate, and the tragic process would repeat itself. Some twenty-six persons in all died in that first summer, and there would doubtless have been more deaths if help had not miraculously arrived, unexpected and unannounced. On July 11, there dropped anchor on the river a ship from London, bringing a number of Jewish families. Among them was a doctor, Samuel Nunis. Sixty people—more than half of the colonists—were ill as he came ashore, with no doctor to care for them. He immediately began his treatments—cold baths, cooling drinks, and other soothing applications, and for all his services he would take no fee.

The Jewish emigrants had raised their own money, fitted out their own ship, and come of their own volition, without consulting with the trustees. News of their arrival caused a furor in London, and Oglethorpe was ordered to load them aboard ship and send them home. Knowing full well how much he owed to Dr. Nunis, Oglethorpe ignored the order. And so began the Jewish community that has contributed so much to Savannah's social and cultural life in all the years since.

Though Oglethorpe gave full credit to Nunis, he never did abandon the idea that it was his own enforcement of the ban on rum that at last brought the fevers to an end. By now, though, the people knew that it was the water drunk from shallow wells and from the river that had been making them sick. As soon as a deep well was dug in the middle of town, and a pump placed in it, the fevers had subsided. With the ending of the sickness the people's spirits brightened. And now, over the seas from England other ships were coming. They were bringing Salzburgers—German Lutherans seeking freedom from religious persecution—who arrived singing hymns and seeking only a quiet place where they could lead peaceful lives in all godliness and honesty. Within a few weeks of their arrival they had found their Ebenezer—Place of Hope—at a site twelve miles up the river from Savannah.

Coming too were the Moravians, of the United Brethren, themselves pious men, and upright in all their dealings, but so gentle of spirit they could not bring themselves to bear arms against any enemy, Spaniard, French, or Indian. They were therefore unable to accept the trustees' requirement that each able-bodied male should be a fighting man, and soon moved on to join their Brethren in Pennsylvania. The Scots who soon were to arrive had no such compunction against fighting. They were brought over to serve as soldiers, and from their post at Darien, they marched with Oglethorpe in his first forays against the Spaniards.

Georgia's first difficulties arose not with an outside enemy but with her own people. In the first year of hard work, of sickness, and of dying, there seemed to come into the colonists' temperament a new element of truculence, of independence, a feeling that the rules the trustees had laid down—as to how much land they could own, and what they should plant, and where they should live, and the restrictions on slavery—bore little relation to reality. What, the haggard settlers seemed to be saying, do those noble lords living in their great houses in Mayfair and Pall Mall know of how life is with us here on the frontier? Oglethorpe, of course, did know, for he shared their hardships with them, and their belligerence annoyed and troubled him. The burden was upon him to get those things done which the trustees wanted—the silkworms produced, the wine grapes grown, the land defended—but he was clothed with no specific authority. He was the trustees' agent, a general overseer. The daily conduct of the business of the colony lay in the hands of those leaders who had been named by the trustees on Oglethorpe's recommendation in the first summer of the colony's founding. These were the magistrates, the bailiffs, the constables, the justices of the peace, the recorders, and clerks of the courts that had been set up. It was their job to keep order in the community, to stimulate the lazy, and control and punish the truculent and contentious, the dissolute and dishonest, judging them under the English law. But these men were not lawyers (lawyers, like rum sellers and slave dealers, were barred from the colony). Peter Gordon, the first magistrate, was an upholsterer. Thomas Causton, bailiff and storekeeper who succeeded him, had been a calico printer. Thomas Christie, bailiff and recorder, was a merchant. Francis Scott, a justice of the peace who sentenced the first Georgian, Samuel Grey, a silk throwster, to the stocks for suspected mutiny, was a military officer who had been reduced in rank. Another Conservator of the Peace was Richard Hodges, a basket maker. Noble Jones, who as surveyor, constable, guardboat commander, register and captain of militia, seemed to carry the weight of the whole colony on his shoulders, was by trade a carpenter.

The trustees recognized that by reaching into a group which started out as equals and choosing certain ones to be set above their fellows it was inevitable that they would "create some future uneasiness among them." [7] The uneasiness was not long in manifesting itself. Peter Gordon turned into a common scold. William Waterland, the second magistrate, turned out to be a drunk and soon left for Carolina—a route that many discontented Georgians would follow in the rough years to come. Thomas Causton, the third magistrate and storekeeper, was described by Peter Gordon as being so arrogant and dictatorial there was no living with him. Gordon also charged Causton's clerks with dispensing from the trustees' supplies molasses that had been spilled on the floor and had dirt in it. The recorder Thomas Christie sold rum, Gordon charged, and surveyor Noble Jones had been so slow in laying out tillable land for the freeholders that many were forced to live in town and pay high prices for food.

Squabbling among the chief magistrates had its counterpart at all levels of early Savannah society. One project highly prized by the trustees was the so-called trustees' garden, a ten-acre plot east of the town in which not only native plants, but useful specimens from all over the world would be tested for their capacity to thrive and grow in the coastal climate. It was hoped

7. Temple, Coleman, *Georgia Journeys*, p. 20.

that the garden would become what its gardener, James Fitzwalter, called a "nussary" [8] for baby plants, including cotton, from which the freeholders would be allowed to take all sorts of cuttings, seeds, and seedlings for their own gardens and orchards. Unhappily, the area chosen for the garden was dry and sandy in parts and swampy in others, and despite the most assiduous watering, draining, and tillage, nothing seemed to thrive there. This was puzzling to the trustees. To the earl of Egmont and to his colleagues, dirt was dirt, whether it be the sandy soil and salt marshes of Tybee, the rich mulch of the Ogeechee River bottom near Fort Argyle, or the deep black loam of a new-cleared field in the little settlements at Abercorn or Highgate or Hampstead. You treated it the same way. You put a seed in the ground and you tended it, and it grew, reproducing itself manyfold. The anguished colonists who had been given land at Tybee or at Skidaway or Thunderbolt, where Oglethorpe set up ten-family outposts, knew well that this was not so, and though they did their uttermost, they could not make the land produce enough to feed their families. They died or gave up, returning to Savannah to work for hire, or moved on to Carolina and were forgotten or went back to England, disenchanted with their dream of a new life in Georgia. The fields they cleared quickly grew up and the guardhouses they had manned fell into ruin.

Mr. Oglethorpe soon had more to trouble him than unhappy farmers on outlying islands, and Mr. Causton, the public storekeeper, had more weighty matters on his mind than the charges that his clerks had sold dirty molasses. On the ship that arrived from London in the spring of 1735 was the Reverend John Wesley, his brother Charles, a Reverend Delamotte, and a young Church of England clergyman named Ingham, all of them men of overwhelming piety and all obsessed with the idea of going into the wilderness to convert the Indians. Charles Wesley, whose special job was secretary to Oglethorpe and commissioner of Indian Affairs, soon became so displeased with everything he saw around him that he went back home some five months after his arrival. John Wesley, who discovered no

8. Temple, Coleman, *Georgia Journeys*, p. 124–125.

Indians who showed any interest in being instructed in the Christian faith, soon found himself focusing his attention on the non-Indian parishioners of Savannah, particularly upon one of them. She was a Miss Sophia Hopkey, niece of the chief magistrate and storekeeper, Thomas Causton, a friend and stout supporter of General Oglethorpe and all his policies. Just what transpired between the solemn young clergyman, a bachelor of thirty-three, and Miss Sophia is still a puzzle to historians. All that is known is that Miss Hopkey at first took religious instruction from him, studied French under his tutelage, and on occasion went with others to his house where he administered private communion, after a session in which they would all reprove, instruct, and exhort one another.

Upon one occasion he is said to have told Miss Hopkey that he would like to spend the rest of his life with her, and was much wounded when she somewhat curtly told him to put such talk aside. Wesley was hurt, but not discouraged, and not trusting his own feelings, he turned to his friend the Rev. Delamotte for advice, who told him to forget it. He then conferred with the Moravians, who prayed over the issue and came up with the same advice. Whether or not this caused a chill in his attitude toward Miss Hopkey is not known. At any rate, on March 12, 1737, Sophia Hopkey was married to William Williamson by an Anglican clergyman in Purrysburg, South Carolina. And not long after that, John Wesley refused to administer the sacrament of communion to Sophia Hopkey Williamson, his reason being that she had not, before coming to the holy table, satisfied him that she was, as the scriptures required, in love and charity with her neighbor.

The religious and political squabble that followed split the town. Storekeeper Causton was outraged that his niece had been so treated, and husband William Williamson brought suit against Mr. Wesley for a thousand pounds sterling. The colony was soon divided into factions; one supporting Causton, Williamson, and Sophia; the other taking the side of Wesley. Charges that Causton's clerks gave short measures again were bandied about, and dark stories were told that Wesley was actually a Papist, his mission to destroy the Anglican faith. Even the grand jury which heard the charges was divided, but strongly enough on Sophia's side to bring a true bill of ten indictments against Mr. Wesley. Of these, only the first accusation, that he had spoken and written to Mrs. Williamson without her husband's consent, was of a civil nature—the others, including the charge that he had "repelled" [9] her from Holy Communion, had to do with his activities as a clergyman. He was ordered not to leave the colony pending trial, and he in turn demanded immediate trial. When it was not forthcoming, he posted notice in Johnson Square that he was leaving, and Causton and the magistrates ordered him arrested. Before the bailiff could lay hands on him, he slipped off at night, by boat to South Carolina, losing his way in the woods as he walked to Beaufort. From there he went on to Charleston where he took ship for England. So ended the brief Georgia sojourn of the great clergyman who was to become the founding father of the Methodist Church.

Georgia, indeed, had trouble keeping ministers. Many died of fevers, others suffered both spiritual and physical malaise. Following the departed Wesleys came the Reverend George Whitefield, the great evangelist, who sought first to found a college at Bethesda, and failing in this, established an orphanage. He soon found Georgia too small a parish for his prodigious talents as a preacher, and moved on to wider fields. There were many problems other than those connected with keeping ministers, however. Causton and his fellow magistrates were soon to find themselves confronted with an angry populace determined that at least two regulations laid down by the trustees should be honored only in the breach. When Oglethorpe in 1736 came back from his first trip to London, he brought with him strong affirmation of the rule that there should be no black slaves in Georgia, and no rum should be sold there. The Georgians got around the ban on rum by ignoring it. South Carolina happily smuggled rum to public houses across the river, and when arrests of rum sellers and rum drinkers were made, only rarely could a jury be found which would convict. The judges, who were fond of rum themselves, were reluctant to pass sentence even on those found guilty. The ban on slaveholding was

9. Trevor Reese, ed., *The Clamorous Malcontents* (Savannah: The Beehive Press, 1973), p. 68.

equally vulnerable. Georgians who could afford it "rented" black men and women from South Carolina slave dealers, paying a lifetime "rental" in one lump sum. A restriction even more annoying to the colonists, and one which could not be circumvented, was the rule of "tale male," under which land could be inherited only by a male heir who could bear arms in defense of the colony.

The trustees from the beginning had been disappointed in the progress made in Georgia—and horrified by the size of the bills Oglethorpe and, in Oglethorpe's absence, his agent Causton were sending back to London for them to pay. Soon the colony was in deep financial trouble, and the trustees were in a mood to abandon the whole project. Neither Oglethorpe nor his magistrates, they complained, knew how short of cash they had become. The truth seems to be that there was in Oglethorpe's mind one goal that transcended all others. Let the trustees worry about silkworms and wine making and Causton's too lavishly stocking the company store. Oglethorpe was a compassionate man and a philanthropist, but he was first of all a soldier, and his mission in life was to fight; thus he was determined to turn his infant colony into an armed camp, surrounded by strong outposts, and able to defend itself against all comers. It was the private belief of some of the trustees that Oglethorpe had given Causton, his chief magistrate, orders to spend whatever was necessary to further this end, sending the bills to the trustees for payment. Whatever they might have felt about Oglethorpe being basically responsible, though, their wrath fell upon Causton's head. They called Oglethorpe back to London and laid down the law to him. He came home to Savannah in 1738, and to a thunderstruck citizenry gave the doleful word. Causton was to be relieved of his post as magistrate and storekeeper and sent to England to answer charges. He removed Noble Jones as surveyor and suspended him as constable and dismissed Fitzwalter, the gardener. He ordered the store closed. This meant that those people whose food crops had failed that year would have nothing to eat, an unmitigated disaster to those who had discovered that they could not feed their families, no matter how hard they might labor, on the lands assigned to them.

The speech by Oglethorpe marked a turning point in the colony's history. There was a great murmuring in the streets, and slowly there boiled up in the hearts of the people the angers that had been simmering there. Representations were drawn up to send to the trustees, in the first head-on confrontation between the settlers and their well-meaning but somewhat befuddled landlords. The papers were signed by 121 "malcontents," including the three magistrates, a representative cross-section of the freeholders. They pointed out what the trustees had heard often before—and had in great degree ignored—that the colony could not survive on agriculture or industry in competition with other colonies, South Carolina in particular, where the burden of the work was borne by slaves. No freehold family alone could clear and fence the land, build barns, and protect growing crops from crows, turkeys, squirrels, and other small animals, which must be guarded against night and day. And even if all these tasks were performed with the greatest industry, drought or storm might wipe out a crop and the farmer at the end of the year would have to apply again to the trustees for supplies to tide him over. At the end of a year, the writers claimed, many a farmer owed more to the doctor than he had made from the land. The colony therefore must depend on trade. And here again rose the question of labor. All Georgia had to export was her timber, and without slave labor, she could not compete with South Carolina. The signers of this bold paper also did not agree that men must work as they were forced to work under trustees' orders, only to improve land which they could not sell, but could only pass on to their sons, and not to their wives and daughters. (If there was no male heir, the land reverted to the trustees to be granted again to an arms-bearing male.)

Oglethorpe's answer to this statement was blunt and to the point. If Georgia was to become a slave state, or if the land tenure was changed, he would have nothing further to do with Georgia. Nor were the trustees sympathetic to the colonists' complaints. All petitions were turned down. It was, though, the opening gun in a battle that would long continue until the settlers finally got their headstrong way. By 1748 even the Salzburgers—those good and gentle folk—had changed their minds and supported the importation of slaves, with their leader Martin Bolzius pleading strongly for the laws to be changed. The Rev.

George Whitefield joined his German friends, urging that he be allowed slaves to work his orphanage lands at Bethesda. Finally, in 1749, the trustees capitulated. Slaves could be brought in but for every four slaves in a household, there had to be one white male indentured servant. The next year the trustees took one more step in retreat. The "tale male" was abolished, along with quitrents and the limitation on land ownership.

Even though these limitations were at last removed, Georgia's colonists had many other reasons for discontent. The reputation Georgia was to maintain throughout its history as a place where punishment of miscreants was brutal and prison life was hard, began in the colony's earliest days. For no worse an offense than missing his every-fourth-night guard duty, a weary farmer might be tied neck to heels by his tything-man. Georgia juries and magistrates soon got a reputation for the severity of their sentences, which ranged from long hours in the stocks, to ducking in the river, to lashes on the bare back at the tail of a cart pulled through town, to hanging in a public square. Small offenses were punished under English law by fine, imprisonment, or burning on the hand. It is little wonder what wrongdoers were quick to cross the river into South Carolina, and Causton, until the trustees stopped him, sometimes would sentence them to this exile. His motives were compassionate. His colonists had no money to pay fines. If jailed, they could do no work for the colony and their families would starve. And whipping and burning in the hand seemed too ignominious for a freeholder.

Despite all his other troubles, Oglethorpe was successful in his main endeavor, which was to turn Georgia into a bastion, guarding Carolina and all the older colonies to the north from Spaniards, roving Frenchmen, and enemy Indians. Once Savannah was laid out and the first houses were completed, the effort to protect the little town with a chain of outposts was begun. The first of these log forts, manned by ten families, was at Fort Argyle, forty miles west of Savannah on the Ogeechee, where an Indian trading path crossed the river. The Salzburgers were set up at Ebenezer on the Savannah. Though they were not primarily fighting men but gentle, deeply religious Lutheran farmers, their presence in the hinterlands could serve as a warning post. At Darien, on the Georgia coast, the Scotch High-landers, who *were* fighting men, set up their settlement guarding the mouth of the Altamaha. And on St. Simons Island the key fortress of them all was laid out—Frederica—which was to become the main bastion on the water route leading from St. Augustine to Savannah. It did not matter to Oglethorpe that it lay south of the Altamaha and therefore was not truly Georgia's at all. Once he had his coastal defenses lined up, in 1736 he went up the Savannah River one hundred and fifty miles and es-tablished the inland fort of Augusta, which quickly became more Carolina than Georgia in its orientation as the Charleston traders flocked there to barter with the Indians for the thousands of deerskins they brought in each year. It was to become one of the most picturesque places on the Georgia frontier and the scene of some of the bloodiest affrays in the Revolution that was to come. His next move was a long reconnaissance to the south, to determine, he said, just where the king's domains joined lands claimed by the Spaniards, and to pick out outposts south of Frederica where garrisons could be established—one at Fort Andrew on Cumberland Island, another at Fort King George, at the mouth of the St. Johns.

All this activity on Oglethorpe's part made the Spanish ex-tremely nervous, and while Oglethorpe was in the area, they held in prison at St. Augustine an English delegation that had come down by sea from South Carolina to see if some agree-ment could be reached as to boundaries. When Oglethorpe turned back without attacking, the Spanish captain general in Florida, Don Francisco Moral Sanchez, seemed mollified. He turned the Englishmen loose and sent his own commissioners back with them to Frederica to continue treaty discussions there.

And now, it seems, the Spaniards were deceived by a little play-acting on Oglethorpe's part. At every little fort he had scat-tered along the coast, he ordered all guns fired in salute as the Spanish boats went past, giving an impression of much greater strength than the outposts actually could muster. At Frederica, the drama reached a climax when yelling Indians, apparently enraged, burst in upon the conference, denouncing the Spanish for their cruel ways. With apparently great difficulty Oglethorpe quieted the Indians. He then went on to explain that his forts' activities were for the protection of the Spaniards from Indians who wished to do them harm.

The agreement that resulted—that neither side would occupy the mouth of the St. Johns, and that all boundary disputes would be left to the home governments—so enraged the Spanish king that he called Don Francisco Sanchez home in disgrace. His replacement was Don Antonio Arredondo, a captain of engineers, who brought word to Oglethorpe that the treaty previously signed at Frederica was now void. The Spaniards would not pull back to the mouth of the St. Johns. The English, instead, must withdraw beyond the Savannah River, abandoning all Georgia.

This put English-Spanish relationships in a new and dangerous light. The string of little forts down the Georgia coast, manned by heads of households who were farmers first and soldiers second, could not stand against a Spanish attack. If Georgia was to survive, Oglethorpe had to have professional fighting men of his own. In the fall of 1736 he made his second trip to England, this time not to show off a group of friendly Indians, but to raise a regiment. He came back with six hundred men—and a new title, General of all the military forces in South Carolina and Georgia. The troops he brought with him to Frederica were a rude and brawling lot. Some were Papists; others were openly critical of the king and all his works. There was a generous sprinkling of Spanish spies among them, for many of them were from the Gibraltar garrison. A company of the regiment that Oglethorpe stationed at Cumberland Island was particularly troublesome. When Oglethorpe went there to inspect the troops, a group of them set upon him and attempted to assassinate him. The ringleader was seized and shot. The officers, too, were a rowdy bunch, fighting each other with fists and sticks and now and then fighting duels. Many of them were so unruly that Oglethorpe had to send them home.

From now on Oglethorpe's role in Georgia was more and more that of the soldier, less and less that of the administrator. His rank as commanding general—the only official title he ever held in Georgia—was from the king, not the trustees, and his first concern had now become security, not philanthropy. The trustees recognized he would be less and less their agent and named William Stephens, another "decayed gentleman," to take over as secretary for the affairs of the trustees. Stephens's main job, which he carried out faithfully, was to write the letters Oglethorpe had not time to write, reporting in minute detail everything that went on in the colony, including gossip, rumor, and scandal.

The War of Jenkins' Ear, as it was called in Georgia, was the outgrowth of bitter commercial rivalry between England and Spain, a contest for world dominion, for command of the seas and of world trade. Oglethorpe saw it coming, and knowing how desperately he would need allies, in the summer of 1739 he made a long journey across wild lands to the Creek town at Coweta on the Chattahoochee. There he renewed his treaties with the Indians, who promised to send a thousand fighting men. He also asked South Carolina to send money, men, and supplies, but the Carolinians now were jealous of this upstart state that was throwing its weight about so arrogantly in the disputed land, and they were slow in responding. With the outbreak of war in October, though, he finally got the promise of six hundred men to come south on a four-month enlistment, and by the late spring of 1740 he was able to make his first strong move. With nine hundred troops, regulars and militia, two hundred of them Georgians, and eleven hundred Indians under his command, he moved on Florida, the South Carolinians and Highlanders by land, Oglethorpe's army by water. Spanish outposts fell easily, and by late May Oglethorpe's force had taken Fort Moosa, two miles from St. Augustine. Unhappily, the nine small gunboats provided by the British navy could not get past the Spanish galleys at the harbor's entrance, and the plan for headlong attack on the city from land and sea had to be abandoned in favor of a long and profitless siege. Disease came with the heat, the Indians found no honor and excitement in such waiting, watching warfare, and the whole expedition was a colossal failure. The South Carolinians blamed the Georgians and Oglethorpe; the Georgians blamed the South Carolinians—a pattern of mutual recrimination that was to be repeated in times of stress for generations thereafter. Oglethorpe marched his miserable and fever-ridden forces back north. The Carolinians went home; the Georgians stopped off at Frederica, where for two months Oglethorpe himself lay desperately ill of fever.

And now the Spaniards began their move. In Havana, fifty ships manned by a thousand seamen took aboard eighteen hundred soldiers and headed for the Georgia coast. By early July of 1742, they were off St. Simons, moving in to land a few miles up the inward passage toward Frederica, where Oglethorpe lay in wait with his small force of Highlanders and Rangers. In confused fighting of fire and fall back, ambush and counterambush, the battle went on. One Spanish force of several hundred, weary of marching and fighting, stacked arms in an open glade beside a marsh and prepared to rest. Here, at the signal of a Highland cap raised upon a sword, the Scots attacked, driving the Spaniards into the marshlands and killing or capturing some two hundred men. It was a small engagement, this brief clash that was to go down in history as the Battle of Bloody Marsh, but in its effect it was one of the world's historic battles, for it ended fovever any further Spanish threats to the British colonies on the eastern shore. Oglethorpe, with the two platoons he commanded, was not present at the affray in the marsh, but as the Spaniards fell back upon their ships, he, with all the men he could muster (some five hundred, for South Carolina had ignored his second plea for men), followed hard upon their heels.

His plans were frustrated by a deserter, a Frenchman spying for the Spaniards, who carried to the demoralized and disorganized Spaniards a full report on the weakness of Oglethorpe's forces. This was disastrous, for if the Spaniards had rallied and counterattacked, Georgia might be speaking Spanish today. Again, though, Oglethorpe proved himself a master of subterfuge and deception. He sent a Spanish prisoner with a letter to the Frenchman which indicated that the Frenchman was, in reality, a double spy, sent now to lead the Spaniards to their doom. The letter told the Frenchman to lead the Spanish ships back toward Frederica so that hidden gun batteries could be brought into play. First, though, he was to persuade the Spaniards to stay on St. Simons three more days, for by that time two thousand men and six armed ships would arrive. Mention was also made in the letter of a supposed attack on St. Augustine from the sea, by British naval forces in the Caribbean. None of this, of course, was true, but the Spaniards in their dejection and defeat no longer trusted each other. The Spanish commander, though he still outnumbered Oglethrope's forces four to one, made sail and ran for home. It was the last foray of the Spaniards into Georgia. The land that had been "debatable" for nearly a hundred years was no-man's-land no longer. Praise poured in on Oglethorpe from the governors of all the colonies to the north—including South Carolina—which he modestly shared with Lieutenants Sutherland and MacKay, who had laid the winning ambush at Bloody Marsh.

In March of 1743 Oglethorpe took a small force and marched once more to the gates of St. Augustine. The Spaniards would not come out and fight, and he turned for home. For him the wars were over. Turning over his regiment to Major William Horton, he went home to England. It had, in a way, been a harsh ten years for a man whose deepest motives had been compassion for the unfortunate and their physical protection in a wild and dangerous land. Many of those in his charge had proved to be as feckless and whimpering in Georgia as they had been in England. The trustees and the British government had not always agreed on what should be done in Georgia—and Oglethorpe had been caught in the middle. South Carolina, which had so warmly welcomed the first Georgians, was unfriendly now, and the war which to him was absolutely essential to the survival, not only of Georgia, but of South Carolina, had been but feebly supported by the British crown and even more feebly by the trustees.

Back in England Oglethorpe, now approaching his sixtieth birthday, married the beautiful and wealthy Lady Elizabeth Wright, and settled down to write an occasional romantic verse and live the life of an old soldier turned country gentleman. Across the world the state he founded and nourished through its earliest days would see him no more, though his name there would never be forgotten. What he felt of his decade of service in Georgia is difficult to surmise. Nothing had quite turned out as either he or the trustees had hoped. Georgians, on the verge of starving as they tried to carry out the trustees' requirements regarding what crops to raise, began to prosper as the Spanish threat ended. But they prospered in ways that the trustees had not foreseen. The "money crops" which thrived were not mulberry trees and grapevines, as had been hoped, but timber, furs, clay products, potash, and cattle. As the laws against slavery were weakened, rice began to come in, and here and there some settlers had noted how peaches and tobacco seemed to thrive. And up at Ebenezer the Salzburgers were planting a little cotton—the crop which in the future would come to use all the black man's labor and all the best Georgia land, building the great plantation empire which, in time, emancipation would destroy.

There was a different feeling in the air now—a different attitude on the part of the people toward the trustees. By the time Oglethorpe went home, half of Georgia's nearly two thousand white inhabitants were not charity wards of the trustees, but men who had come over at their own expense, bringing indentured servants which permitted them to receive grants of up to five hundred acres of land. These "adventurers" as the trustees called them, had not clustered in the little towns as Oglethorpe had encouraged, but had laid out their plantations along the rivers, growing there what crops they willed. Thus Georgia, which had been founded by special people carefully chosen to live under a special set of rules laid down by men of good minds and warm hearts, but who lived far away and sometimes lacked understanding, became much like its sister colonies in its goals and attitudes and ambitions.

In the days of Mr. Oglethorpe, he had been the law in Georgia, the voice of the trustees. After his departure, the trustees gave the people themselves a modicum of self-government. A colonial assembly was created in 1751, to be made up of delegates from towns and groups of families numbering ten or more. They could pass no laws, but they could report on conditions and recommend and suggest what legislation was needed. Now that Oglethorpe's regiment was gone, a militia was needed, and one was formed under the command of Noble Jones, with all owners of six hundred acres of land or more being designated as cavalrymen.

When in 1752 the weary trustees gave up at last and King George took over, he sent into the colony a new lawmaker, harsher far than Oglethorpe, less wise even than the trustees, less aware by far of what the young colony needed and wanted than the people themselves. He was the royal governor, and his title was almost Spanish in its grandiloquence—Captain General and Governor in Chief of His Majesty's Province of Georgia, and Vice Admiral of the Same. His power was nearly absolute, for he could convene the assembly or dissolve or veto what it had done. He was the court of final appeal, and grants of land were under his control. He ruled through a royal council of twelve, which served as the cabinet, court of appeals, and upper house of the legislature.

There was one power, though, that was granted to the people. The lower house, of nineteen men, was elected by them—and through it for the first time Georgians were given a voice in their own government—even though their acts could be disallowed by the governor or the king.

And now began in Georgia that bitter contest, long since latent in the older colonies, between the king's royal governors and the people whom they tried to govern. In less than a quarter-century it would lead on to bloody revolution, and the final freedom from kings forever of Georgians and all the American people.

2

From Royal Rule to
Revolution

$\mathcal{O}$NCE her people learned to function under the general form of government in effect in the other colonies, Georgia began to stir and grow with a greater flourish, economically, than she had shown under the benign but sometimes bemused administration of the trustees. The admission of slaves and rum and the change in the land laws caused the people to look with a blither heart upon their prospects. Soon, however, it became clear that the edicts of a royal governor could be more frustrating than the burdens imposed by the trustees. And when the royal edicts began to interfere with the economic well-being of the colonists, the seeds of revolution long dormant in the American soil quickly began to sprout.

Georgia was particularly unhappy with the king's first choice for a governor. He was a sailor, Captain John Reynolds of the Royal Navy, and his idea of governing was to conduct himself like a ship's master, bellowing orders from the quarterdeck to a crew of cowed and chastened seamen. Georgia's legislators were inexperienced but not cowed, and the first elected assembly ever held in the state spent a lot of time in controversy with the governor. Despite this, though, the assembly did pass a number of laws, some wise, some foolish. One of the first laws passed was a barbarous one which was soon repealed; it offered a bounty to the Indians for the scalp of any slave killed while

33

running away. This "Black Code," upon which all later Georgia laws pertaining to slavery were based, is of interest here because of the relationship it revealed between the races in the beginning—the haunting fear of the black man, which still persists today, particularly in our cities. Under the code no slave could leave his home plantation without a permit (Many an old Georgia family still treasures these written passes as proof of family prosperity *ante bellum*). They could not assemble in large numbers, nor travel at night in groups of more than seven. They could not possess beer or liquor, or own a boat or cattle of their own. They could attend church, but they must not be taught to read or write, nor were they permitted to beat a drum or blow a horn, or make any other unusual noise. Ten crimes were made punishable by death, among them murder, rape, poisoning a white person, setting fire to property, or inciting to insurrection—all a reflection of the outnumbered white man's fear of a slave uprising. Yet not all the slave code was cruelly restrictive. Other laws were meant to protect him against a cruel master. He could not be made to work on Sunday; he must not be worked more than sixteen hours a day, and he should be properly clothed and fed. Whoever killed a slave would be fined fifty pounds, and if the government had to put one to death, the owner would be paid fifty pounds, and so would the injured party. Another law, designed to encourage white artisans to come to Georgia, forbade slaves to become carpenters, masons, and bricklayers. This was not strictly observed and each plantation, in time, trained its own skilled craftsmen.

When Governor Reynolds arrived by warship to take office in 1754, the people greeted him with bonfires and rejoicing. They celebrated his departure two years later with equal joy. Showing an incredible disregard for law and the rights and duties of the elected assembly, he had highhandedly dissolved that body and sought to replace it with one made up of his supporters, hand-picked by his secretary, William Little, who had been his ship's surgeon. His regard for the courts was minimal, and he once ordered a man hanged two days before the date set for his execution. He quickly became extremely unpopular in Savannah by trying to move the capital fourteen miles westward to a town on the Ogeechee which he founded and called Hardwicke, naming it for the Lord High Chancellor of England who was his kinsman. It must be admitted that Reynolds had some reason quickly to become disenchanted with Savannah. The building where he held his deliberations with the council and the assembly fell in soon after he arrived, and he had to move to a kind of shed behind the courthouse.[1]

The people, for their part, had paid little heed to Governor Reynolds. When he tried to raise two regiments of Georgians to fight in the French and Indian War then raging in the northern colonies, the Georgia assembly politely declined. Georgians were more interested in trading with the Indians than in fighting them. Reynolds, like Oglethorpe, laid out a system of forts along the Georgia coast, which the king refused to pay for, and Georgia could not afford. Reynolds, left holding the bag, was called home to England, where he was promoted to admiral.

His successor, Governor Henry Ellis, was received joyfully, for he was a man of diplomatic and amiable disposition as well as of high character. Educated in the natural sciences, in 1746 he had led an expedition deep into the Hudson Straits in search of a passage to the Pacific, for which he had been made a Fellow of the Royal Society, England's most prestigious scientific body. Georgians were glad to build a chain of forts when such a man requested it, and they were pleased when he settled Mary Musgrove's claim that she owned St. Catherine's Island. She in turn helped him obtain a treaty of friendship with the Cherokees. Unhappily, Ellis soon fell ill and in 1760 he returned to England, leaving Georgians much distressed for they had come to look upon him as a friend and as a man of honor.

Ellis turned over the reins of government to James Wright—who in the stormy twenty-two years to come would be successively the iron-fisted ruler, exasperated but affectionate advisor, unhappy prisoner and parolee, and at last the disenchanted refugee from the place and people he had done his uttermost to govern for the king. This third and final governor of Georgia, though South Carolina born, was educated in England and was a Loyalist to the core, a truly devoted servant of the British crown.

1. E. Merton Coulter, *Georgia: A Short History* (Chapel Hill: University of North Carolina Press, 1933, 1948, 1960), pp. 82–86.

Yet he was wholly committed to the colony and its people, seeking constantly a reconciliation between them and their king while at the same time sturdily carrying out his own duties as the king's agent. And even as the monarch lost the power to control, he made Georgia and its people more prosperous and productive than they had ever been before. His task in his first three years was to keep the peace with the Indians, a chore made easier when, in 1763, the French by the Treaty of Paris gave up all their holdings in America, and the hapless Spaniards at last were forced to abandon their claims in Florida north of the St. Marys River. When this happy news reached Georgia, Wright on the king's orders brought seven hundred Indians, representing the Creeks, Cherokees, Chickasaws, Choctaws, and Catawbas, together at Augusta to meet with him and the governors of the two Carolinas and Virginia. A treaty of friendship was signed, and the Creeks at this conference ceded to Georgia all the lands lying between the Savannah and the Ogeechee rivers, and to the north beyond Augusta to the present area of Lincolnton. Along the coast the Georgia boundary was extended to the south from Altamaha Sound to the St. Marys.

Now, for the first time in Georgia's troubled history, the Indian threat had receded, and Governor Wright could get on with his business of making money for His Majesty. The French and Indian War had been very expensive, leaving the royal government deeply in debt. Since the war had been fought to protect the colonists as well as to defend territory, it seemed reasonable to the king that they should be called upon to help foot the bill. Herein, though, in his efforts to collect, the frugal and greedy George III set the fires of rebellion to flickering. The Stamp Act of 1765 was the first revenue measure to bring about an open breach. This measure taxed newspapers, most legal documents, dice, playing cards, and ships' sailing orders. In Georgia it was opposed by the people, though not as violently as in other colonies, where the king's stamp agents were manhandled roughly. Georgia only burned hers in effigy, frightening him so badly that he fled Savannah. This was enough to bring down upon the objectors the wrath of Governor Wright, and he forced the legislature to vote its support of the act. Georgia, in fact, became the only colony to use stamps—not on all official documents, by any means, but in clearing ships out of the harbor at Savannah. Even this small concession to royal edict so enraged the South Carolinians that they threatened to stop doing business with Georgia, calling her action a betrayal of the colonists' cause. The Stamp Act was repealed in 1766, but the damage was done. A fabric had been torn that could never be mended. Wright still commanded a powerful faction of Loyalists, but he never again would govern a united colony.

For a while, though, political differences were put aside as population growth increased and times grew prosperous. His South Carolina plantation background led Governor Wright to urge Georgians to bring under cultivation the rich lowlands along the rivers, a practice which he personally demonstrated could make them very rich. Among those coming in to share in Georgia's new prosperity was a group of New England Puritans who had lived for several generations in South Carolina. They settled at Midway in St. John's Parish in 1752, and the old church, which they built there in 1792—the fourth on that site—is still standing under the ancient oak tree, a serene and handsome landmark reminiscent of a New England meeting-house. The Puritans, like the Salzburgers, added a sober, industrious, and pious element to the sometimes dawdling and feckless English population, many of whom by now were becoming inmates of Georgia's own debtor prisons. The Puritan aptitude for commerce was soon manifest. The port which they developed at Sunbury for a while threatened to replace Savannah as Georgia's busiest entrepôt.

The greatest effect their coming was to have upon their adopted colony was not in their commercial genius, though, nor in their piety, but in the fierce urge for freedom that motivated one of them. Dr. Lyman Hall, Yale-trained minister turned physician and rice planter, was a big, likable, long-nosed man with deep brooding eyes. Born and raised in Connecticut, he had brought with him to Georgia, which was in effect a British frontier outpost with heavily Loyalist leanings, the fierce spirit of independence long felt in his native Connecticut. He therefore became Georgia's first "rebel," a delegate to the Continental Congress, a signer of the Declaration, and in time, governor.

For a time in the early days, unhappy Georgians, chafing

under the trustees' demands, had fled from Georgia into South Carolina or the colonies to the north. Now the flow was reversed. Virginians and Carolinians began drifting down the Appalachian Valley to find homesteads in the newly opened Indian lands. New settlers continued to come in from over the sea. More Germans came in to join the Salzburgers, making Germans the second largest ethnic group in Georgia. Scotch-Irish Protestants from Ireland came in the 1760s and 1770s, moving from Savannah to settle at Wrightsborough on the Ogeechee.

The entry of new settlers into Georgia brought increased pressure on the Indians, who by now were in no strong position to resist. Their hunger for the manufactured goods of Britain had got them deeply into debt to the Indian traders—the furs which they had brought in failing by some two hundred thousand pounds to cover what they owed. So, in 1773, to wipe out this debt, they were persuaded to give up two other huge tracts, one continuing up the Savannah north of Augusta to the headwaters of the Broad River, and westward through what is now Wilkes County. This land was ceded by the Cherokees. Another tract, ceded by the Creeks, lay to the southwest between the Ogeechee and the Altamaha, the two grants totaling some two million acres. As these Indian lands became available, Governor Wright lost no time in passing the word up and down the eastern seaboard that more new lands were to be had. And from Virginia and the Carolinas the settlers poured in at an even more furious rate, most going into the northern cession, settling around what are now Elberton, Washington, and Lincolnton.

By now Georgia and Georgians had greatly changed, in area and in attitude, and all that survived of the trustees' dream of an ideal state was the commercial aspect. Georgia was proving to be almost as productive as its promoters had predicted. It proved easy to grow rice in the coastal swamps, and wheat, corn, peas, and indigo further inland. Timber, tar, pitch, and turnpentine were in endless supply in the forests, and hogs and cattle in great numbers roamed the uplands. Tobacco came in with the Virginians. Tiny "coffee pot" sawmills stayed busy, turning out boards, scantlings, and barrel staves, but this was about the only industry the province could boast. Georgia bought in England and in the northern colonies everything she needed in the way of manufactured goods, which took all the money she could lay hands on by the sale of her raw products to the West Indies. These islands were her best customers, trading slaves, rum, sugar, and molasses for Georgia rice, pork, and barrel staves, and giving gold and silver for the excess. Elsewhere Georgia sold rice, indigo, cow hides, deer skins, beef, lumber, and naval stores, but there was little she produced that the northern colonies wanted, except money. So here began an economic pattern that Georgia after two hundred years has only recently begun to break—the dependence on others for things she could well produce herself out of her own raw materials.

The royal era was the time of the development of the great plantations, as Georgia changed from a land of small freeholds worked by yeoman farmers to a slave-based agriculture. James Habersham, partner with Francis Harris in the first successful import-export house to be established in Georgia, found time on the side to operate plantations on which two hundred slaves produced more than seven hundred barrels of rice a year. Governor Wright on twelve plantations totaling nineteen thousand acres worked five hundred slaves whose labors brought him in six thousand pounds a year, and John Graham, his lieutenant-governor, owned twenty-six thousand acres.

Cheap land, low taxes on property, and a seemingly endless supply of slave labor in the years before the Revolution saw the quick creation of a small but powerful ruling class—rich plantation owners who built themselves great houses in the country and equally handsome seats in town. Some of them remained blunt and simple men, but many, in these last years before the Revolution, lived like royal princelings, elegant in dress and equipage. They sniffed smelling salts from crystal bottles, carried silver toothpick cases, opened their fine Madeira with pearl-handled silver corkscrews, and wore silver-mounted small swords. They kept track of time with sand glasses as they danced, played cards, or merely sat about conversing on handsomely designed furniture of mahogany and walnut, or listening raptly while their ladies in silks and satins played the spinet. They were open to fresh ideas in the field of science and the arts, collected the paintings of Hogarth, read books borrowed from the Library Society of Savannah, and were among the first in America to protect their houses with a marvelous device called the lightning rod.

Their twenty thousand Negro slaves—half the state's population in 1778—did not share in the good things, and there was a considerable middle class which had no great yearning for silver snuff boxes and silken breeches. But many Georgians felt they had good reason to be grateful to England—and to England's royal governor—as Wright cajoled and shepherded and prodded his colony on to higher levels of prosperity. Thus Georgia moved more slowly and reluctantly to the final break than did the older, bolder, and angrier colonies to the north.

There was, though, far more at stake here than commercial prosperity and civil order or loyalty to a monarch or friendship for his proconsul. There were certain new and disturbing ideas—of human rights and freedoms and individual liberty—that, in the minds of a little group of Georgians now took precedence over all other things. They called themselves the Sons of Liberty, or Liberty Boys, and they were not a mob of idle malcontents, though their loyalist enemies referred to them derisively as "bonfire brethren" [2] for their habit of holding clamorous night meetings lighted by bonfires around rallying points called Liberty Poles. Governor Wright, with surprising sharpness of tongue for a man noted for his public manners, called them Sons of Licentiousness, and in truth there were among them men too quick with tar and feathers and public humiliation for those who disagreed with them. Among these radical Patriots, though, were solid Savannah artisans, conservative small merchants, and, somewhat surprisingly, a number of quiet Puritans from St. John's Parish at Midway and Sunbury. Their leaders were young men, Georgia-born, and some of them were the sons of distinguished Georgians who in the fullness of their years could not turn their backs upon their king. One young Patriot was Dr. Noble Wymberley Jones, son of Noble Jones the carpenter who came over on the *Anne* and became surveyor, captain of militia, and bulwark of Georgia second only to Oglethorpe. Others were Joseph Habersham and his brothers John and James. Their father, James Habersham, had been the

2. Coulter, *Georgia*, p. 111.

loyalist-patriot who served as stand-in governor for Sir James Wright when Wright went back to England on a leave that turned into a two-year stay, and he could never turn against his king. The brothers Telfair, rich merchants of Savannah dealing in every import from silk to slaves, were a house divided. Edward was a Patriot, William a Loyalist.

Though Georgia's protest against the Stamp Act took the form of little more than shouting, and the hanging and burning in effigy of a stamp agent, there was a continuing row over the passage in 1767 of the Townshend Acts, which laid import duties on glass, tea, lead, and painters' colors, and there was an uproar of protest in Georgia, as in other colonies, over Parliament's edict that each colony should provide supplies and quarters for the troops stationed on its soil. In the beginning, though, the Patriots in their rallies were careful to direct their criticism toward Parliament while strongly proclaiming their loyalty to the king and his family. Nor was there any sudden rallying to the cause of the radicals on the part of a majority of Georgians. In the summer of 1774 two rallies, called by the radical Patriots Noble W. Jones, Archibald Bulloch, John Houstoun, and George Hailey, were held at the Tondee Tavern. They set up a committee to correspond with other colonies, set up another committee to collect rice to send to the beleagered citizens of Boston (it soon had 579 barrels), and passed resolutions boldly condemning the British government. Governor Wright, on his part, had no trouble arranging countermeetings at which Noble Jones, father of Noble Wymberley Jones, and James Habersham, father of three radical sons, managed to bring together fully a third of the people, to whom Wright made the eloquent argument that Georgia owed its very existence to the British Parliament, which had contributed more than two hundred thousand pounds to its support in the early days, and now was protecting it from the Indians and the Spaniards. As a result, the conservative group passed a resolution decrying any criticism of England whatever.

Undisturbed by the doubts of their fathers or by Wright's threats to arrest them, the young radicals went ahead with plans for a more formal organization that their loose network of committees. They organized what came to be known as the First

Provincial Congress—which Wright had the power to adjourn. What he could dissolve he could not put back together again, though, for when he sought to reconvene the assembly, he couldn't get a quorum. Most assemblymen now belonged to the congress. It was the provincial congress, then, instead of the now dormant elected assembly, which named Bulloch, Jones, and Houstoun as delegates to the Second Continental Congress. They refused to go, however, since they represented only four out of twelve parishes. The seemingly quiet and pious Puritans of Sunbury in St. John's would have no part in such shilly-shallying. When Georgia in its first provincial congress refused fully to endorse the stand the northern colonists were taking— that no colony should henceforth have any trade whatever with England, or with any other colony which did not observe the same ban—the Puritan group walked out. Next they tried to secede from Georgia and join South Carolina. When denied this privilege, they sent their own delegate, Dr. Lyman Hall, as the representative from Georgia to the Second Continental Congress. He went off taking 160 barrels of rice and fifty pounds in money to be given to the people of Massachusetts. The argument over banning trade with England brought Georgia and South Carolina so near to warfare with each other that Carolina broke off trade relations with Georgia, saying that Georgians were "unworthy of the rights of free men." [3] Such hot words were passed that Governor Wright asked for British troops to protect him from his once cordial friends and neighbors.

Though Georgia's actions up until the spring of 1775 had been confined largely to angry words and the occasional tarring and feathering of a critic of the Patriot cause, the news of bloodshed at Lexington, Massachusetts, set off an emotional explosion. On the night of May 12 a group of Patriots, among them Joseph Habersham, Noble W. Jones, Edward Telfair, and John Milledge—all members of the Council of Safety created by the Patriots earlier—broke into the buried powder magazine at Savannah, stole 500 pounds of powder, sent part to Beaufort, S. C., and hid the rest in their own garrets and cellars. The gov-

3. Coulter, *Georgia*, p. 122.

ernor offered one hundred fifty pounds reward for information leading to the culprits who stole the powder, but, though everybody in town knew who they were, nobody came forward. A month later, on the night of June 2, other unknown miscreants spiked the cannon to be fired in honor of the king's birthday on June 4, and pushed them off the bluff. Angered but undaunted, the governor had the spikes drilled out and the guns hauled up again. Paradoxically, though, on the next day, when the first Liberty Pole was set up in Georgia, the yearning of all Georgians to heal the unhappy division between king and colony was revealed. The first toast drunk by the young Patriots was to "the King," the second to "American Liberty."

It was humiliating to Georgia, and a loss to her merchants, to be shut off from commerce with other colonies belonging to the association, the economic union that by forbidding trade with Great Britain had forced repeal of the Stamp Act. To ameliorate the local situation, the Council of Safety, under William Ewen, was ordered to take Georgia's case before the Congress and the other colonies. By summer of 1775 the whole province was seething with discontent and in the second provincial congress, which met on July 4, all the one hundred delegates, representing all the parishes, were present. Archibald Bulloch was elected president and George Walton secretary, and after their session at Tondee's Tavern they gathered at the Meeting House, where the Reverend John Joachim Zubly, a Presbyterian minister, preached a fiery sermon on the alarming state of American affairs. The story of the Rev. Zubly is one of political tragedy. In the beginning, he had been one of the most eloquent spokesmen for American liberties, but when it came time to sunder all ties with the British crown, he could not bring himself to do it. The anti-British talk he heard at the Second Continental Congress, to which he was a delegate, so alienated him that he began to speak openly against independence and the Liberty Party. Once the Patriots' hero, he now became despised as an enemy, and in 1777 he was banished from Savannah and half his estate was taken from him. He died in 1781, at fifty-six, broken in spirit and in fortune. Savannah, remembering the Patriot hero he was in the beginning, still has two streets named for him.

At the Second Continental Congress, which had so alarmed Dr. Zubly, Georgia at last had fully committed herself to the cause of liberty and independence and was with her sister colonies to the end. Her fidelity was quickly tested. The ban on any export or import trade with Britain and her possessions in the Caribbean worked a dreadful hardship on a state so deeply dependent on others, not only for her manufactured goods, but for a market for her own raw materials, and all industrial progress in the state came to a halt. Georgia's Patriots did not protest. They took instead an ever more belligerent attitude toward the royal governor and the men around him. The governor's military force of some two hundred men was spread thinly at seven small forts, from Savannah to St. Marys and up the Ogeechee at Fort Argyle, to Fort Augusta on the Savannah. They were supposedly loyal to His Majesty, but the assembly was not loyal to them, and refused to provide support for them. There was also a regiment of foot militia, which to Governor Wright's great outrage proceeded to purge itself of royalist officers and elect Patriots in their stead. With no troops to support him, Wright's rule was at an end. The administration of Georgia was in the hands of a provincial congress which placed all authority in a Council of Safety. This council, headed by George Walton, had carried out the Continental Congress' order to raise a battalion for the defense of Georgia, spending $5,000 in continental currency in doing so. Lachlan McIntosh was its colonel, Samuel Elbert, lieutenant-colonel, and Joseph Habersham, major.

Early in 1776, when two warships and a transport bearing troops from Boston arrived off Tybee, Major Habersham was ordered by the council to arrest Governor Wright and certain of his aides. Going unarmed to the governor's house, Habersham walked boldly past the sentry into the hall where Wright was meeting with his advisors. He marched to the head of the table, laid his hand upon the governor's shoulder, and told him, "Sir James, you are my prisoner." [4] Sir James behaved calmly enough, but his counselors jumped out the windows. Wright was paroled on his promise that he would not leave town or

4. Amanda Johnson, *Georgia as Colony and State* (1938; reprinted Atlanta: Cherokee Publishing Co., 1970), p. 133.

make any contact with the officers of the ships lying off Tybee Island eighteen miles to the south. This arrangement did not last long. Inactivity irked him, crowds gathered in front of the house and shouted insults, and stones were flung through the windows. After about a month of this harassment he slipped past his guards one night and made his way to His Majesty's ship *Scarborough,* lying in Tybee Roads.

Meanwhile, the provincial congress met and elected delegates to the Continental Congress—Bulloch, John Houstoun, Button Gwinnett, Lyman Hall, and George Walton. Their letter of instruction, prepared by Gwinnett, president of the council, gave a clear picture of Georgia's mood of the moment, a combination of concern for safety and determination to be free. Indians, which could only cause trouble, were to the south and northwest; St. Augustine, historically an enemy hideout, provided a rendezvous for British troops. There were blacks and Tories to worry about. These dangers were to be their main concerns. Yet, the letter of instruction pointed out, they should not forget the general good; "remember that the great and righteous cause in which we are engaged is not provincial, but continental." [5] As the delegates departed for the Congress, they carried with them no instructions other than reassurances from Archibald Bulloch that Georgia had all faith in their patience, firmness, and integrity, which would lead them to support all measures for the colonies' common good, and to oppose any that might be destructive.

Houstoun and President Bulloch, busy with important matters at home, did not attend. Thus it was that on July 4, 1776, in Philadelphia, Button Gwinnett—merchant-farmer turned politician, Lyman Hall—theologian turned doctor, and George Walton—carpenter turned lawyer, voted to approve the Declaration of Independence and thus inscribed their names forever on the book of Georgia history. The copy of the document they had signed did not reach Savannah until August 10. It was taken to the Liberty Pole and read aloud there, its imposing message creating wild excitement and the firing of thirteen cannon in salute. Four times it was read aloud before night fell. Then, in a

5. Jones, *The History of Georgia,* 2:215.

great torchlight procession, the people hanged George III in effigy and held a mock burial service over the corpse of royal
government.

As if in anticipation of this day, and the point of no return it
brought, Georgia's Council of Safety had already removed all
restrictions on the import of gunpowder and arms and named Lt.
Col. Elbert, Edward Telfair, and Major Habersham a committee to lay in, from whatever source—French, Spanish or
Dutch—400 stands of arms with bayonets, 20,000 pounds of
gunpowder, and 60,000 pounds of balls, bullets, bar lead,
grape, swan and goose shot. Money to pay for them would be
raised by issuing bills of credit, and anybody in the province
who failed to accept them, or who depreciated their value,
would be jailed. The arms committee was also charged with
seeing that each parish raised and outfitted a defense force, a
local guard of rangers, riflemen, and militia. To protect the beef
supply from rustlers roving the coast, the cattle were ordered
moved off the coastal islands.

While these preparations for possible war were going on, but
well before the signing of the Declaration of Independence had
closed all doors, from his refuge aboard the *Scarborough* Governor Wright had prepared an almost pleading letter by which he
hoped to woo his erring colony back to the right paths. He was
giving them one last chance, he said. He had heard from England, and from General Howe at Boston, and he could promise
that the forces now lying off Tybee would not commit any
hostilities against Georgia, though they could lay waste the colony if they wanted to. All they wanted was "a friendly inter-
course and a source of fresh provisions." As His Majesty's officers, they had a right to these things, Wright said, and he "as
the best friend the people of Georgia have," required that they
comply with the shipmasters' requests. If they would do this,
Wright said, he would go back to England and endeavor to obtain for them "full pardon and forgiveness for all their past offenses." Otherwise he could foresee only total ruin and destruction for them and their posterity. "Let it be remembered," the
governor concluded, "that I this day, in the King's name, offer
the people of Georgia the olive branch." [6]

6. McCall, *The History of Georgia,* pp. 300–301.

The Georgians were not interested in olive branches. They were interested instead in the rice which the British shipmasters coveted. Eleven ships laden with Georgia rice destined for other markets were bottled up in the Savannah River by the British ships off Tybee. When, in March of 1776, the British, getting hungry, decided to capture these boats, they sailed up the river to the five-fathom mark, and great excitement pervaded the town. Orders went out to dismantle the rice ships by removing their rudders, sails, and rigging to prevent the British moving them. Plans also were made to burn the town if any attempt was made to come ashore.

In the light of history the so-called Battle of the Rice Boats had certain ludicrous aspects, but to those involved on either side it was a matter not of laughter but of life and death. Ships were set afire and cut adrift. Boarding parties set off by night with muffled oars to board the British ships—and turned back under British fire so poorly aimed that only one man was wounded. In the end a British ship was set afire, ran aground, and was brought under cannon and musket fire from the shore, causing the British soldiers to flee across the marshes and the half-drowned rice fields, losing their arms and accoutrements. Major John Habersham distinguished himself in this embroglio, as did a young lieutenant named James Jackson.

One good came out of the encounter, however. When the Battle of the Rice Boats broke out, threatening the fall of Savannah, the provincial congress, highly perturbed, fled to Augusta, where it hastily put together the first written document creating a government for Georgia. No formal constitution, but a set of eight rules and regulations, it provided that there should be a president, who should also be commander-in-chief of the state's forces, that the safety council would continue in an advisory capacity, that it could not make laws, but the president must seek its advice and follow it. The congress then elected Archibald Bulloch as president, he being the only man who seemed able to bring the ofttimes quarreling Liberty factions together in some form of agreement. Less than a year later Bulloch, a man of stature equal to either of the three signers, died, and Button Gwinnett was elected Georgia's president and commander-in-chief. It was an act that was to lead to Gwinnett's own death, in a duel with Lachlan McIntosh, and a political division that would torment and weaken the Patriot cause throughout the war.

And so at last, all formal ties were broken between king and colony, and Georgia, stubbornly defiant but with a population still sorely divided in its loyalties, faced a future dark with challenge, bright with hope.

3

War by Bayonet, Noose, and Knife

OR the first three years of Revolution, the formal war was a murmur of agony and a shout of anger out of the north, an anguish shared inwardly, but not personally felt in Georgia. The classic battles that gave their names to Revolutionary history—Trenton, Princeton, Brandywine, and Germantown, Saratoga, and Valley Forge—were all fought far away. Georgia, in contrast, was the site of a bloody, brutal, creeping and crawling guerilla war, in which small groups clashed briefly and ran away. Prisoners were taken and paroled or exchanged, as in the more civilized wars of the past, or they might be hanged on the spot, or turned over to the Indians to be scalped and disemboweled. It was a war that turned father against son, brother against brother; it divided families, destroyed friendships, and the terms "Whig," for Patriot, and "Tory," for Loyalist, had a bitterness of invective, then, that the years have modified.

While waiting for the battered English to turn from their unsuccessful campaigns in the northern states in search of what they prayed would be easier victories in the south, warlike Georgians sought to mount some campaigns of their own. They were tragic failures. Long before Georgia had been founded, St. Augustine was a stronghold of the enemy, a refuge for any who would join the Spaniards against the English usurpers to the north. Now it was a refuge for any enemy of the Patriot cause, from wealthy Tory landowners to Indians and runaway slaves. Out of St. Augustine, raiding bands calling themselves Florida Rangers were probing deep into Georgia, killing, burning, and pillaging, striking by night to murder men, women, and children in their beds. New names come into the records, names of Tory leaders more savage than Indians—Brown, McGirth, Grierson, Schopol—the latter a South Carolina Tory who passed through Georgia en route to St. Augustine, recruiting Tory looters and pillagers all the way. Thomas Brown had been turned irreparably against the Patriots' cause when overwrought Liberty Boys in Augusta had punished him for his allegiance to the king by tarring and feathering him and dragging him at the tail of a cart. Daniel McGirth had turned Tory when a Patriot tried to commandeer his fine horse Gray Goose. What dark angers motivated the barbarities of Colonel Grierson and the guerilla Schopol are not set down. And there were on the Patriot side men of equal malevolence. John Dooley, Patriot leader, was murdered in his bed by Tories, but his son took dreadful vengeance later by murdering nine Tory prisoners. Patrick Carr claimed to have killed one hundred Tories, not all of them in battle, and Col. Grierson, while a prisoner, was killed for his barbarities by a Georgia soldier who was never reprimanded. The Revolution in Georgia, in short, was not alone a war between colonists and king's men. It was a war to the death among men—and women too—who might be little motivated by any spirit nobler than one of vengeance for some private wrong, real or fancied. It was not planned that way by Georgia's military leaders. Backed with $60,000 granted by the Continental Congress to raise and equip two battalions of troops from Georgia, Virginia, North Carolina, and South Carolina, the Georgians prepared to move against the ancient enemy at St. Augustine in the classic formations of European warfare. The expedition was a fiasco, for the troops that straggled down the coast were a rag-tag rabble, poorly trained, ill-armed, and expecting plenty of loot and plunder and no bloodshed. Their overall commander, General Charles Lee, was considered by General Washington to be the wisest and most experienced officer in the American army, but his handling of the ill-fated expedition against St. Augustine did not bear out this estimate. After a month of struggling through the swamps, his leading units turned back at Sunbury, never having seen an enemy.

If this first Georgia expedition was a fiasco, the next was a catastrophe. Colonel Lachlan McIntosh, commander of the Continental Brigade in Savannah, had been one of the three Georgians who had persuaded General Lee that the first campaign was feasible. Its failure gave McIntosh's political enemy Button Gwinnett a chance to do several things that much appealed to him. In early 1777, Gwinnett had succeeded the late Archibald Bulloch as president and commander-in-chief. In this dual capacity *he* now would lead an expedition against St. Augustine, and *he,* of course, would succeed where all the others had failed. Thus he not only would establish himself as a great military commander, he would clearly assert the doctrine that the civil authority should have control over the military. And he would send into military eclipse Lachlan McIntosh, the commander of the Continental Brigade at Savannah, whose troops had done good service in beating back the Florida Rangers south of the Altamaha. None of these happy dreams came true. The Gwinnett expedition turned out to be as poorly planned and carried out as that of General Lee had been. Historians have analyzed Gwinnett's errors and found that they stemmed jointly from ignorance, arrogance, and ambition, resulting in a political as well as a military disaster for Georgia— and for Gwinnett. It not only destroyed Gwinnett's reputation as a military man, it cast strong doubts upon his capacity to function wisely as president. He had been named to fill the unexpired term of the late Archibald Bulloch, and when it came time to run for the full term, he was soundly beaten by his opponent, John Adams Treutlen. Col. McIntosh, whose command of the Continental troops had been usurped by Gwinnett, made no effort to conceal his pleasure at Gwinnett's discomfiture, being heard to say openly that Gwinnett was a scoundrel and that he was glad that Treutlen had won. These, of course, were fighting words. Gwinnett challenged McIntosh to a duel, and at dawn on the morning following the challenge the two met on the field of honor. They fired at almost point-blank range—twelve feet— and each wounded the other in the thigh. McIntosh recovered.

Gwinnett died twelve days later. His death brought into the open the smouldering conflict between the Gwinnett and McIntosh factions. Lyman Hall, a power in politics, sought to have McIntosh indicted for Gwinnett's murder, and McIntosh voluntarily surrendered, was tried and acquitted. George Walton, who felt that the rift between the McIntosh and Gwinnett factions would destroy the patriotic cause in Georgia, persuaded General Washington to send McIntosh off to fight Indians and the British in the Alleghenies.

George Walton had been right. The friction between Gwinnett and McIntosh lighted fires of contention among the Whig leaders that burned throughout the war. Once there were two Whig governments, one headed by John Wereat and the Supreme Executive Council, the other by George Walton, Richard Howley, and George Wells. Arguments between them resulted in a duel between James Jackson and George Wells. Wells was killed, and Jackson went down, shot through both knees. Throughout the war the quarreling Whig leaders had as much trouble supplying the Patriot armies as they had in keeping peace among themselves, and once the Continental Congress had to give General Benjamin Lincoln a half-million dollars to keep the Georgia government going.

In the last days before the British left, Georgia's desperate need was for men as well as money. Many able-bodied men, disgusted with the government's ineptitude, had refugeed to North Carolina and South Carolina and Virginia, there to hide or fight as the spirit moved them. Word was sent out to them that they must either come home and fight, or their property in Georgia would be triply taxed.

By that time, 1778, Georgia desperately needed all the fighting men it could muster. The Loyalist partisans and their Indian allies, made bold by Gwinnett's failure and the earlier fiasco led by General Charles Lee, now were raiding north at will, burning barns and crops in the border areas, driving off cattle, stealing slaves, murdering and scalping men, women, and children as well as whatever militia they could ambush. Another foray toward St. Augustine, led this time by General Robert Howe, who had succeeded General Lee as commander of the southern division of the Continental armies, was as disastrous as those by

Gwinnett and Lee had been. When Howe's commanders firmly refused to take further orders from him, he turned his sick and fevered forces back to Savannah, having met no enemy except a few light skirmishers. From Savannah he went on to Charleston. There he bombarded his superior officer with complaints about the problems he had faced—a seacoast threatened with invasion, all the military works in ruins (Oglethorpe's old Frederica was grown up in brush and trees), a militia that came and went at its own whim, and stubborn, proud, and undisciplined officers who ignored his orders. It is not surprising, then, that when the king's forces did finally make their move against Savannah in the winter of 1778, the city under Howe's command did not long withstand their siege. In the Florida campaign General Howe's subcommanders had refused to take his orders. In the defense of Savannah, Howe refused to take the advice of his subordinates, Col. Samuel Elbert and Col. George Walton, who warned him he had deployed his forces wrongly. Guided by an old Negro man with the remarkable name of Quamino Dolly, the British troops came through the swamps by a secret path to the rear of Howe's forces and harried the fleeing Continentals through the town, driving them into the rice fields where half of them were killed, drowned, or captured. British losses were insignificant—seven killed and nineteen wounded. The American forces lost eighty-three officers and men killed, and more than four hundred noncommissioned officers and privates were captured. The aged inhabitants of the town also were made prisoners, and the private soldiers were induced to enlist in the British army. Those who refused were crowded aboard foul prison ships, where in the heat of the following summer four or five died each day. General Howe was not among those captured. He fled into South Carolina, where he faced a court-martial for misconduct in the defense of Savannah. He was acquitted and, in a duel, he shot through the ear General Christopher Gadsden, who had been one of his harshest critics.

The loss of Savannah presaged other defeats to come. Soon the British forces were stabling their horses in the Salzburger church at Ebenezer—though the pastor was a Loyalist—and Ebenezer never again functioned as a town. Moving on upriver, fighting against the fire-and-fall-back forces of Patriot guerillas, the British took Augusta early in 1779, and from there turned north and west into Wilkes County, driving the settlers into the Carolinas. In July Sir James Wright returned from England to Savannah and under protection of the British military, restored to power a royal civil government; Georgia was the only colony in which this was done. This had no appreciable effect on the Patriot forces still fighting in up-country Georgia. They were taking severe blows, but their cause was far from lost.

Elijah Clarke, John Twiggs, Samuel Elbert, John Dooley, and Benjamin and William Few are the names that ring like iron bells in this dark period. Leading pick-up aggregations of frontiersmen—backed up by South Carolina forces commanded by Colonel Pickens—they fell upon the British at a place called Kettle Creek, killed the commander, a Colonel Boyd, and scattered into the swamp his force of 800 men. Within a month the British had pulled out of Augusta, and with this British retreat there came a surge of hope that Georgia might at last be saved. It was not to be. An American force of some 2,300 men, under command of General John Ashe, was trapped on a point of land lying between Briar Creek and the Savannah River. Surrounded by ponds and streams, with no way to maneuver except across an open field which the British commanded with their guns, this force was quickly annihilated. Trapped Americans, pleading for mercy, were run through with bayonets, an act motivated less by innate savagery, it seems, then by a thirst for alcohol. The British commander had told his troops that any man who took a prisoner would lose his ration of rum. The defeat of General Ashe gave the British access to Indian country in the northeastern part of the state, and the scattered settlers there, finding themselves surrounded by Indians eager to support the English cause, soon found it the better part of valor to embrace that cause themselves.

Twiggs, Dooley, Clarke, and Elbert, however, doggedly kept on fighting their harassing guerilla war, for one ray of hope still shone in the darkness of defeat. The French, whose hatred for the British was deep and long-enduring, had come into the war on the American side, and had dispatched to these shores a fleet under Count d'Estaing, under orders to be of aid to the Americans in any way he could by harassing the British wherever he

found them. Eager for a fight, he arrived off the coast of
Georgia in late August of 1779, and on September 1 he sailed
up the Savannah River and boldly demanded of the British general,
Augustine Prevost, that he surrender the city. Prevost
stalled, knowing that reinforcements were on the way from
South Carolina. The British reinforcements arrived, and General
Benjamin Lincoln came up with his American land forces to
support d'Estaing's seaborne army. The siege began.

As days lengthened into weeks and the hurricane season drew
nearer, d'Estaing became impatient. He decided to attack. Waving
his sword, he led his French troops in three separate assaults
against the devastating fire of the dug-in British until he went
down, wounded so severely he could fight no more. The American
cavalrymen, led by the freedom-loving Pole, Count Casimir
Pulaski, followed d'Estaing into the hottest fighting, where Pulaski
was shot from his saddle, mortally wounded. The South
Carolinians, led by their light infantry, stormed the redoubts in
the face of galling musket and cannon fire, and it was in this
charge that the heroic Sgt. William Jasper, famed for saving the
colors in the battle of Fort Moultrie, S.C., was mortally
wounded. The Georgia column, led by General Lachlan McIntosh,
who had come home from the north to lead again the Continentals
of his native state, was committed late. By the time it
could be brought into action, the battle had already been lost,
and as his men moved up, over ground strewn with the bodies
of French and American dead and dying, the bugles sounded retreat.
The fighting had lasted only an hour and a half. By early
afternoon a truce was called so that the French and American
forces could come under the parapets to pick up their dead and
wounded. The truce was extended until dark, so many were the
dead, for of the 4,000 men d'Estaing led into battle, 1,100 had
been killed or wounded. That night, Governor Wright reported,
many rebel and French deserters came quietly into the city.
Behind them the French moved wearily back to their ships, and
General Lincoln led his Carolinians home in abject defeat.

Savannah was the bloodiest battle since Bunker Hill, and its
loss was a catastrophic defeat for South Carolina as well as
Georgia. Within six months, Charleston was in the hands of the
enemy, and the war in inland Georgia degenerated even further

into a war of extermination, fought under no rules but that of primitive survival. One of the most terrible of these confrontations took place in Augusta. There, in the fall of 1780, Elijah Clarke again had attacked the town, then under command of Tory Colonel Thomas Brown, who had been wounded and was lying in a two-story house known as McKay's trading post on a high hill. Clarke, unable to make a stand against a strong new force which came to Brown's support, was forced to withdraw, leaving some thirty wounded men behind, expecting they would be cared for. But Brown, it may be remembered, was the young Loyalist whom the Liberty Boys had tarred and feathered and hauled through town at the tail of a cart for making slurring remarks about the Patriot cause. And he had not forgotten this. He ordered thirteen of the wounded brought into the house and hanged, ordering his bed moved so that he could see their bodies dangling in the stairwell from a hook set in the rafters. Tradition has it that the thirteen hanged represented the thirteen colonies, and that one escaped by hiding in a closet. The other captives were less fortunate. They were turned over to Brown's Indian allies, who scalped and disemboweled them.

It was the low point of the Patriot cause in Georgia. Then, in the spring of 1781 Lt. Col. Henry Lee, known as "Light Horse Harry," took Fort Cornwallis at Augusta. It was a victory that marked the beginning of the end for the king's cause in America. The British by now had been driven into three seaport enclaves—New York, Boston, and Savannah. A bold soldier named James Jackson, veteran of the Battle of the Rice Boats and now a lieutenant-colonel, was given command at Augusta, and plans were laid for an attack downriver, taking the outposts on the Ogeechee and at Ebenezer. Now many of those who had despaired earlier, swearing allegiance to the British flag and taking refuge in Florida, began to come back to the Patriot cause, joining up with Colonel Jackson's Georgia legion, or Colonel John Twiggs' militia. To give professional direction to this still essentially guerilla army, General Nathanael Greene, commanding in the south, sent General Mad Anthony Wayne to Georgia at the head of some 400 Continental troops. They too moved south, to the Ogeechee River, where they would fight, and win, the last Revolutionary battle in Georgia, defeating the hangman

Loyalist Col. Thomas Brown, who fled to refuge in Savannah. The war in Georgia was to end, not with a bang but a whimper. The king was still in belligerent mood, but the people of England were tired of this tragic colonial war. In October of 1781 Cornwallis surrendered at Yorktown. Late in February of 1782 the House of Commons persuaded the king that a further prosecution of the war against the colonies was useless. By now it was clear that all the money spent and the blood spilled in a period of seven years had in no way weakened the determination of the stubborn American that his country should be free and independent. But though the fighting stopped, the war did not officially end. Hoping to salvage something from the wreck, the British stalled, offering terms of peace that did not specifically spell out that the one-time colonies were now truly free and independent states. Finally, though in May of 1782, word came to Governor Wright in Savannah that the troops there would be evacuated. Ships would come to take them off, and anyone else who wished to go. This caused mixed feelings among Savannah's citizens—relief that the fighting was over, deep anxiety about what would happen to them. About the first of July Savannah merchants sent to General Wayne a deputation seeking to learn what would happen to those who had stayed in Savannah, loyal to the king to the last. Wayne announced that his troops would protect the citizens from all disorder, but what happened to them in the long run was up to the civil authorities.

What happened was amazingly gentle, in a situation where feelings had run so high. The rules, as laid down by free Georgia's first governor, John Martin, were these: Those who wished to stay after the soldiers left would be allowed to remain in the city for a reasonable time, in which they could dispose of their property and settle financial matters. They then would be guaranteed safe passage to wherever they wanted to go. Those who had served in the British army would be allowed to come back after two years, if they so wished. Only those charged with murder or some other heinous crime would not be allowed to leave but would be held to face the Georgia courts. If the terms seemed generous rather than vindictive, it was the purpose of General Wayne and Governor Martin that they be so. Both knew that the entire merchant class of Georgia, and nearly all the trade goods in the state, were concentrated in the city of Savannah. It would do neither the state nor the nation any good for them to be shipped off to England or some other British port. The terms, in fact, were so reassuring that many of the loyalists stopped packing, took the oath of allegiance to the United States, and stayed on.

On July 11, 1782, the evacuation of the city was begun. By July 25, 7,000 persons had taken ship—5,000 of them Negro slaves, most of whom had been plundered from their Patriot masters by the British and the Loyalists. Of the others, 1,200 were British regulars and Loyalists, 500 were women and children, and 300 were Indians. Fewer than 300 in all were banished from the state, their property confiscated, and a number of these came back, swore allegiance, and were restored to citizenship. Their property was returned when they paid a percentage of its value into the public treasury. Many, of course, were not forgiven. The properties of Governor Wright and other Loyalist leaders were confiscated, and the proceeds were used to reward the victorious Whig generals. Colonel Jackson was given a town house in Savannah. Mad Anthony Wayne received an 840-acre plantation, and General Nathanael Greene was given two plantations totaling more than 3,000 acres. Elijah Clarke was given the lands of Thomas Waters, a notorious Tory looter and plunderer, and Count d'Estaing was granted 2,000 acres, which he never lived to enjoy for he died on the guillotine in the French Revolution.

On the day the first troops sailed, Colonel James Jackson received the keys to the city in a formal surrender and marched in at the head of his army, his men looking smart in their new issue of clean linen. Savannah, and Georgia, at last were free. But all around the city and far into the northern reaches of the state, fields, barns, and houses lay in ashes, desolate. Now would come the great task of healing not only the physical wounds the war had left upon the land, but the deep political differences that had scarred the hearts of the people.

4

From Revolution to Rebellion

*T*HERE were four fixed ideas which the citizens of Georgia brought with them out of the Revolution: the conviction that all men should be free and independent (except, of course, slaves); that every man be given an opportunity to earn a living for himself as best his talents and energy could provide; that every man should be free to worship in his own way, in any form that he saw fit; and finally, that all white Georgians, male and female alike, should have the opportunity for an education. But these were idealistic goals, and before they could be realized, problems must be solved that were closer at hand. Before a fledgling state government could be formed which represented all the people, the political divisions growing out of the bitter angers between Whig and loyalist must be healed. And before anything of lasting worth could be done, the permanent boundaries of Georgia must be established. The War of the Revolution was over, but along the unmarked borders frontiersmen and Indians still fought desultory battles with knife and tomahawk. Peace obviously must be established between white Georgians and the aboriginal warriors, the Creeks and the Cherokees. It was not too difficult to achieve at least the forms of peace. The Indian admired a winner at war, and the Americans had won.

Early in 1783, Governor John Martin called together the Cherokee chiefs at Augusta, where they established the boundary line between Georgia and the Cherokee nation to the north. Soon after, the Creeks surrendered to the state all the lands east of the Oconee. In these tracts later were laid out the two huge counties of Franklin and Washington, and from them came the forty thousand acres of land which would be granted the first state university, chartered in the following year, but not organized until fifteen years later.

Problems other than Indians faced the young government. From the fall of Savannah in 1778 to the departure of the British in 1782, the government literally had been wandering in a wilderness from one temporary backcountry hideout to another. Now, back in its old seat at Savannah, it must get the courts going again, schools established, soldiers mustered out, confiscated property disposed of—and hundreds of the hungry and homeless must be cared for under some sort of welfare arrangement that would provide to the destitute such necessities as corn, rice, and salt. It was these, as well as the famous generals, whom the new government wanted to care for, and for them the gifts were generous—not only to soldiers, but to civilian families who had stayed in the state, loyal to the cause, when it was almost completely overrun by the British. The grants actually had begun as the war began—one hundred acres to anyone who would enlist for three years, or the duration of the war. The next year this was increased to two hundred acres for every head of a family, plus fifty acres for each family member, including slaves. Nominal pay was expected for lands granted, but this was to be long delayed. This was an effort not only to bring in men who could carry a musket, but new settlers with desperately needed skills. A man who would build a grist mill on his land would get an extra one hundred acres; a sawmill or an iron works was worth two hundred acres. A town was even planned, around which these new men would settle. It would be located in Wilkes County and it would be called Washington.

In the years immediately after the war, more than four thousand Continental soldiers who had served Georgia, and the sailors in the state navy, received these grants of Georgia land. The distribution was not always an orderly process. The ex-soldiers were not polite and patient men, and when the first land courts opened to distribute the warrants, drunken crowds stormed the clerk's office, grabbing warrants by the handfuls. Under such loose controls, by 1789, warrants had been issued for three times more land than was available. So confused and disorderly was this "head right" system that in 1803 the land lottery was adopted, as being fairer to all and more easily administered.

The war had been a great economic and social leveler. The Tories who had been banished, their lands confiscated, were for the most part the well-to-do, the educated, the slave-owning gentlefolk of the big coastal plantations. The new class arising out of the land distribution were in the main the hill countrymen and piney-woods farmers who cultivated a little patch around their houses and let their hogs and cattle roam wild in the woods. Out of this group, in the fluid democracy of the next half-century, a new wealthy class would arise as acquisitive men gathered to themselves the land granted to their more hapless brothers—a class made up of the slave-owning cotton farmer, the small-town banker, lawyer, merchant, and landholding doctor. And out of this new democracy too in time would sink the poor white—called "po' white trash" in Georgia. As tenant farmer and sharecropper, his life was less secure than that of the slave, who had his necessities provided. All the poor white had to sustain him was a fierce and angry pride in the color of his skin.

The war had made of Georgia a dark and dangerous ground, and for a while after formal strife had ceased, there was no change in this lawless atmosphere. Highwaymen roamed the forest paths and the wagon roads, robberies and murders were common, and the man was foolhardy who did not go armed.

Despite the hazards of travel, though, there was heavy immigration into upper and central Georgia throughout the 1790s. Virginians pouring into the Broad River country and North Carolinians filling up the area around the little settlement of Washington soon shifted the center of population from the coastal area to a point in Wilkes County, north and west of Savannah. It was natural, therefore, that the frontier-dwelling Georgians should wish the capital moved nearer, and in 1786 this was done. The seat of government was moved temporarily to Augusta and in this year Scotch-born Edward Telfair, one-time Savannah merchant, was elected governor. He became one of the state's most notable chief executives—particularly remembered for his handling of the ever-threatening Indian problem, but his first act sorely outraged his former friends and neighbors in Savannah. He ordered the early records of the state moved from Chatham County to Augusta. Strong protests arose, but Telfair got his way, by dismissing the chief justice and all the associate justices of the Chatham County superior court. The records were loaded on covered wagons and brought to Augusta under armed guard.

Georgia, while struggling to place her internal affairs in order, was also quick to enter, though with certain reservations, into confederation with the twelve older states. During the brief period when the Articles of Confederation were the law of the land—which lasted from 1781 to 1789—she maintained the attitude of a little nation within an association of little nations, signing official documents in the name of "the State of Georgia by the Grace of God Free Sovereign and Independent." [1] Exercising this right of self-rule, in 1784 she passed a number of acts designed to bring in revenue, one a tariff law that applied not only to foreign countries but to trade with other states. The new young state might be free and independent but she quickly found herself desperately short of money. First revenues had come from the sale of confiscated property, which amounted to something over one hundred thousand pounds in pre-war currency, and when this ran out, land and property taxes became the main source of income. They began reasonably enough—twenty-five cents for each hundred acres of land, town lot or slave, soon to be raised to thirty-five cents for each one hundred dollars worth of land—classified as to its nature. The surface of Georgia was of infinite variety—sea island, salt marsh, tidal swamp, river swamp, pine lands, pine barren lands, and oak and hickory land—and each paid a different impost. There were also head taxes. A free Negro had to pay one dollar poll tax, and idlers paid two dollars, an idler being defined as a male

1. Coulter, *Georgia,* p. 168.

over twenty-one years of age who did not follow a lawful occupation or trade, nor farm five acres of land.

For the Constitutional Convention of 1787 Georgia elected six delegates, but being short of cash, she managed to send only four, and of these, only two, William Few and Abraham Baldwin, signed the Constitution. The next year, as cannon boomed in triumph, a convention met to ratify the act. To Georgia, this hopefully would be insurance, bringing her under the sheltering wing of the federal government against the Spaniards, who were still troublesome in Florida, and against the Creeks and Cherokees, who were growing extremely restless under the strong pressure of new settlements on their borders. Ignoring treaties signed five years earlier, the Creeks had gone on the warpath in 1787–1789, killing eighty-two people on the Georgia frontiers, and burning eighty-nine houses. The old Confederation of States had done nothing to prevent or punish this, and Georgians hoped that the new government, created under the Constitution, would take a different attitude. It did, sending General Benjamin Lincoln to Georgia to treat with the Creek leader, the Scotch-French-Indian Alexander McGillivray. Unhappily for Georgia, McGillivray turned out to be such an able trader that the treaty made the next year in New York so favored the Creek cause that it thoroughly outraged Georgians. In effect, it handed over to the Creeks all of Georgia except a small eastern strip. Furthermore, it committed the federal government to settle the Creeks forever on the land by furnishing them free tools and cattle, thus making husbandmen of them instead of wandering hunters. Georgia would not accept this. Her governors ignored the treaty, and her land-hungry people pressed relentlessly westward, shooting Indians on sight, until finally President Washington himself intervened. Georgians' regard for Washington, however, did not apply to other federal officials who favored the Indian cause, and the distrust of the central government implanted in the minds of Georgians in that time persists today.

In 1792, Georgia found herself locked in forensic battle with the government at Washington over matters other than Indians. The issue was state sovereignty. In 1794, the U. S. Supreme Court decided that Georgia had acted illegally in confiscating debts owed to one Brailsford, a British merchant, and ordered the money refunded. In 1793 in a far more famous case, a South Carolina loyalist named Chisholm brought suit against Georgia for confiscating his lands during the war. Georgia argued that no individual had the right to sue a sovereign state without its consent. The Supreme Court disagreed, in a decision which so angered the Georgia assembly that it passed an act providing that anybody who tried to carry out this judgment should be hanged. No one was hanged, and the row in time subsided, for the Eleventh Amendment to the U. S. Constitution, passed in 1798, confirmed Georgia's point of view.

In 1789 Georgia had adopted a new constitution of her own, a document which provided for a strong chief executive and a two-house legislature. Any citizen twenty-one years of age, who had paid taxes in the previous year, could vote—including women, if they so wished. Nine years later, in 1798, what was in effect a new constitution was written, mainly by the old soldier-duellist James Jackson, for whom a new up-country county had been named the year before. This document removed the property qualification as a requirement for service in the legislature, but the choice of representatives—one from the smaller counties, four from the largest, based on the "federal" population (in which five slaves were counted as three whites)— weighted the assembly heavily in favor of the slave-owning coastal planters. This constitution, which forbade the further importation of slaves, lasted, with only twenty-three amendments, until just before the Civil War. The weighting of the lawmaking powers in favor of the plantation counties, and the efforts of up-country Georgians to break it, created a political and social dichotomy that marked Georgia politics for generations. It was the clash of wills between the conservative coastal counties and the free-swinging, fast-growing up-country Georgia, whose frontiersmen had their eyes fixed on the limitless and profitable future. It was this conflict which brought about the removal of the capital from Savannah to Augusta. It was expressed, too, in the rapid proliferation of new counties—for each new legal entity brought new representatives from upper and middle Georgia to balance off the influence of the old staid coastal centers. In 1793 seven new counties were formed, all bearing the names of

Revolutionary heroes. In these raw new frontier counties, justice was rough and heavy-handed. Juries frequently met under a tree or in a private house. In the absence of a jail, prisoners were chained to trees or penned in a house while awaiting trial, and a tree limb served as a convenient gallows. Men frequently settled their differences without reference to the courts. Gentlemen killed each other in duels, and common men fought with fists and booted feet, teeth and horny thumbnails, the object being to gouge out an eye, bite off an ear, or knock an opponent down and stomp him to death. Laws were harsh and brutally applied. The pillory and the lash were common punishments. Vagabonds who wouldn't work could be arrested and hired out, their wages given to their families or to churches. If they still wouldn't work, they would be given thirty-nine lashes on the bare back. The realities of these raw, rough days were portrayed with only modest exaggeration by Augustus Baldwin Longstreet in his classic, *Georgia Scenes,* describing gander pullings, horse races, shooting matches, and wrestling bouts.

In 1794, the next year after the flurry of county-founding, Elijah Clarke, who proved as relentless in pursuit of gain as in the pursuit of Tories, sought to establish his own fiefdom, something he called the state of Trans-Oconee. He and a motley array of land-hungry speculators laid out several forts and towns and prepared to welcome settlers. Unhappily, their land across the Oconee still belonged to the Creek Indians, and President Washington asked Georgia to bring Clarke home. It was not an easy task, and the militia had to be called to force the old soldier to capitulate. Clarke's was not the only land speculation that marked these exciting, and inevitably corrupt, days. Nearly every political leader seemed to be affected by the speculative schemes that swept the state. Though Georgia ostensibly had abandoned its plans to claim everything from the Altamaha westward to the Mississippi, the ancient grant from Charles II was still on the minds of Georgia leaders, and they were eager to make something for the state, and for themselves, out of Georgia's supposed ownership of what is now Alabama and Mississippi. Out of their ambition came the greatest speculation of them all—known to history as the Yazoo Fraud. There were actually two separate speculations involving land along the

Yazoo River. In the first, in 1789, three syndicates, formed in South Carolina, Virginia, and Tennessee, sought to buy about twenty million acres of Georgia's western land for $207,000. This fell through when the Virginia Yazoo Company sought to pay Georgia in Georgia's own paper currency, which she didn't want.

Georgia in 1795 was back in the business of selling Yazoo lands. This time the groundwork for the scheme had been more carefully laid, its goal to sell from thirty-five million to fifty million acres at a price of about one to one-and-a-half cents an acre, or a total of $500,000—an obvious giveaway of rich, though still unsettled lands. A Georgia Yazoo Company had been formed, allied with a Georgia-Mississippi, an Upper Mississippi, and a Tennessee firm, and bribes, it later was discovered, were freely handed out to Georgia legislators in return for their votes to pass the enabling Yazoo Act. Land—as much as seventy-five thousand acres for one person—*or* barrels of rice or slaves or money were offered. The state itself was proffered what was in effect a bribe—two million acres allotted to the citizens of Georgia, to be distributed on a sliding scale to each county. Honest legislators whose moral scruples would not allow them to sign the Yazoo bill were persuaded not to attend the session at which the enabling act was passed, and Governor Mathews, a man not averse to questionable land deals, first vetoed, then after some minor changes, signed the bill. It is highly likely that neither he nor many of the legislators knew exactly what was in the bill. Some Georgians, though, realized the state had been swindled, among them William H. Crawford, just beginning what was to become a great career in national politics. Riots broke out, the corrupt legislature was turned out of office, and one or two members were run out of Georgia. The new legislature, meeting in 1796, quickly rescinded the Yazoo Act, declaring it null and void. To drive their point home, both houses met to publicly burn, with solemn ceremony, the act and all the documents connected with it—using, symbolically, fire from heaven—the sun's rays focussed through a magnifying glass. In addition, so ashamed was the state of the perfidy of its representatives, that it ordered that every reference to the act be obliterated from the records. So enraged was General James

Jackson, now a senator, at the rascality of his fellow Georgians, that he came home from Washington to fight four duels growing out of quarrels over the fraud.

The Yazoo frauds remained a tangled national issue until 1810 when the Supreme Court finally rendered a decision in the case of *Fletcher* vs. *Peck*. Speaking for a unanimous Court in what was the first case in which the Court declared a state law unconstitutional, Chief Justice John Marshall wrote that the motives of the legislators who voted for the sale were irrelevant, and that their grant was a contract within the meaning of the Constitution which a later legislature could in no way impair. Trying to untangle the knot, Georgia in 1802 ceded to the federal government all her territory west of the Chattahoochee River for $1,250,000. From it the holders of Yazoo warrants could receive five million acres, or the proceeds from the sale of five million acres. In addition, Georgia would receive from the federal government those lands ceded by South Carolina lying east of Georgia's western boundary. Reversing its stand about establishing the Creeks as farmers in western Georgia, the U. S. in turn promised to buy the Indian lands and give them to the state "as soon as it could peaceably be done on reasonable terms." [2] The Yazoo Fraud was the greatest, and fortunately the last, of the great land scandals that marked the early history of the state.

Though frauds and scandals, duels and desperadoes, Indian troubles and the rough justice of the frontier marked the history of Georgia in its first quarter-century of independence, there were less dramatic events taking place that would have their effect on the minds and hearts of Georgians forever. For it was in this period, roughly spanning the years from 1783 to 1825, that two of the ideas that Georgians had brought with them out of the Revolution—freedom of worship and the opportunity to get an education, began to take on tangible form. In 1783 Lyman Hall became governor, and in his inaugural message the concept of the university system of Georgia was born—a state-chartered school to be supported by endowment of state lands. Two years later, under Governor Samuel Elbert, a charter, written by three

2. Coulter, *Georgia,* p. 205.

Yale graduates, Abraham Baldwin, John Milledge, and Nathan Brownson, was accepted by the legislature. It provided not only for a university, but for elementary schools and academies, and a board of trustees was named. It was sixteen years later, in 1801, that this *Senatus academicus* finally got around to choosing a site for Franklin College, the first log-and-shingle university building. It was to sit on a small plateau above the Oconee River in newly formed Jackson County, amid 130 acres of rolling pine-clad hills. Here, President Josiah Meigs, another Yale graduate, held his first classes in the open, under the trees, while puzzled Indians peered from the bushes. Three years later, in 1804, on a stage under a brush arbor, the first ten graduates received their AB degrees, a ceremony witnessed by the residents of a new little town now proudly calling itself Athens, the classic city. Surrounded by still almost primitive wilderness, such dedicated men as Meigs, Moses Waddell, and Alonzo Church taught Greek and Latin to an unruly student body made up mainly of planters' sons. From their classrooms were to come the orators, the debaters, and the fighting men who would lead Georgia in the rebellion, and through the bloody Civil War, and the Reconstruction that followed. From them too came Crawford Long, whose discovery of ether as an anesthetic made bearable the pain of battle wounds. And thus was planted in Georgia's psyche a feeling of affection for the university, and an admiration for its graduates, which still exists today.

The university, though, was not the first institution of higher learning to open its doors in Georgia. In Augusta, Richmond Academy, created by the legislature in 1783, held classes in private houses until its own building opened in 1802. And in Savannah, Chatham Academy had been charted by the legislature in 1784.

While Georgia's Yale-trained intellectuals were struggling to put together a system of statewide education, other less learned but equally earnest men were seeking to bring the word of God to the lonely backcountry. As soon as the Revolution ended, itinerant evangelists, chiefly of the Baptist, Methodist, and Presbyterian faiths, began roving the state, vigorously competing for the souls of Georgians. There had been no restriction on religious worship under the king—except on Papists—and though all Georgians were taxed to support the established Church of England, sects of many denominations flourished. In 1772 a South Carolina Baptist named Daniel Marshall had organized the first Baptist congregation in Georgia, on Kiokee Creek, twenty miles from Augusta. This became the mother church of the Baptists in Georgia. By 1785, four more Baptist churches had been organized, under such noted ministers as Jesse Mercer, Silas Mercer, Abraham Marshall, and Sanders Walker. From this beginning the Baptists in time became the dominant denomination in the state. Close behind them, in 1786, came the Methodists, equal in fervor if fewer in numbers, a faith brought in by the Virginians and Carolinians who poured into Georgia after the Revolution. Two wandering preachers, Thomas Humphries and John Major, came into Wilkes County in 1786, going from cabin to cabin preaching and praying and making many converts. The Methodists introduced the soulful experience of camp meeting, which combined socializing at dinner-on-the-grounds with religious exhortation, and by 1788 there were enough of them to foregather with their wandering bishop, James Asbury, to form the first Methodist Conference in Georgia. The Presbyterians, whose faith came into Georgia with the Scottish Highlanders, were concentrated mainly at Darien, at Midway, and in Savannah, but when settlers began to come into up-country Georgia, Presbyterian evangelists moved out of the coastal area to form strong little churches near Washington in Wilkes County. The Episcopalians, the Lutherans, and the small group of Catholics who had come into Georgia after the Revolution, remained in their Savannah redoubts, not venturing forth for many years to join the evangelistic crusaders in upper Georgia.

The churchmen of all faiths were as firm believers in education as they were in religion, and their ideas along this line fitted exactly with those of Georgia's political leaders. In 1833 the Baptists established Mercer Institute, in Greene County, a modest layout consisting of two double cabins with a garret above. Two years later, in 1835, both the Presbyterians and the Methodists established schools of their own—each stressing manual labor. The Presbyterian school, Midway, near Milledgeville, later became Oglethorpe University. It did not survive the Civil

War, but the name still lives in Oglethorpe University in Atlanta. The Methodist school was Emory College, at Oxford near Covington, the parent school of Emory University in Atlanta. The Methodists in this same year founded the Georgia Teachers College at Macon. In addition to these church-supported institutions of higher education, each county had its "academy," roughly the equivalent of today's high school. They stressed Latin, Greek, and mathematics, and though some of them were excellent, most were little more than elementary schools. The elementary schools were known in Georgia as Old Field Schools, and they were for the most part pitiful institutions. Spelling, reading, and arithmetic, with some geography, made up the curriculum, and study was done out loud in a clamor of many voices. The school building was usually a one-room log cabin with a dirt, or puncheon, floor and homemade benches. The teachers were men usually poorly educated themselves. Many were given to drink, and all were quick to use the hickory switch. It was frequently their custom to collect a few fees from the parents and then drift on. Parents too poor to pay even the small fees charged by the wandering pedagogues were permitted to draw from a state fund called, naturally, the Poor School Fund. Any parent who paid taxes of fifty cents a year or less was declared poor, and his child was entitled to three years of free education, provided he wanted to go no further than reading, writing, and arithmetic. The judge of the county courts had to decide who was entitled to this help. Many Georgians didn't want to be pointed out as paupers in such a way, and many others did not care enough to send their children to school. As a result, by 1860, out of a white population of roughly 577,000, there were more than 40,000 men and women in Georgia who could not read or write. Around 1840, all school endowments were put in one Common School Fund, to be distributed to the schools on the basis of the number of white children enrolled between the ages of five and fifteen, but this plan didn't last long. The state soon went back to its old plan of helping only the poor.

All that had happened in Georgia since the Revolution ended—the in-surge of immigrants, the growth and prosperity, the defeats, the scandals, and the establishment of schools and churches, could hardly have had a greater effect on the future than an event taking place at Nathanael Greene's old seat, Mulberry Grove, seven miles upriver from Savannah. There, in 1793, Eli Whitney, a young New England tutor, acting on an almost casual suggestion from the general's widow, devised an "engine" for separating the short lint fibres of upland cotton from the seed, a task hitherto laboriously performed by hand. According to legend, Whitney, visiting in the Greene home, had fixed Mrs. Greene's watch. When a neighboring planter, holding a handful of seed cotton, discoursed on the fame and fortune to be earned by anybody who could make a device to separate the fibre from the seed, Mrs. Greene turned to Whitney and said, "You can do it." Whitney set to work, and in ten days had his "gin" in operation.

Whitney's achievement was to shape the future not only of Georgia but of all of what was to become the "Cotton South." It made the short-staple upland cotton a profitable crop and extended the cotton belt over a vast inland area, reaching deep into the Piedmont hills, and westward toward the Chattahoochee, where the long-staple Sea Island cotton, easier to separate by hand, could not be grown. In 1791, two years before Whitney's invention, Georgia produced 1,000 bales of cotton. Within a decade that figure had increased to 20,000, and by 1826, to 150,000 bales, making Georgia the leading cotton producer in the world. By 1860, production had reached 701,840.[3]

In expanding the plantation system beyond the boundaries of the old rice country, it extended, and more deeply imbedded, the economic necessity and the moral evil of slavery. Georgia in the years after the war had at first forbidden importation of slaves from foreign nations, and in 1817 a law was passed requiring that all foreign slaves be brought to Milledgeville, to be sold for the benefit of the state, unless someone could be found to pay their passage back to Africa. It had followed that by a ban on the import of slaves from other states for sale in Georgia. And in the minds of many Georgians slavery was an evil that in the name of common humanity must in time be ended.

The cotton gin changed all that. In 1824, the law against

3. Mills Lane, *The People of Georgia, An Illustrated Social History* (Savannah: Beehive Press, 1975), p. 150.

bringing in slaves from other states was repealed, and the trade in domestic slaves became a lucrative business. The importation of slaves from foreign countries had been prohibited by the Constitution after 1808, but just as their colonial forbears had ''rented'' black men for life from their South Carolina owners, Georgia cotton planters were soon buying all the foreign slaves that could be smuggled in. The state government tried to stop the traffic, offering as a reward one-tenth the price of a slave brought in to anyone giving information and, though a number of people collected rewards, nothing prevailed to stop the foreign trade. The slave smuggling continued until the beginning of the Civil War. As late as 1858, a slave ship, the *Wanderer,* slipped into Brunswick with 420 Africans. The ship was confiscated, but nobody was found to send them back to Africa, and the black men and women went on the Georgia market at more than a thousand dollars each. In 1800 there were fewer than 60,000 slaves in Georgia; in 1860 there were more than 460,000, and the price for an able-bodied man had risen from $300 to $1,800.[4]

Fear of the free Negro possessed the people of Georgia—there were 3,500 of them in the state by 1860—and the laws governing them were almost as rigid as those controlling the slaves. They could not vote, carry weapons, practice medicine, set type, or be taught to read and write. To preach, a free Negro had to have a license from a justice of the peace, and in Augusta, unless he was blind, he could not carry a cane or stick. He could not smoke in a public place, or follow a parade, and he had to be off the streets by 9:15 p.m. Despite these restrictions, which were often ignored, some ambitious blacks accumulated land and slaves of their own, and one became a physician of such repute that he had a white doctor as a partner. A slave owner could not give a slave his freedom without an act of the legislature, and this was rarely done—though for valiant service as a soldier in Elijah Clarke's forces during the Revolution, a mulatto boy named Austin Dabney was accepted as a freedman so that he could serve in place of his white master, and after the war was given 112 acres of land in Walton

4. Lane, *The People of Georgia,* p. 157.

County. A slave named Sam was freed by the legislature when he saved the state capitol from fire.[5]

The vast expansion of the plantation system brought increasing pressure upon the Creek Indians, and bloody retaliation by them on the Georgians pushing steadily toward the Chattahoochee boundary. There were more than 163,000 people living in Georgia in the first decade of the 1800s, and to many of them the War of 1812 offered the opportunity to settle once and for all the question of who should own and use the land, the white man or the Indian. It also held out the possibility that with federal help the nest of freebooters, hostile Indians, Spaniards, and British sympathizers who harassed south Georgia and her coastal islands from St. Augustine, might at last be destroyed. And in time this did come to pass. Georgia's Creeks, counting on the federal government to protect them, remained fairly quiet throughout the war. But the tribe in Alabama, stirred by a fiery old orator named Tecumseh, who dreamed of an Indian empire, massacred four hundred people at Fort Mims on the Alabama River. Georgia sent a force under John Floyd to support Andrew Jackson's Tennessee troops as they moved out of New Orleans to retaliate. In a bloody fracas at Horse Shoe Bend, the Creeks' main forces—armed with British weapons—were destroyed, though the Georgians themselves were pretty well chopped up as they wiped out two Creek villages. Out of this victory came a treaty under which the Alabama Creeks gave up their lands in southwest Georgia, and in nearly all of Alabama. Unhappily for Georgians still determined to push on to the west, it left all the lands from the Ocmulgee to the Chattahoochee—the Georgia heartland—in the hands of the seemingly friendly Georgia Creeks, many of whom had fought with Jackson against their Alabama brethren.

The end of the war marked the beginning of the end for Spain's interests in Florida. When Georgia's coastal islands after the war continued to come under harassment of freebooters and Indians out of north Florida, the U. S. warning to Spain was blunt: Control your people or get out. In 1818 Andrew Jackson moved in, took two Spanish forts, hanged two British

5. Coulter, *Georgia,* p. 260.

subjects, and raised the American flag over the province. In 1821, the victory was complete. Florida became a territory of the U. S., and Georgia's southern border at last was secure.

The treaty did little, though, to resolve the question of the Indian lands in Georgia. It had been nearly twenty years since 1802, when Georgia had given up to the federal government her crown-granted territory lying westward to the Mississippi, on the government's promise that the Indians would be moved out as soon as it peaceably could be done. Since that time, two states, Alabama and Mississippi, had been created out of these lands. And still in Georgia the Indian remained. The federal government, seeking to placate the angry Georgians, did buy certain lands from the Creeks—but not enough to push the Georgia borders all the way to the Chattahoochee line. And that might have been the end of it—with Georgians and Creeks and Cherokees sharing the land forever—if a strange stern man named George Troup had not come to the governorship. His words and actions were blunt and ominous. Under two U. S. presidents, James Monroe and John Quincy Adams, he threatened to take Georgia out of the Union and into war with the U. S. unless the Indians were bought off and forced to move. Finally, in 1827, under heavy pressure, the Creeks ceded the last of their lands in Georgia and moved on to lands, said to be of equal value, beyond the Mississippi.

There still remained the Cherokees of the Georgia mainland, a far more civilized and domesticated tribe than the Creeks. The Cherokees had early abandoned the life of the wandering hunter for that of the farmer and herdsman. They had their own organized and functioning nation, their own school systems, developed with the help of the federal government, their own churches and preachers, backed by the American Board of Commissioners for Foreign Missions. One of their members, a youth named Sequoyah, had performed the stupendous intellectual feat of creating an alphabet for the Cherokee language. They had a capital city, New Echota, where they printed their own newspaper, the *Cherokee Phoenix,* both in English and in the new tongue. They thought of themselves as a nation in their own right, and when their leaders visited Washington, they were accorded the courtesies due to foreign diplomats.

Their presence in the hills was not of great concern to Georgians, for the mountain land was not good cotton country. Then, in 1827, gold was discovered at Dahlonega. Now, following in the footsteps of Governor Troup, Governor John Forsyth in 1828 persuaded the legislature to extend the rule of Georgia over all the Cherokee country, and the next governors, George Gilmer and Wilson Lumpkin, followed his lead in moving against the Indians. Actually a strong legal hand was needed in Cherokee country, not to control the Indians but to protect them. The discovery of gold brought in a flood of rough and lawless men. There were also missionaries, stubbornly continuing their work in the Cherokee nation despite Georgia's law that their presence there must be registered with the state. The Supreme Court twice ruled against Georgia, holding that it had violated treaty agreements in its dealing with the Cherokees. Georgia's government ignored the Court's rulings and continued to do as it pleased. In 1831 it ordered the Cherokee lands to be surveyed, the next year it laid them out in ten new counties, and in 1833 it held a lottery and gave the land away—to whites. In 1834 it let the whites come in to take over their holdings, and warned the Cherokees they had only two years to move out of the way.

Some went, others held on. The holdouts, led by half-breed John Ridge, Major Ridge, and Elias Boudinot, finally agreed to give up their land and leave, in return for five million dollars, paid not by Georgia but by the federal government. Another group, led by John Ross, refused, and in 1838 these were rounded up by U. S. troops led by General Winfield Scott and marched away to the west. In one of the saddest migrations in all history, fourteen thousand men, women, and children were moved overland on foot on a journey that took five months, and more than four thousand of them died of illness, accident, or sorrow. One small group escaped the roundup and fled into the mountains of North Carolina. There they found sanctuary under a friendly state and federal government and there they have remained since, clinging doggedly, until recent years, to their ancient tribal customs. It was not one of the most glorious moments in Georgia's history, this period when incoming settlers were pushing with stubborn anger against her frontiers.

The years after the War of 1812 were a time of great growth and prosperity for most of the nation. Steamboats moved up and down the rivers, a national road was under way, canals were being built, and the first railroads began to crisscross the land. In 1820 the Missouri Compromise, a detente worked out between the slave states and the free states as to which new states coming in should be slave or free, had postponed for at least a generation the final bloody confrontation between North and South. But the 1820s brought the threat of economic trouble to the Seaboard South, particularly to Georgia. There were many causes. The old lands that had been under cultivation for generations were beginning to wear out. The tobacco and rice markets were on a decline; men who owned slaves were moving west to the newly opened cotton lands in Alabama and Mississippi, and much money was being spent on slaves to work these lands, instead of going into the organization of the banks, shipping lines, railroads, insurance companies, mines, and factories the region needed. In this period, almost unnoticeably, the national dichotomy, the social and psychic drifting apart, the separation of the industrial North from the agricultural South, began to intensify. From now on an unbridgeable gulf would swiftly widen between the slave state and the free. In population, per-capita wealth, mechanical horsepower, in all skills other than farming, the Southern states, Georgia among them, began slipping behind the rest of the nation. It was not a painful process in the beginning, nor was it highly visible at first. Growth and expansion went on steadily, particularly in Georgia where the new lands, taken from the Indians, could be distributed to the incoming settlers.

Even before the Indian removal, the steady flow of settlers into upper and central Georgia had shifted the population center so far to the west that the old capital at Louisville was now considered to be in the backwash of the in-migration. Milledgeville, nearer to the center of the state, was laid out as the capital, and in October of 1807 fifteen horse-drawn wagons, guarded by a troop of cavalry, transferred the treasury and the state records to the new town being created around four twenty-acre squares. One of these was called Penitentiary Square, an indication that even so early as the first decade of the 1800s, Georgia was thinking with compassion as well as concern of the control of a growing criminal element. The penitentiary was a first move away from the harsh punishments of the earlier days—when a horse thief, for example, might be given thirty-nine lashes on three separate days with an hour per day in the pillory, and twenty days to a month in jail. For a second offense, hanging was the penalty. The penitentiary was not finished until 1817, and two years later there was strong effort made to abolish it as a failure. Those incarcerated, it seems, were not being turned into good and decent law-abiding men overnight—and what was more—the simple trades they could work at while in prison did not pay the expense of running the place. No better system, however, was devised, and the prison system continued, drawing harsh criticism for its faults—as it still does today. Some modifications of the codes did make prison life a little easier. By 1818 sheriffs were required to furnish prisoners with blankets, clothing, fire, and medical attention, and in 1823 the jailing of debtors was forbidden. In 1837, Georgia began taking care of its insane at Milledgeville, in an institution that still exists.

While the tide of immigrants rolled on westward, leaving dead towns in its wake, the old fortress town of Augusta, on the Savannah, was continuing in its role as a great trading post. Dominated in the beginning by a shrewd Irishman named George Galphin, it carried on a trade that reached from Charleston to St. Augustine and Mobile. Established in 1735, just two years after the founding of Savannah, Augusta served the dual role of fort and market. Here, in the early days, from all of north and central Georgia, the Indians brought bales of deerskins and beaver fur, much favored by English gentlemen for hats and breeches; and here the Charleston traders came with their packhorses loaded with the blankets and the ornaments the Indians loved. During the Revolution Augusta had been a bloody battleground which changed hands a half-dozen times, and at the end of the war its people were so destitute that the planters had to pole supplies upriver to keep them from starving. The town literally had to start all over again, and, with the fur trade dwindling, its salvation this time was tobacco. Virginians coming in to take over newly opened Indian lands brought with them their knowledge of growing tobacco. Soon the huge rolling hogsheads, turning on axles and standing high as a man's head, were being pulled by mules and oxen into town, and well into the next century Augusta was the state's leading tobacco market. Slowly the rude frontier town began to take on the aspects of civilization; Richmond Academy was founded; the *Augusta Chronicle and Gazette* began publishing, surviving to become today the oldest newspaper in Georgia; a Thespian Society and a Library Society were formed, and the foundation was laid for the opening of the Medical Academy of Georgia, first medical school in the state.

As the century moved on, cotton supplanted tobacco, and the laden cotton wagons rumbled into Broad Street, bound for the wharves where fifteen steamboats and a fleet of flatboats waited to load on 800 to 1,000 bags—each containing 250 pounds of lint cotton—for the trip downriver to where the sea-going vessels waited at Savannah. Augusta's status as a cotton market made opportunity for another "first" which, for good or ill, was to mark the face of the South for generations. Twelve miles north of Augusta on the Carolina side, William Gregg in 1845 set up a little textile mill and around it laid out the first mill village in the South. The mill village as a social institution had its faults. The hours in the mill were long and pay was low and the working conditions, especially for children, were fearful. But the simple houses, the schools and churches, the job for cash wages, did create equality of status and opportunity for men and women for whom the slave-supported plantation had no place. The "lint head" of the mills might be no landed gentleman, but he was far from "po' white trash."

From 1840 to the mid-fifties recurring epidemics of yellow fever raged in the city, carrying off the citizens in such numbers that vehicles to take away the dead were lacking, and wheelbarrows were used to trundle them to the cemeteries. Augusta was not alone in being the victim of this pestilence. Savannah was severely stricken in 1820 and again in 1854. Children were particularly hard hit in all Georgia cities, both with the fever and with a dreadful dysentery.

Despite recurring plagues of illness, Indian troubles, and the wasting of the land that was a grim by-product of the cotton economy, the early decades of the 1800s were promising times in Georgia, particularly in that area lying west of Augusta across the state via Macon to Columbus on the Chattahoochee. It was a time of steamboats on the rivers, of cotton factories springing up where falling waters offered power, and the coming of the first steam train. The era of the traveler on horseback was ending, the transport of people and freight by oxcart and mule-drawn wagon was coming swiftly to a close. Typical of the development taking place in central Georgia was the city of Macon, laid out in 1823 on the plan of the ancient city of Babylon. It took Georgians ninety years to move from Savannah to a point on the Ocmulgee River, some two hundred miles northward as the crow flies. But there on the fall line which marked the boundaries of an ancient sea, there was quickly created an inland port, linked first by flatboats, then, after 1829, by steamboats on the Oconee and the Altamaha, with the coast at Darien. Within a year of its founding, Macon had become a retailing and distributing center for middle Georgia, with the combined characteristics of the agricultural region between the fall line and the red clay hills to the north where industry was developing. Its climate, as its soils, was mixed—sultry summers, crisp falls, mild winters, and cool, flowery springs. No other Georgia town until Atlanta's founding demonstrated more clearly than did Macon the hunger for new land, for new opportunities to work and earn and pile up wealth. By 1828, five years after its formal founding, nearly forty thousand bags of cotton came into the town, and from then on, from fall to spring, the roads leading to Macon from both banks of the Ocmulgee were filled with wagons, bringing in the cotton and carrying back supplies to the plantations. Columbus, founded five years later on the Chattahoochee, soon was to show the character of a vigorous manufacturing center.

Georgia, with its deep, slow-flowing rivers draining nearly every area of its terrain, was a vigorous pioneer in the development of the steamboat, and once pushed for a series of canals that would link the main river basins laterally between the fall line and the Piedmont hills. The canal project failed, due to the lie of the land and the porous nature of the soil, but a series of turnpikes soon connected all the main cities with the capital at

Milledgeville. It was the rivers, though, and the steamboats that plied them, which interested Georgians most. Hardly had the war cry of the Indian died out before the steamboat whistle was blowing. The state worked earnestly to keep the channels clear of snags and sandbars, but Georgia's confidence in the steamboat was not confined to navigation of inland rivers. In 1819, the Savannah Steam Ship Company sent the *Savannah,* under sail augmented by steam power, across the Atlantic to Liverpool. This was the first ship ever to cross the ocean aided by steam, and in 1834 Savannah registered another seagoing "first." Gazaway B. Lamar, a Savannah banker and cotton merchant, had iron plates made for him in England which were riveted together in Savannah into the first iron ship ever seen in America.

The rowdy and raucous riverboating days did not long survive. In the unending search for a better way to move raw materials to market and bring manufactured goods to the hinterlands, the steamboat in the 1830s began to give way to the steam train, and by 1860 and the beginning of the Civil War, a network of railroads covered the state. And not Milledgeville, but a new and brash and bustling little town known first as Terminus, then as Marthasville, for Governor Wilson Lumpkin's daughter, and later as Atlanta, was the hub of this network.

As had been the case in other matters in the past, Georgia's fierce railroad-building drive had been prodded into action by the South Carolinians. Charleston promoters in 1833 had built a line to the Savannah River opposite Augusta which tied in with the first road to be built in Georgia—the Georgia Railroad organized by an Athens man, James Camak, running between Augusta and Athens. Augusta interests soon got control of this line, and pushed it west from Union Point to the Chattahoochee. This vastly annoyed the Athenians, who felt themselves isolated at the end of a branch line. It also alarmed the citizens of Savannah, who felt that this would serve as a feeder line to the Charleston road, enabling the Carolinians to drain off to their own docks and wharves shipping that had been coming downriver to Savannah. Savannah therefore began building her own road, the Central of Georgia, to Macon in the heart of the state. It reached there in 1843—thus tapping the rich central area of Georgia with its profitable cotton trade.

And now the transportation pattern that was to shape and influence Georgia's economics, and the personal lives of millions of Georgians until the truck and the interstate highway network came, began to fall into its final form. The Georgia Railroad out of Augusta pushed westward from Union Point toward the Chattahoochee. The Central of Georgia moved northward from Macon to somewhere in the pinelands of the Georgia Piedmont; and where these two lines would intersect, a state road, the Western and Atlantic, would start its route to Chattanooga. Here would be driven the stake that would mark the zero mile post, and around this stake there would grow up the city that soon was to become the transportation center, the political capital, and the thriving commercial entrepôt, not only of Georgia, but of all the Southeast. There was nothing but the lie of the land, the geography, that brought about the crossing of the rail lines here. There was no population, no commerce, to draw the railroad to this spot. There was only the little fort at the old Creek village known as Standing Peachtree, on the Chattahoochee; the rude log house of Hardy Ivy, a pioneer settler of the newly opened Cherokee lands; the farm of his brother-in-law; and to the west on the stage coach route, a new tavern and post office called White Hall. To the east in the pine-clad hills near a great mountain of grey granite lay the young town of Decatur, its citizens already showing concern that the new railroads would bring with them noise and soot. And of course they did bring noise, and soot, but they brought vast prosperity too. It took time, but new wealth was inevitable. For, if a straight line were drawn on a map from Boston, through New York to New Orleans, and another from Chicago to Miami, they would intersect at a point only slightly northeast of Atlanta. The northeast leg would serve a vast region lying along the eastern slope of the Appalachians, and stretching from the St. Lawrence Valley in Quebec to the Alabama coastal plains. The northwest leg, from Chicago to Miami, would serve the rich Ohio Valley and the upper Mississippi, passing through the gap in the Appalachians at Chattanooga from where there was easy grade to Atlanta.

Thus Atlanta, standing where these lines crossed, became in a partial sense the combined counterpart of the cities lying at the end of the line. There was something of Chicago's raw, rude hustle about her—her mule market was in miniature a counterpart of Chicago's stockyards. There was something of New York's concern with the complex forms of exchange and their concomitants, with banking and the law, and with communication and the clerical and managerial skills. There was a violent divisiveness in her politics, which divided her citizens into two factions designated as Moral Men and Rowdies. And there was a trace, though not much more, of the grace and leisure of old New Orleans and Savannah, where gentlemen walked home for lunch and a postprandial snooze.

And now, as steel rails began to link Georgia with the rest of the nation, other matters began to draw her deeper into the web of national politics. The issue of admitting Texas to the Union brought on fierce contention between the national Whigs and Democrats. The Northern Whigs, and Northern men in general, opposed Texas's admission on two grounds—it could bring on war with Mexico and it would disturb the balance in Congress by bringing another slave state into the Union. But Georgia's Whigs and Union men alike had deep ties with Texas. There was hardly a family which did not have a younger son or an uncle or a cousin who had gone to Texas to seek his fortune, and many of them had become leaders there, in war and politics. Mirabeau Bonaparte Lamar, a native Georgian, was the second president of the Texas Republic. James W. Fannin led a Georgia contingent to its death in the Goliad massacre in 1838, and a Georgia woman, Joanna B. Troutman, of Crawford County, fashioned out of white and blue silk the first Lone Star Flag.

Texas came into the Union as a slave state, in December of 1845, and as the fighting started in 1846, Georgians volunteered eagerly. Ten rifle companies, totaling some 910 men, were recruited from communities all over the state, but the role they played was minor. They were used, in the main, to guard supplies and money trains, and none ever got within earshot of the enemy. Their casualties from disease, however, were heavy. When they mustered out in June of 1847, 145 men had died, and more than 300 had already been discharged.

Though the war with Mexico linked Americans geographically in a country that now stretched from sea to sea, political

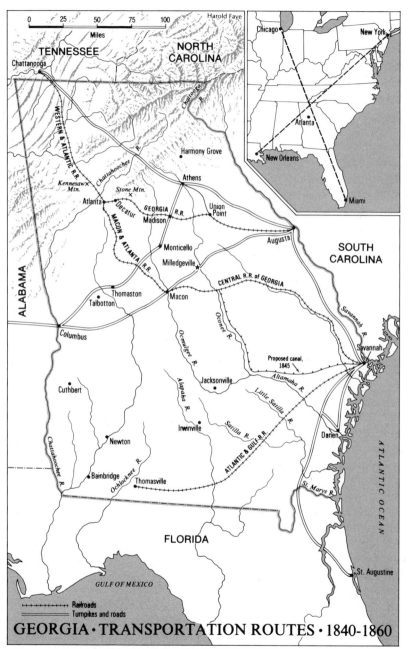

Harold Faye

0   25   50   75   100

Miles

TENNESSEE

NORTH CAROLINA

Chattanooga

Chattooga R.

WESTERN & ATLANTIC R.R.

Chattahoochee R.

Harmony Grove

Kennesaw Mtn.

Stone Mtn.

Athens

Atlanta

Decatur

GEORGIA R.R.

Union Point

MACON & ATLANTA R.R.

Madison

Augusta

Monticello

SOUTH CAROLINA

Milledgeville

CENTRAL R.R. OF GEORGIA

Savannah R.

ALABAMA

Thomaston

Talbotton

Macon

Ocmulgee R.

Oconee R.

Savannah

Columbus

Alapaha R.

Jacksonville

Proposed canal, 1845

Altamaha R.

Cuthbert

Little Satilla R.

Irwinville

Satilla R.

Darien

ATLANTIC OCEAN

Newton

Chattahoochee R.

ATLANTIC & GULF R.R.

Ochlocknee R.

Bainbridge

Thomasville

St. Marys R.

FLORIDA

St. Augustine

GULF OF MEXICO

⊢⊢⊢⊢⊢⊢⊢ Railroads
———— Turnpikes and roads

GEORGIA · TRANSPORTATION ROUTES · 1840-1860

Chicago

New York

Atlanta

New Orleans

Miami

and economic issues that had been growing for three decades further divided them psychically and emotionally, and sorely exacerbated sectional differences. In 1816, to protect New England manufacturers, Congress had imposed tariffs against foreign imports. These were, in effect, indirect taxes levied upon the agricultural South, causing Southerners to pay more for clothes and shoes, and to receive proportionately less for their raw products. Outraged Georgians and South Carolinians soon resolved to wear their own homespun rather than buy cloth from the North, but the imports increased, year after year. Finally, in 1828, the South Carolina legislature adopted eight resolutions, drafted by John C. Calhoun, which declared the tariff laws unconstitutional. His arguments rested on the long-disputed doctrine of nullification, refuge of the discontented since the early days of the Republic, which held that any state could declare null and void within its own borders any act of Congress the people of the state itself believed to be unconstitutional. There were those, of course, who held that nullification could be neither a peaceful nor a constructive remedy and would eventually lead to strife and disunion, but Calhoun's ideas caught on strongly in the South, and his home state in 1832 went one step further and adopted an Ordinance of Nullification. This led President Andrew Jackson to push for a law—called the Force Act—which would hold nullification to be an act of treason. Under this act, federal law would be enforced by federal troops. A new and less offensive tariff act, however, made it unnecessary to invoke the Force Act. Earlier in the same year the Georgia legislature, after bitter debate, had refused to pass a nullification act. The argument, though, caused serious dissension within the two political parties that, since the early 1800s, had ruled the state. The Troup party, voice of the planter class, was founded by James Jackson, supported by the highly regarded William H. Crawford, and named for George Troup, the foe of the Indian. It favored nullification. The other faction, supposedly representative of the frontiersman, and named for John Clarke, the son of Elijah, opposed it—as did such distinguished former Troupers as Wilson Lumpkin and John Forsyth. The quarrel over nullification changed the pattern of politics in Georgia, from parties owing their allegiance to personalities, to parties more closely tuned to national issues. The Troupers became a states-rights party, owing allegiance to the Whigs, opponents on the national scene of Andrew Jackson and his theories of strong central government. John Clarke's faction gravitated to the Union cause, out of which came the Jackson-supporting Democrats. Thereafter, until the Civil War, the governorship was swapped back and forth between Whig and Democrat until the Whigs, for their attitude on slavery, passed from the political scene.

Thus there began more than one hundred years ago the conflict over states' rights versus federal authority, which survives today. Nullification was a legal concept used by both sides in the Civil War, and was revived again in the mid-1950s, when several Southern states declared null and void the Supreme Court's action in desegregating the public schools. The quarrel over tariffs also indicated the economic gulfs that separated Yankee trader and Southern planter. The slavery question, moral as well as economic, was part of this pattern of regional division, and was the illness for which there was no cure.

In the wake of the Mexican War, though, there was a brief time of respite. Congressman David Wilmot of Pennsylvania ceased introducing in Congress his Wilmot Proviso, forbidding any territory taken from Mexico to enter the Union as a slave state, a piece of legislation that had angered Georgians to the point of threatening to secede from the Union. Under the Compromise of 1850, California, bought from Mexico at the war's end, was brought in as a free state. It was left up to the citizens in the territories of New Mexico and Utah to decide for themselves whether they should come in as states slave or free. The compromise, to quell the growing talk of secession in the South, also included a strong Fugitive Slave Act which set up fines for anyone who would help a slave to escape. This caused outrage in the North, as the Wilmot Proviso had insulted and outraged the South. But the compromise on the whole served to stem for a little while the onrushing tide of partisan anger that was leading on to civil war. Georgia in the long run was the state which swung the South to acceptance of the compromise, and stilled, for a little while, the talk of secession. Representative Alexander H. Stephens and Robert Toombs and, notably, Howell

Cobb, Speaker of the House, were three Georgia leaders on the national scene who joined with Henry Clay and Daniel Webster to work out the compromise. At a meeting in Macon, in the fall of 1850, Stephens and Toombs joined Cobb in one desperate, last-minute effort to save the compromise—and the Union. They persuaded two radical firebrands from other states, Robert Barnwell Rhett of South Carolina and William L. Yancey of Alabama, to go along with them. The Macon meeting led to another in December at Milledgeville at which the conservatives succeeded in passing what came to be called the Georgia Platform. Written by Charles J. Jenkins, this document pointed out that the South had been greatly provoked, and would be pushed no further, but that the compromise was the only alternative to the dissolution of the Union and therefore should be supported. The Georgia Platform held the Union together as the other Southern states—even fire-eating South Carolina—supported the compromise, but all political party lines in Georgia began to crumble.

With the California-Utah-New Mexico issue seemingly settled, at least temporarily, there now came upon the national conscience the question of Kansas and Nebraska. The act which created these two territories provided that they decide for themselves whether slavery would be permitted, a compromise arranged by Stephen A. Douglas, to the vast delight of the South. Proslavery settlers rushed in to found communities at Leavenworth and Atchison, and the free-state forces rushed to populate the state with antislavery votes. Guerilla fighting broke out and "Bleeding Kansas" became a preview of the savage civil war that was to come.

Georgians were left relatively untouched by this. Few of the slave-owning settlers came from Georgia, but the state did provide money and free transportation over the state railroad to any slave-owning migrants passing through en route to Kansas. Proslavery feeling ran high in the state, but it expressed itself in less violent ways than warfare. Many Georgia planters and merchants, for example, resolved to cut off all trade with the North and deal directly with Europe instead, sending Georgia cotton and timber to Europe in Georgia-owned ships, and bringing back the goods Georgians did not themselves manufacture.

Affairs other than the slavery question also concerned them—notably state politics. The planter, whether the rice-growing coastal aristocrat represented by James Jackson, or the upland merchant-doctor-lawyer who raised cotton on the side, whose spokesman was William H. Crawford, had more or less dominated Georgia politics since the Revolution. Now came a man of Andrew Jackson's mold to challenge the white-columned mansion set. Joseph E. Brown, a yeoman farmer, a plainspoken young judge from the hills of north Georgia who in his youth drove a team of oxen to Dahlonega to sell wood and corn, in 1857 was chosen Georgia's governor over Benjamin H. Hill. His nomination startled many, including Robert Toombs, who when he got the news, is alleged to have said in genuine puzzlement, "Who in the hell is Joe Brown?" [6] Brown himself was probably equally surprised. He was at home shaving, after shocking wheat in the fields all day, when word came to him of his nomination. Brown proved to be a good choice. A strong states-righter who was born in South Carolina, he was also an able executive, a businessman who straightened out the state's slipshod bookkeeping, increased the income from the state railroad, and for the first time gave to the Georgian of the hill country and the pine barrens the feeling that he had a friend in the statehouse. The state which Brown took over was one whose leaders were moving swiftly toward seccession and inevitable war. In 1854, as the Kansas civil war began, the old Whig party, its Northern and Southern adherents sorely divided over the slavery question, went out of existence. Some Georgia Whigs, like Alex Stephens and Robert Toombs, joined the Democrats. Others, among them Benjamin H. Hill, became part of a strange coalition called the Know-Nothing Party. And in the North rose a new political group calling itself the Republican party, which had for the principal plank in its platform an absolute and irreversible opposition to the extension of slavery, any time, anywhere. Its candidate for the presidency in the election of 1856 was John C. Frémont, Savannah-born of a French émigré, Western explorer—and implacable foe of slavery.

Now Georgia's oratorical big guns began to thunder. No

6. Amanda Johnson, *Georgia as Colony and State,* p. 352.

longer in a mood to compromise, Robert Toombs, speaking of the Republicans, called them public enemies who had only one motivating force—hatred for the people of the slaveholding states. Toombs expressed what many Georgians felt about Republicans, and his views were echoed. Governor Herschel Johnson and Howell Cobb were both devoted to the idea that the Union could and must be saved, and both foresaw secession if Frémont were elected. And to Joseph E. Brown—if the Constitution could no longer protect the states in their right to own slaves—then the time had come to dissolve the Union.

Secession fever grew even stronger shortly after Brown was elected for his second term. In the Kansas civil war a fanatic abolitionist named John Brown, with four of his sons, brutally hacked to death five proslavery settlers at a place called Pottawatomie Creek. Unpunished and unrepentant, he sought to put in action an even bolder plan three years later, at Harpers Ferry, Virginia. He and a handful of followers raided the federal arsenal, Brown's idea being to arm the slaves on the surrounding plantations and set off a South-wide slave revolt. He and his men were still in the arsenal when Col. Robert E. Lee arrived with a company of Marines. In the fight that followed, ten of Brown's men, including two of his sons, were killed, and Brown was captured. He was tried, convicted, and hanged, and on his death became a martyr.

John Brown's deed struck terror into the hearts of Southerners who since colonial days had lived in fear of a slave rebellion. Governor Joseph E. Brown, seeming to feel that conflict was now inevitable, began to speak of putting together a defense force, shifting Georgia's trade completely away from the North to European markets, and calling for a convention of the slaveholding states.

The event that made secession inevitable, so far as the South was concerned, was the election of Abraham Lincoln, Republican candidate for president. His opponents were Stephen A. Douglas, candidate of the Northern Democrats, earnest seeker after formulas which would allay passions and bring about compromise on the slavery issue; John C. Breckinridge, candidate of the Southern Democrats, who pushed for the extension of slavery; and John Bell of the Constitutional Union Party, a Tennessee slaveholder who sought to hold the Union together by ignoring the problem of slavery entirely. Georgia split its vote between Breckinridge and Bell, ignoring the fact that a Georgian, Herschel V. Johnson, was running for vice-president on the Douglas ticket.

Lincoln was no hot-eyed abolitionist of the John Brown stripe. His personal feeling was that slavery was morally wrong, but it was not worth the destruction of the Union even to bring an end to so great an evil. He had opposed expansion of slavery into the territories in the profound belief that the nation could not exist half-slave, half-free. And his goal first and foremost was to save the Union, to find some bridge of understanding across which North and South could meet.

Almost alone among Georgia's leaders Alexander H. Stephens seemed to understand this. At the convention to decide what the state should do, called by Governor Brown at the urging of Robert Toombs, Thomas R. R. Cobb, and other fiery secessionists, Stephens argued with squeaky but earnest eloquence against hasty action. A Republican president could do little harm to the slave-owning states in the face of a Democratic Congress, he pointed out, urging that Georgia wait to see what Lincoln would do before going off half-cocked. Let the Southern states all meet, he urged, and decide on a joint action. In this he had the support of Benjamin H. Hill. Herschel V. Johnson also joined with Stephens in arguing that the alternative to precipitate secession would be war, bloody and long drawn out. They could do no good against the oratory of the secessionist firebrands. Howell Cobb, Robert Toombs, and Thomas R. R. Cobb volleyed and thundered in a verbal onslaught against the Northerners' arrogant interference with the Southerners' way of life, and the ill and aging Wilson Lumpkin wrote an impassioned letter. Three fire-eaters from other states, W. L. Harris of Mississippi, Robert Barnwell Rhett of South Carolina, and Edmund Ruffin of Virginia, demanded that Georgia stand up and be counted. It was a state's right to secede, they argued, when it felt itself no longer treated as an equal in the Union of States; and if the state at some future time might wish to rejoin the Union, it would be in a much better position to bargain. The slave owners, of course, needed no warning of the threat against their property, but Governor Brown hit upon a device designed to convert to secession's cause the little farmer who owned no slaves. In the years before the war, in many counties, the small farmer and the big planter had worked out a symbiotic relationship profitable to them both. The plantation, specializing in growing cotton or rice, provided a steady market for the little farmer's small grains—oats, wheat, rye, and corn. In return, the little farmer would have his one or two bales of cotton ginned at the plantation gin. Now, Brown argued, if the slaves were freed, the taxpayers would have to shell out two billion dollars to pay their owners for them. The former slaveholders would then use the money to buy up all the little farms, and the little farmers would be made tenants. It would cost equally as much to send the Negroes back to Africa, as some advocated, the governor argued. And if they were freed and not sent away, they would become competitors for the jobs now held by the white laboring man. Brown's warning of the planters' moving in on the little farmer was not too farfetched. The pattern was well established. As the cotton culture wore out the land, the planters who could afford it moved westward, often buying out the little farmers, who in their turn moved on into the woods of northern and western Georgia, clearing new land. More persuasive even than these arguments, though, was a feeling that the poor-white who owned no slaves had in his bones. All that set him above the black man on the economic and social scale was the fact that he was free and the black man was a slave. He must be kept that way.

These arguments, spoken and unspoken, prevailed. The vote was for immediate and drastic action, and at Milledgeville on January 19, 1861, Georgia followed South Carolina, Mississippi, Florida, and Alabama out of the Union. The secession ordinance was offered by Judge Eugenius A. Nisbet and the vote was 208 for, 89 against. Two days later those against, including Ben Hill and Alex Stephens, signed the ordinance to make it unanimous. Georgia was now a sovereign and independent state. The national flag was taken down from the capitol building and the state flag of Georgia, a red star on a white field, was raised. Clicking telegraph keys carried the news throughout the state, and everywhere—in the cities and the towns—there was wild excitement. Cannon boomed, bonfires flared, torchlight processions passed through the streets, and frenzied oratory rent the air. And the young men began to come in from the countryside to form rifle companies and elect the commanders who would lead them to death or glory. Two months later, in a convention at Montgomery, Georgia voted to join another Union, the Confederacy of the United States. Here Georgia played a leading role. Howell Cobb was president of the convention, Robert Toombs was seriously considered for the presidency of the Confederacy—before the choice fell upon a military man, Jefferson Davis—and Toombs was made secretary of state instead. Alexander H. Stephens, the hopeful conciliator dragged reluctantly into secession, was chosen vice-president.

Actually, Georgia's first act of aggression against the Union had been committed even before this final breaking of the ties had taken place. There was an element of the ludicrous about it. South Carolina had withdrawn from the Union, and Governor Brown had heard "on good authority" that the federal government would take military steps to force a seceding state back into the Union, by moving first to man the old forts along their coasts. This meant that Georgia, for her own protection, should take over and garrison Fort Pulaski, which commanded the sea approach to Savannah. Brown therefore ordered Col. A. R. Lawton, a West Pointer commanding the First Regiment, Georgia Volunteers, at Savannah, to take Pulaski and "hold it against all persons." This order from the governor threw Savannah into a fever of excitement, for here at last was an outright act of war—a step that would bring state and federal governments into armed confrontation. Aglow with warlike zeal, and with flags flying and drums beating, on January 3, 1861, three companies of volunteers marched into Pulaski—to find that its defense force consisted of one elderly U. S. sergeant, who surrendered without a struggle. The guns were rusty, the powder magazines nearly empty, but the citizen-soldiers immediately began making ready to repel, if need be, an attack by the entire U. S. Navy, which they expected to come at any minute. Governor Brown's action in taking the fort before the Union forces could occupy it deprived Georgia of a place in history that her more rabid anti-Unionists would have coveted—for the quiet takeover meant that Fort Sumter, instead of Fort Pulaski, would be the site where the first shot was fired and the Civil War began.

The near unanimity with which Georgians supported these acts which would plunge them headlong into war is somewhat surprising in view of the economic and social stratification which had grown up in the state. It was the slave-owning planters whose voices had been most loudly heard in the push toward secession, but the state actually was a land of yeoman farmers, three-fifths of whom owned no slaves. Of some 118,000 families in Georgia, 41,000 were slaveholders, 69,000 were not. Yet except for a few mountain communities where loyalty to the Union remained steadfast, hardly a voice was raised in warning or protest. Nor did any protest come from Georgia pulpits, in churches linked, if not by politics, at least by ties of faith with their brethren in the North. The Southern preachers were as ardent in their defense of slavery as any planter-politician. Long before the state had resigned its membership in the Union, both the Methodists and the Baptists had broken their ties with their Northern churches. The Methodists broke away in 1844 to form the Methodist Episcopal Church South when the general conference of the church demanded the resignation of Bishop James O. Andrew, whose wife had inherited slaves. Since in the Georgia of that day all a wife's property became the property of her husband, this made the bishop a slave-owner. He refused to give them up, as a matter of conscience, on the grounds that this would be a cruelty to such helpless creatures. In 1845 the Baptists left the national fold to form the Southern Baptist Convention, the long smouldering issue becoming an open break when the Foreign Mission Board refused to appoint slaveholders as missionaries. The wrangle with the Yankee church did nothing to weaken the churches in the South. As the war began, there were 2,393 churches in Georgia—2,000 of them about equally divided between Baptists and Methodists.

Georgia went into her role as a state of the Confederacy with high heart and vast enthusiasm. Where evangelists preaching secession had been coming into Georgia, Georgia now began to send its own exhorters into the still uncommitted states. It offered the Confederacy ten square miles of territory on which to establish its capital, and it turned over all its forts and war materials to the central government. It also pledged to supply two regiments of troops to the Confederacy. Governor Brown immediately began taking what steps he thought necessary to put Georgia in a strong defensive position. The arsenal at Augusta was under federal control, an affront to Brown, to whom the U.S. was now a foreign power. He demanded its surrender and sent 800 Georgia troops to show that he meant business. Since the U.S. commander, Captain Arnold Elzey, had only eighty troops with which to defend the place, he immediately surrendered the arsenal with its 22,000 rifles and its other weapons and ammunition to Brown's representative, Col. W. H. T. Walker, who gave Captain Elzey a receipt for all that was taken over. The two men, to seal the bargain, drank toasts and embraced each other, after which the U.S. flag was hauled down, and the Georgia flag, white with a red star in its center, was raised over the arsenal. The governor also took over the U. S. mint at Dahlonega, which netted the state $20,000 in gold coin.

Georgia's hostile actions had not gone unnoticed in the North, of course, and out of an understandable desire that they should not in future be shot at by guns of their own manufacture, the Northerners took certain steps. The New York police seized 200 rifles ordered by a business firm in Macon, and refused to give them up even after Governor Brown had written Governor Morgan of New York, demanding their release. When he heard nothing from Morgan, Brown ordered that every ship in the harbor at Savannah belonging to a citizen of New York to be seized and held. The guns were released.

The taking of Fort Pulaski, of the Augusta arsenal, and of the Dahlonega mint had been accomplished with no gunfire and no bloodshed. The taking of Fort Sumter on April 13, 1861, was a different story. The war of words was over. The shooting war had begun.

5

Georgia at War

EORGIA'S entry into the Civil War was to bring to an end nearly eight decades of fairly steady progress. The Indian problem had long since been solved—brutally and brusquely, truly, but solved. And now from the mountains to the sea the traveler could move about without fear of losing his scalp or having his horses stolen. Twelve hundred and twenty-six miles of railroad had been built by 1860, penetrating every section of the state. Roads, though still incredibly bad in rainy weather, were improving as each local farmer gave his yearly due of work to keep passable the road that went by his house. Though the cost of slaves and plantation land had drained off much of the money that might have gone into factories, the state on the eve of rebellion was not entirely without manufacturing resources. The War of 1812 had taught Georgians the necessity of supplying themselves other than by agriculture. The first cotton mill was set up in Athens in 1829 by Augustin S. Clayton, and in the next thirty years textile mills sprang up wherever there was water power to turn a mill wheel. Augusta and Columbus became textile towns, and Macon, in addition to its cotton mills, boasted tanneries, shoe factories, and machine shops. Athens, for all its concern with the things of the mind, had many small industries. As Sumter fell and the war began, there were 1,890 manufacturers of all kinds in Georgia, and Governor Brown began making use of every resource at his command to convert them to war production. The penitentiary at Milledgeville was turned into an armory turning out 125 rifles a month. Munitions works sprang up in Augusta, where the Confederacy's largest powder factory was soon at work. In Macon, Columbus, and Athens, factories made rifles and sabers. Columbus, in fact, became so busy a manufacturing center that it was to furnish to the Confederate quartermaster more clothing, hats, shoes, cooking utensils, harnesses, and spades than any city in the Confederacy except Richmond. Atlanta the rail center became the headquarters for the Confederacy's quartermaster and commissary supplies. Little factories sprang up everywhere in the city, making buttons, belt buckles, guns, saddles, canteens, railroad cars, Bowie knives, cannon, and gun carriages. Churches contributed their iron bells to make cannon barrels and plates for iron-clad ships. Governor Brown, anticipating the day when powder and metal for muskets and bullets would be scarce, designed a weapon of his own and had several thousand of them made. It was a dagger, fastened to the end of a pole, and it was called a "Joe Brown pike."

All over the state, except in the remotest mountain communities where Union sentiment was still strong, young Georgians flocked to join the battalions that were forming everywhere. When President Davis asked for volunteers to defend Norfolk, companies in Macon, Columbus, and Griffin quickly formed a battalion and headed north. No state in the Confederacy was more eager for war, nor more active in preparing for war, than was Georgia. Troops were organized into companies, drilled, and held ready for the call to battle. Soon, though, there grew up a bitter antagonism between Governor Brown and President Davis. Brown held to the view that the governor of a state was the commander-in-chief of that state's troops and he alone should say how and where they should be used. A Savannah brigade, the Oglethorpe Light Infantry, commanded by General Francis S. Bartow, went north without the governor's permission, carrying weapons provided by the state, and their crossing the state line with these arms deeply angered Brown. Brown's criticism of Bartow was bitter, and the acrimonious exchange of letters between them was still going on when Bartow was killed, leading his troops at the first battle of Manassas. Brown was willing enough to send Georgians off to fight—but only if they were first mustered into state service—an attitude that got him into vociferous argument with his own legislature. President Davis, however, refused to accept state troops in units larger than regiments, which meant that Brown could not appoint officers of higher rank than colonel. Brown, then, as fast as his state units were requisitioned by the Confederacy, began building up his own ten-thousand-man force of boys and older men. Their job was to defend the state within its borders and they were known as "Joe Brown's Malish." Particularly offensive to Brown was the Conscription Act, passed by the Confederate Congress in 1862, which exempted from military service owners of twenty or more slaves. To Brown this not only outraged the principle of state sovereignty, it was an arrant discrimination against the common people in favor of the well-to-do, and in letters to Davis he made strong protest. Actually, Georgia herself, with Brown's full approval, exempted a number of professions. Planters, millers, and blacksmiths, Brown argued, did not belong under arms for their job was to supply the fighting men, and the home front, with food and arms. Also exempt were legislators, state officials, mail carriers, telegraph operators, college professors and presidents and teachers with twenty or more pupils, superintendents of woolen mills and cotton mills, machine shop workers, tax receivers, and ministers of the gospel. Nor were all of those ineligible for deferment quick to spring to arms. Many failed to appear for induction, many deserted; so many, in fact, that a $500 fine was imposed on anyone harboring a deserter, and desertion was made grounds for divorce. And the rich, of course, could avoid service by hiring a substitute to serve in their place.

Brown's disagreement with Davis was only one of many controversies that grew up between the state government and the Confederate government—and between Georgians themselves. Alexander H. Stephens, secretary of the treasury in Davis's cabinet, opposed the president's policies in many areas. Howell Cobb held that the Confederacy could never succeed under Davis's command, and Robert Toombs roared his arrogant discontent with Confederate policies. Yet Brown, who shared these views, often found himself at odds with Toombs and Cobb. Benjamin Hill, who supported Davis, was not on speaking terms with Stephens, who was also at odds with the wartime Georgia legislature. As the war went on, however, and Georgia and the South's desperate condition became clear, Cobb, Stephens, and even Toombs at times began to come to the defense of Davis's administration, and they joined with Hill and H. V. Johnson in agreeing that Davis, for all his faults as an administrator, was a true and faithful defender of the Southern cause.

Brown, like many another Confederate leader, at first had believed that the North's need for cotton was such that a war which would shut off the supply would never be allowed to happen. When that idea proved a wishful myth, Brown created two shipping companies to ship cotton to Holland, France, and England in exchange for weapons. The North immediately set up a blockade to stop this trade, while some Georgians bought ships and became fabulously rich running the blockade. Brown's business instincts were offended by this private enterprise. He persuaded the state to charter four blockade runners, so that the state itself could make the profits. The state ships ran only to Nassau, in the Bahamas, where the cotton was transferred to European bottoms, while the blockade runners loaded war materials from vast new warehouses there for the fast journey home. Georgia even had its own navy of sorts, a mosquito fleet put together under command of Commodore Josiah Tattnall for the purpose of attacking Yankee gunboats blockading Georgia and South Carolina waters. It fought with valor but was in the main ineffective.

The blockade grew tighter and tighter, the market for cotton more restricted. Soon it was clear that Georgians must either start growing the food they once had bought with cotton money, or go hungry. It became patriotic *not* to grow cotton, and laws were made restricting its cultivation to three acres per field hand. Cotton land went to grain and feed crops, sustenance for both people and cattle. Much of the cotton that was raised went into homespun fabrics, made into cloth for the army's uniforms and the civilian populace. Old spinning wheels and looms gathering dust since pioneer days came into service again, and it became a badge of honor to wear the homespun—a fact which Governor Brown dramatized when he was inaugurated in a homespun suit.

Coffee and tea, which could not be produced in Georgia, disappeared and salt came to be in such short supply that people dug up the floors of their old smokehouses and boiled the dirt to get the salt. "Coffee" was made from parched corn, rye, or potatoes, and "tea" from sassafras, with sorghum syrup used as a sugar substitute. Since corn was desperately needed for food and cattle feed, its distillation into whiskey was forbidden by law, but a great number of Georgians ignored the law and became rich on the profits of their hidden distilleries. As the war went on, laws were made forbidding Georgians to make alcohol of potatoes, pumpkins, peas, and dried fruits.

The hardships the civilian population endured were minor, though, in comparison with those that the Georgia troops who had gone north to fight were suffering. In nearly every great battle of the war, Georgia cavalrymen, infantrymen, and artillerymen fought with gallantry under Georgia generals holding their commissions from the Confederacy. Prominent political figures such as Robert Toombs, Howell Cobb, and A. H. Colquitt, all led troops in battle, and Brigadier General T. R. R. Cobb was killed as his brigade took the brunt of the Federal attacks at Fredericksburg. (A tragic irony: the bullet which killed him was fired from Federal Hill, where his Virginia mother had been born.) Prominent among Georgian field commanders were Lieutenant General John B. Gordon, who commanded a wing of Lee's army at Appomattox, and Lieutenant General James L. Longstreet, who fought at Gettysburg.

Another Georgian who distinguished himself at Gettysburg was General Ransom Wright. Gettysburg is the battle which many historians look upon as the turning point of the Civil War, and Pickett's charge with his Alabamans is considered the moment when the Confederate battle tide crested, broke, and began to ebb. This was on the third and last day. But on the second day, at six o'clock in the afternoon, the destiny of the Confederacy rested for a moment on General Wright's brigade of Georgia infantry whose red banners waved from the wooded crest of Cemetery Ridge. To many students of the Civil War, this was the high moment, the crucial skirmish, when for a little while, 1,450 raw-boned Georgians held the fate of the South in their hands. In terrible hand-to-hand combat over the rocks and through the trees, they fought their way to the top of the ridge, drove the Federals down the back slope, and held the high ground. Then Union guns from right and left brought them under a raking crossfire and they had to retreat.

To Georgians at home the war was at first merely a headline in the *Augusta Chronicle,* the *Columbus Sun,* the *Atlanta Intelligence,* the *Milledgeville Union,* the *Athens Banner,* the *Macon Telegraph.* It was a murmur of pain and weariness and boredom, expressed in the sweat-stained letters written by their soldier sons by the flickering light of campfires in Virginia. Within Georgia's own borders there was little actual combat for the first three years of war. In early 1862 Federal warships forced their way up the Savannah River, set up gun batteries on Tybee Island, and brought Fort Pulaski under fire. The usual demand for surrender was made. The usual defiant answer was given from the commander of the besieged garrison, Colonel Charles Olmstead. For two days the cannonade went on, and on the evening of the second day the surrender came. The strong brick walls had been breached, proof that the masonry of traditional forts could not withstand the fire of the new-fangled rifled guns. Unable to move further up the Savannah, the Union gunboats next tried to take Fort McAllister on the Ogeechee, but were driven off after an eight-hour bombardment, the parapets of earth and sand standing up better under fire than had Pulaski's bricks. Union forces then were content to raid the plantations up and down the coast, and to burn Darien.

Georgia's second experience with war's more violent aspects was a bold adventure that has lived in history as "The Great Locomotive Chase." In April of 1862, a Federal captain named James M. Andrews and twenty-one of his men, all in civilian clothes, boarded a Western and Atlantic railroad train at Marietta, their purpose to seize the train and tear up track, thus cutting off the Confederate states from their sources of supply in Georgia. At Big Shanty, now known as Kennesaw, about twenty-five miles from Atlanta, the train stopped so that the train crew and passengers could have breakfast. Seeing their chance, Andrews and his men uncoupled the engine—the General—and three empty freight cars, and headed north, hotly pursued by the conductor, William Fuller, the engineer, Jeff

184282

Cain, and Anthony Murphy, the foreman of the W&A shops in Atlanta, who was on his way to Allatoona to inspect a water pump. First on foot, then in a flat-car, then on another engine, the Texas, running backward, the pursuers followed the raiders, pressing them so that they had no time to carry out their plan of tearing up the tracks. Finally, two miles north of Ringold, the General died, out of wood, out of water, out of steam. Andrews and his men took to the woods, but he and seven of the raiders soon were captured, brought back to Atlanta, and hanged. Their bodies now lie in the National Cemetery at Chattanooga, in a semicircle around a granite pedestal bearing a bronze effigy of the General. The locomotives still exist. The Texas was rescued from the scrap pile, refurbished, and placed on permanent display in the basement of the Cyclorama building at Grant Park in Atlanta. The General, after standing for years on exhibit in the Union Station at Chattanooga, was returned to Georgia after a court fight, and now can be seen at Kennesaw, the "Big Shanty" where the great chase started.

A year after Andrews's raid, another effort was made to cut the Western and Atlantic, the Confederacy's lifeline. Fifteen hundred Federal troops, under command of Col. A. D. Streight, came raiding into north Georgia, pursued by General Nathan Bedford Forrest, with a force about one third as large. Forrest overtook Streight near Rome and by a stratagem which convinced Streight he was outgunned and outmanned, brought about his surrender. Whatever elation Georgians might have felt over this first small triumph of Confederate armies on Georgia soil was tempered by grave concern. The Yankee forces were coming closer. The Atlanta City Council took note of Streight's raid and asked the mayor to request all citizens to organize into companies and arm themselves so they could protect the city from raids.

When the "raid" did come, it came with such force and power that no citizen army, nor even the South's finest fighting men, could stand against it. In September of 1863, Georgia at last became a battleground. General Braxton Bragg, no longer able to hold Chattanooga under mounting pressure from Union forces under General Rosencrans, pulled back down the W&A

railroad to take up position along a winding creek with the Indian name of Chickamauga, meaning River of Death. It was an appropriate name, for in the two-day battle that occurred there, between two blind armies groping for each other through thickly wooded hills along a six-mile battle line, the Federal forces lost 16,000 men killed or wounded, the Confederates, 18,000.

Atlanta's new hospitals at last began to fill with wounded, and the first Yankee soldiers the city had seen passed through en route to prison at Andersonville. The Union now held Chattanooga, the gateway to Atlanta and the heart of the Southeast, Vicksburg and Jackson, Mississippi, and Knoxville, Tennessee. And now, with Chattanooga in Federal hands, the noose was drawing tighter around Georgia. But what U. S. Grant and William Tecumseh Sherman were planning for Georgia was not a slow death by strangulation but a spear-thrust at the heart.

Two Confederate citadels still remained to be destroyed. At Richmond, seat of the Confederate government, Lee's armies before the capital had now begun to feel the hammering blows by which Grant, taking over at Chickamauga, had driven Bragg back from Chattanooga in bloody battles at Lookout Mountain and Missionary Ridge. And in Atlanta, rail center through which food and guns and fighting men still flowed in a steady stream to the armies in Virginia, slave laborers commandeered from all the counties of Georgia worked with pick and shovel from dawn to dark, throwing up a ring of earthworks around the city.

In north Georgia, at Dalton, thirty miles south of Chattanooga, a new Confederate commander entrenched his 62,000 men, waiting the onslaught he knew soon must come out of Chattanooga, where a grim, redheaded general named William Tecumseh Sherman now commanded an army of 99,000 men. After the defeat at Lookout Mountain and Missionary Ridge, General Bragg had asked to be relieved of his command. His replacement was General Joseph E. Johnston, a West Point graduate, who had learned his trade fighting Indians and Mexicans. A small man, gray, soldierly in bearing, with a certain gamecock jauntiness about him, he was a topographical engineer, skilled in the use of terrain in war. He soon was to be given full opportunity to make use of this talent. He took command in December 1863, with orders to reorganize Bragg's shattered forces and set them upon the offensive.

The opportunity never came. Somewhere outside Richmond, in the spring of 1864, Ulysses S. Grant sat down on a log and composed a telegram to William Tecumseh Sherman in Chattanooga. His orders were blunt, their meaning clear. Sherman was to "move against Johnston's army, to break it up, and to get into the interior of the enemy's country as far as you can, inflicting all the damage you can against their war resources." [1]

Here then was the beginning of Sherman's march through Georgia to the sea, still the most poignantly remembered event in the state's history. Thousands of Georgians now would learn, by bitter firsthand experience, what Sherman never said in so many words, but which his troops thoroughly demonstrated —that war is Hell.

From Dalton to Cassville, to Allatoona, to New Hope Church—at last to Kennesaw, Johnston fought, and fell back along the railroad as Sherman tried to encircle him. And finally, at Kennesaw, Sherman changed his tactics. His orders from Grant were to move strongly against Johnston's army and break it up, and so far, he had failed. Johnston's lean, gray troops had fought as gray wolves fight, with slash and cut and quick retreat. From creek-bank thickets, from the crests of hills, from the high crags of mountains, they had fought a running fight. Now they had gone to earth again, on the flanks of Pine Mountain, Lost Mountain, Brush Mountain, and Kennesaw. And Sherman knew that somehow they must be destroyed in this place before he could safely move on to Atlanta, the dusty, busy little city of twelve thousand that lay on the horizon just twenty miles away.

Here, Sherman decided, he would make his first headlong frontal attack. His men were tired of chasing a retreating enemy. They were ready for a showdown. Two weeks of rain made circling maneuvers difficult over muddy roads and paths, and his own lines of communication were growing dangerously

1. *"War is Hell!" Sherman's March Through Georgia,* edited by Mills Lane (Savannah: The Beehive Press, 1974), p. 24.

extended. There were political pressures, too. President Lincoln was running for re-election, and needed a victory to still the rising tide of antiwar sentiment in the North.

On the ninth of June Sherman hurled his forces against the ten-mile-long Confederate line. Almost daily, for twenty-three days, the attacks were repeated, and time after time the Union troops were thrown back with heavy losses. Whenever they got a toehold, the Confederates would counterattack, the men on both sides fighting in every possible style, but using clubbed muskets more often than the bayonet. In the fierce hand-to-hand fights that raged through the rocky hillsides, both sides were badly hurt, and it was not only the common soldiers who were getting killed. The bishop-general, Leonidas Polk—who only a short time earlier had baptized John B. Hood in services at Dalton—was killed by an artillery shell as he stood atop Pine Mountain surveying the battlefield below. Sherman lost two generals, Harker and McCook, and soon, in the fighting around Atlanta, Union commander James B. McPherson and Confederate W. H. T. Walker were to go down, mortally wounded.

The fierce Confederate resistance at Kennesaw forced Sherman to go back to his old tactic of encirclement, but Johnston was too quick to be outflanked. Pulling his battle-weary forces back, he crossed the Chattahoochee over bridges and fords guarded by 3,000 old men and young boys of Joe Brown's state militia. In seventy-four days of battle, he had held his command together while fighting a force twice his own. It was a weary, but not a beaten, army that "Uncle Joe" Johnston led across the muddy river to take up position south of Peachtree Creek, its back against the outer line of breastworks defending Atlanta. And there he was waiting, making his battle plans, when the Confederate high command, disappointed that somewhere in the hills he had not divided and cut to pieces Sherman's army, relieved him from command. Hood took over, John B. Hood of Texas, who was himself a slugger, as Sherman was, but who lacked Sherman's genius for maneuver. Brash where Johnston was careful, bold where Johnston was shrewd, he came to the command of an army which Johnston had used as a rapier, which he was to use as a club—until the club was shattered in his hands.

So they lay on that bright day of July 17, when the hosts of
Sherman came pouring across the Chattahoochee and on toward
Atlanta, rumbling cannon shaking the earth from north and east
down Pace's Ferry, Powers Ferry, Peachtree Road, and the red,
dusty strip of the Doraville road. And so they lay through the
long, hot days of the 18th and 19th as the right wing of the blue
hosts came on from the river to the creek and across the creek,
to spread out their crescent battle line south of the wide and
shallow stream.

Sherman's right was the pivot of the great "right wheel" that
was his first maneuver, with McPherson, so soon to die, swing-
ing wide on the eastern flank to strike behind Decatur and to destroy the railroad line. Successful, he turned back, and as he
turned (to face the harrying onslaught of Fighting Joe Wheeler's
cavalry), far on the western end of the battle line, along the
banks of Peachtree Creek, on the afternoon of July 20, Hood
struck with his left and center one crushing blow at Sherman's
right. The bugle called at 3 o'clock, and, under the shock of the
Southern charge, the blue ranks wavered. Fiercer and fiercer
raged the fight, and for a while it seemed the Confederates
would prevail. But numbers told the story, and the men in blue,
fighting like madmen with the creek to their backs, held, broke
the Southern line, and then surged forward.

That day the first shell from Sherman's guns fell in Atlanta,
killing a little girl, and a trembling city knew for the first time
the horror of what was to come. Atlanta had seen wounded men
before, from Kennesaw and battles to the north, but nothing like
the bleeding wagonfuls which rolled down the red-clay roads to
the hospitals within the city that night. There was little fighting
on the following day, though sniping casualties were heavy, and
on that night General Hood withdrew his forces from the Peachtree line. He had lost nearly 5,000 men, to 1,500 for the Federals. Atlantans huddled on their porches watched part of that
weary army as it tramped down Peachtree Street, moving si-
lently in the darkness with only the muffled thump of feet and
the clink of gear to tell of their dark passing, on a march of
fourteen miles, from Peachtree Creek to a position in the east
Atlanta area that was to become the blood-soaked terrain of the
actual Battle of Atlanta—the battle depicted in the great painting
now housed in the Cyclorama.

The dread day dawned, July 22, 1864. Hood struck this time at Sherman's left, at McPherson's army, beating its way back from Decatur in the face of Wheeler's cavalry. His plan was to strike at the same time at Sherman's right flank, which had swung down from the bloody ground along Peachtree Creek to take up position in the new theater. But that attack came too late, at four o'clock in the afternoon. And, though McPherson himself was killed and a famous Yankee battery was taken, again the superiority of numbers told, and the gray forces fell back from the field defeated.

Hood struck once more, six days later, at Ezra Church. Six times from midmorning to midafternoon his crippled legions charged. Each time they fell back, shattered. Sherman now held the high ground to the north and the east. The black snouts of his cannon pointed toward the town with no answering gun to silence them. The battles of Atlanta were over. The siege of Atlanta, the forty days of torment that was Sherman's brand of war, had begun. The men whom bullets could not kill from Chattanooga to the Chattahoochee, lay dead in every thicket, in every open field. The bulldog at last had found the gray wolf's throat. The city that could not fall was crumbling into rubble. And south, ahead of Sherman, stretched the broad road to the sea.

For more than a month, the Federal troops ringed the city with their guns, pouring a sporadic harassing fire into the town, using as their targets the tall spires of churches, high chimneys, the railroad yards, and fires set by incendiary shells. Citizens moved warily in the streets by day, and lived in pits dug under their houses and in their yards by night. On the 25th of August, the guns fell silent. Sherman was ready to give up his siege tactics and once again sent his blue crescent circling Hood as it had circled Johnston. Hood's reaction was the same as Johnston's had been. On the night of September 1, he withdrew, to the sound of great explosions and flames that lit up the night sky. This was no work of Sherman's but of Hood's own cavalrymen, left behind to blow up his ammunition trains. He fell back to Jonesboro, and there Sherman's forces fell upon him in the fourth and final battle for Atlanta—a shattering defeat for the Confederate forces. In the silent city men stayed home to guard their wives and daughters, while through the downtown streets began to flow a shabby tide of stragglers and deserters, Negroes half-crazed by their strange new sense of freedom, and lean and haggard looters, men and women alike, who plundered stores and vacant dwellings of anything they could carry away.

So lay Atlanta on the morning of September 2, between two armies, abandoned by one, with little hope of mercy from the other. Hood had made no formal surrender, so the mayor, James M. Calhoun, set out on horseback with members of his council to perform the sad chore. They rode out under a flag of truce until finally, far out war-shattered Marietta Street, they came upon a Federal patrol. Mayor Calhoun took a notebook from his pocket, and addressed a message to the nearest Union general. It said, "Sir: The fortune of war has placed Atlanta in your hands. As Mayor of the City I ask protection to noncombatants and private property." [2] An hour later a blue river of Federal soldiers was flowing down Marietta Street in the heart of Atlanta. Defiant small boys watched them pass, and whistled "Dixie" and the "Bonnie Blue Flag." Three days before he himself entered the city, Sherman ordered all civilians not connected with the Union army to leave. They could go north or south, as they pleased, and they could take whatever movable property they could carry along, as well as their servants. But they must leave. Few moved north, for most Union sympathizers had long since gone. Those who chose to go south— some 450 families—were moved to the little Clayton County community of Rough and Ready. There two detachments—one hundred of Hood's soldiers, one hundred of Sherman's men— took care of them, the soldier guards, so late at bayonet's point, laughing and joking with each other.

Sherman's occupying forces stayed in Atlanta until mid-November when they departed, shouting, dancing, drinking, singing, setting fires behind them that left the city a smouldering ruin. With the flames of the burning city at his back, Sherman moved out on the night of November 14–15, striking through the heart of the state to Savannah, birthplace of Georgia. His army moved in two columns, roughly parallel—spread out some

2. Franklin M. Garrett, *Atlanta and Environs,* 3 vols. (New York: Lewis Historical Publishing Co., 1954), 1:635.

five to fifteen miles apart on a flexible front that might vary in width from thirty to sixty miles. The total force, about equally divided, was some 62,000 men, including 5,000 cavalry. The left wing moved south through Decatur, Covington, Madison, Eatonton, and Milledgeville to Sandersville where it joined forces with the right, which had come down by way of Jonesboro, Monticello, Gordon, and Irwinton. Feinting motions only were made towards Macon and Augusta, and Columbus was ignored until later.

The march to the sea, though a terrible and never-forgotten disaster for the Georgians in its path, was a stroll in the open air for the Yankee soldiery. There was no unified opposition in front of them—a few cavalrymen under Joe Wheeler harassing the picket lines, a few militia, some 3,000, under G. W. Smith, who fired a shot and quickly fled—and now and then, as at Griswoldville, stood and fought and died. In the 100-odd miles between Atlanta and Chattanooga, Sherman's losses had numbered more than 25,000. From Atlanta to Savannah, some 300 miles, they were counted at 567 killed, wounded, and missing. It was, as one soldier called it,

> . . . a glorious tramp right through the heart of the state, [we] rioted and feasted on the country, destroyed all the R.R., in short found a rich and over-flowing country filled with cattle hogs sheep and fowls, corn meat potatoes and syrup, but left a barren waste for miles on either side of the road, burnt millions of dollars worth of property, wasted and destroyed all the eatables we couldn't carry off and brought the war to the doors of Georgians so effectively I guess they will long remember the Yankees.[3]

In fairness it must be said that Joe Wheeler's Confederate cavalry, which harassed the Yanks, and the militia which skirmished with the pickets, were almost as destructive of Georgia property as were the Federals, for they too were living off the land.

Actually, Sherman himself had sought to spare the state the plundering and the devastation he had ordered. Shortly after the fall of Atlanta, he had sent a message to Governor Brown at the

3. Lane, *"War is Hell!"*, p. xxi.

capital in Milledgeville, through a go-between who believed that the Southern cause was lost. The gist of Sherman's message was that if Brown would remove his state troops from the armies of the Confederacy, he, Sherman, would spare the state the devastation he had planned for it. He would confine his armies to the main roads and would pay for all the food and forage needed in his passage to the sea. A similar message was sent to Alexander H. Stephens, who was known to be bitterly disenchanted with President Davis's conduct of the war. Both Brown and Stephens ignored the messages.

With Sherman's cavalry only a few miles away from Milledgeville, Governor Brown and the legislature hastily abandoned the city, fleeing frantically toward Macon and southwest Georgia by train, carriage, horseback, and afoot—after calling to arms all able-bodied Georgians except murderers in the penitentiary and the state officials themselves. Sherman did not destroy the capitol building, or the governor's mansion, but the capitol did undergo a certain degree of desecration. Soldiers broke into the legislative chamber, which the fleeing lawmakers had left with papers still on the desks, held a mock session of the legislature, and repealed the ordinance of secession.

By December 13, Fort McAllister, guarding Savannah, had fallen. Sherman had reached the sea at last, his army still intact. The old city of Savannah, where General William Hardee's army of 10,000 and a garrison of 1,500 tensely waited, fell without a struggle. There was no formal surrender. Like Hood at Atlanta, Hardee had suddenly withdrawn, leaving the city by way of a pontoon bridge over the Savannah River. The next day, Sherman rode down Bull Street to the customshouse, climbed to the roof, and looked out over the city, the marshlands, and the vast rice fields on the Carolina side, into which Hardee had disappeared with all his men. All was calm except for the smouldering ruins of the navy yard, which Hardee had destroyed. He left behind, Sherman noted approvingly, "all the heavy guns, stores, cotton, railway cars, steamboats, and an enormous amount of public and private property." [4] On December 22, 1864, Sherman sent his famous message to Presi-

4. Lane, *"War is Hell!"*, p. 178.

dent Lincoln, who received it on Christmas Eve: "I beg to present you as a Christmas Gift the City of Savannah, with 150 heavy guns and plenty of ammunition, also about 25,000 bales of cotton." [5]

Behind him in the heart of Georgia, he had left the wasteland he had promised, blackened chimneys stark against the sky, ruined fields and pillaged barns and corncribs, dead animals and wrecked wagons. He had torn up 200 miles of railroad, making bonfires of the crossties, and on them heating the iron rails so that they could be twisted around trees and telegraph poles into knots that the soldiers called "Sherman's neckties." His troops had taken, in his passage, thousands of head of cattle, mules, and horses. Great numbers of these were shot, by Sherman's orders, because his footsore soldiers would ride them and he did not approve of this. And he had left behind a people living off what fruits and nuts and berries they could find, and meat skins, and even the gleaning of the corn that Sherman's horses had dropped. And he had left behind, too, a people who would not smile again for many years, and who for many generations would not forget him.

Just before leaving Georgia on February 1, 1865, he summed up, in a letter to his wife Ellen, what he believed he had done that will "survive the clamor of time," describing to her, as if addressing a West Point class in tactics, the way he had handled his troops from Chattanooga to the sea.

> . . . Like one who has walked a narrow plank, I look back and wonder if I really did it, but here I am in the proud city of Savannah, with an elegant mansion at my command, surrounded by a brave, confident, and victorious army. Negroes and whites flock to me and gaze at me as if at some wonderful being, and letters from great men pour in with words of flattery and praise, but I still do more than ever crave for peace and quiet, and would gladly drop all these and gather you and my little ones in some quiet place where I could be at ease. [6]

But the "quiet place" was not yet to be found for Sherman as he moved on, fighting, into the Carolinas, nor for the Georgia

5. Lane, *"War is Hell!"*, p. 181.
6. Lane, *"War is Hell!"*, p. 187.

brigades still fighting in Virginia. On April 9, at Appomattox, General John B. Gordon of Georgia led the last attack of the Army of Northern Virginia, a battle in which his ragged, starving veterans were still fighting furiously at the very moment General Lee rode out to find General Grant to discuss the terms of surrender. Four days later, General Sherman's old enemy Joseph Johnston, again commanding a Confederate army, surrendered to him at Hillsboro, N.C. But Georgia's agony was not yet quite over. A week after Appomattox, a Union general named James M. Wilson came raiding out of Alabama into the heart of Georgia, striking with his cavalrymen at Columbus and Macon. At Macon he accepted the surrender of Governor Brown, who first exacted the promise that he would not be jailed. Instead, he was arrested and sent off to Washington, where he was held in prison for a week before President Andrew Johnson pardoned him and sent him home.

Other Confederate leaders were also seized in the first days after the war, briefly imprisoned, then paroled. Alexander H. Stephens was arrested at his home at Crawfordville and was imprisoned at Fort Warren in Boston Harbor, where after five months he was paroled. Benjamin H. Hill, Confederate senator and brilliant spokesman for the Davis government, was arrested at his home at Lagrange, and Howell Cobb, who in the face of invasion had organized a home guard of 18,000 men, was taken in Macon. Both were soon paroled. Robert Toombs, Georgia's original and perpetual "unreconstructed rebel," escaped to France. He came home, under the informal protection of his old friend Andrew Johnson, in 1867, but he never asked for pardon, and amnesty was never granted.

Not long before Robert Toombs made his escape, Jefferson Davis, fleeing from Richmond, arrived in Washington, Georgia, with General Bragg, his military advisor, and his quartermaster-general and commissary general. With them came a train of wagons, bearing all the gold and silver that the Confederate treasury possessed. Instruction for distributing this money to as many soldiers as could be reached, in increments of $26.25 per man, were the last orders of the now shattered Confederate cabinet, holding its last meeting in the Wilkes County courthouse. Moving on by wagon into the interior of Georgia, Davis was captured by pursuing Union cavalry near Irwinsville, in Irwin County, and on May 10, 1865, old and sick and feeble, he was taken in chains to prison at Fort Monroe. For two years he was held there, shackled at first, then allowed to move freely about the grounds. Finally he was released under $100,000 bond, under a technical charge of treason, which was never prosecuted, though he insisted that he be tried. The indictment was dropped in 1869, and Jefferson Davis entered into Southern history, a marytr and a legend.

Paradoxically, for all the suffering, physical, economic, and psychological, that Georgia endured in the war that culminated in Sherman's march, the total effect in the long run proved beneficial. It destroyed the institution of slavery, to which all Georgians themselves had been enslaved. It left deep wounds in the heart, but along with an enduring hatred and distrust of Yankees which only in recent generations has begun to diminish, it created a feeling of confidence, born of real achievement, in what Georgians could accomplish on their own. Georgia at the beginning of the war had made some small beginnings toward industrialization, but she was still a rough frontier, dependent upon the North for the amenities of life. With her wealthy citizens putting their money more often into land and slaves than into mills and mines and factories, she had to buy from others the glass and finished furniture, the ink and paper, the matches and medicines and farm machinery that she needed to create a viable economy. In the war, forced by necessity, she began to produce these manufactured goods. Mines were opened, and foundries started, to make weapons for the army, but these were easily converted to peacetime uses after the war. During the war, too, there had begun a movement, of men and women from the farms to the towns to serve the burgeoning factories. Thus, in the smoke of "the first modern war, the Industrial Revolution came to Georgia . . . and gave political power to the middle class for the first time—two exhilarating, constructive social developments." [7]

It also brought in its wake what to many a Georgian was war in a different form, the agony called Reconstruction.

7. Lane, *The People of Georgia*, pp. 192–195.

6

Reconstruction—and Its Aftermath

IF the election of Abraham Lincoln in 1860 was the fuse that detonated a civil war, the assassination of Lincoln by a crazed actor, John Wilkes Booth, in April of 1865, gave sudden impetus to a war of revenge which, by every means except actual combat, forced upon Georgia and the South far-reaching social, political, and economic changes. Lincoln was for a generous peace, "with malice toward none, with charity for all," he said in his second inaugural on March 4, 1865. In a conference with Generals Sherman and Grant, he urged that Lee and Johnston be offered generous terms. In his last public address, before a company at the White House on April 11, two days after Lee's surrender, he spoke of reconstruction being carried out in a spirit of generous reconciliation. And on the afternoon of the day he died, in a cabinet meeting he expressed the wish that there would be no persecution of the South after the war. As early as 1863 he had announced his own plan of reconstruction, based on the presidential power to pardon. Its terms were generous, providing that all white male Southerners, with the exception of Confederate officials, could return to full citizenship by taking a simple loyalty oath. As soon as ten percent of the state's voters had taken this oath, a state government could be formed and send representatives to Congress, provided only that they support the freeing of the slaves. Andrew Johnson, sworn in as president on the death of Lincoln, held these same generous views. But Radical Republicans in the Congress, led by the grimly vengeful Thaddeus Stevens, who looked upon the Confederate states as conquered provinces, to be treated as such, did not share his support of Lincoln's policies; and though Lincoln might have been skilled enough in politics to handle his Congressional opposition, Johnson was not.

He did, however, at first make a strong attempt and good progress toward the kind of moderate Reconstruction that Lincoln had in mind. He offered amnesty to all white male voters except high Confederate political and military leaders, and certain large property holders (Johnson, a North Carolina-born hillbilly and son of a bank porter, felt no warmth toward the planter aristocracy). Once amnesty had been asked and granted to a sufficient number, each state could call a state convention, abolish slavery, repeal their acts of secession, and repudiate their Confederate and state war debts. Then they could come back into the Union. Though the repudiation of war debts was hard to accept, since this meant financial ruin to many a Southerner whose total wealth had gone into Confederate bonds, by December of 1865 all the states except Texas had accepted Johnson's rules and were seeking readmission to the Union. Seventy-five Confederate war leaders, both civil and military, were given individual pardons by Johnson, among them Alexander H. Stephens of Georgia, former vice-president of the Confederacy.

There was no mass punishment of "war criminals" as since has befallen those who made war against the U.S.—though Henry Wirz, commander at Andersonville prison, was hanged. Nor was there any wholesale confiscation of property, except the loss incurred in the freeing of the slaves. The Radical Republicans instead sought their revenge by political means. The return to Congress of a new host of Southern Democrats would destroy or greatly dilute Republican supremacy in the House and Senate, and this could only be prevented by giving the Negro his full rights of suffrage, so that around him the Republican Party in the South could be built.

In this view the politicians were joined by many people of good heart in the North. During the war the freeing of the slaves had made but little change in their status. Outside of the relatively few who had gone off with the Union armies, being fed by them, working for them, or simply tagging along in their wake, the great majority of slaves had stayed on their home plantations. With their masters away at the war, though under no compulsion to stay other than their own affection for their "white folks," most of them had continued to serve the mistress and her children as they had always done. And throughout the South there had been no general uprising, no slave rebellion. With the end of the war, however, and the disintegration of the plantation system, with the flocking together of thousands of new freedmen without work—the white South's old fears came back—of a slave revolt, of a black labor force that would do no labor, of the thing unthinkable in the South—black political rule. This resulted in the enactment in 1865 and 1866 of Black Codes in nearly all of the new Southern state governments. The effect of these was to place the Negro again in bondage. They legalized his status as a free man (the states had to satisfy the Thirteenth Amendment before they could be readmitted to the Union), but so restricted him in other ways—in freedom of speech, freedom of movement, conditions of employment, the right to vote, to serve on juries, to testify against whites in court—that they returned him very nearly to that status from which he had been emancipated. Georgia's laws were less repressive than other Southern states', but the implications were the same. The Negro was to be given, superficially, the equal protection of the laws, but he was still to be denied political and social equality.

The adoption by state after state of the Black Codes nullified all that the North had hoped to do for the Negro in the establishment of the Freedmen's Bureau in 1865. In 1866, Congress passed a civil-rights act invalidating the Black Codes, and later the Fourteenth Amendment guaranteed to the Negro equal protection of the laws. Georgia, like all the Southern states except Tennessee, refused to ratify this amendment and the Radical Republicans in Congress took harsh revenge. They wiped out the governments established under the Johnson administration and divided the South into five military districts, each ruled by the army. Georgia, after two years of precarious democracy within the Union, was now back under bayonet rule.

The state must have some form of government, of course, and the Radicals in Congress made sure that the governments formed gave full and complete recognition to the black vote. Under a series of Reconstruction Acts, military commanders were authorized to organize new governments, control registration and voting, and appoint or remove state officials. Since the whites, by not going to the polls, could forestall ratifying a new state constitution providing the Negro with equal rights, an act was passed making a simple majority of those voting sufficient to ratify. As fast as these Reconstruction acts were passed President Johnson vetoed them, and his veto was as promptly overridden. This led to his impeachment by the House, but the Senate, by one vote, cleared him in the trial that followed.

Historians looking back on this period see Republican actions as a curious mixture of progressive aims and corrupt means. These military governments were in the main supported by the Negro vote, by carpetbaggers from the North, and by Southerners known as scalawags, who supported the carpetbaggers. These were the real rulers of the post-war South, and their goals were often laudatory though their methods were sometimes venal. Many of the social-welfare programs we know and accept today, for example, were first tried in these times, by the Freedmen's Bureau. Voting qualifications were changed to take some of the power from the big property owners, ancient barbarisms such as dueling and imprisonment for debt were outlawed, and public school systems began to replace the old private academies. In Georgia, as in all the South, carpetbag legislatures wrote into new constitutions laws of positive democratic value which "achieved reform in the organization of the courts, in judicial procedures, in the systems of county governments and school administration, in the manner of electing public officials and in methods of taxation. In a period of political, economic, and social upheaval they laid the groundwork for reform." [1] But along with these good things came certain evidence of human weakness—corruption and theft in high places and extravagant spending that sent state debts skyrocketing. The carpetbaggers and their friends, in short, were a blending of lofty idealists promoting great moral concepts, and sharp-witted

---

1. Francis Butler Simkins and Charles Pierce Roland, *A History of the South* (New York: Knopf, 1972), p. 277.

wheeler-dealers determined to miss none of the spoils of victory.

Georgia shared full measure in both the good and the bad of Reconstruction. Under the first state government, as formed under President Andrew Johnson's fairly lenient rules, Charles J. Jenkins was inaugurated as governor, and Alexander H. Stephens and Herschel V. Johnson were sent to the U.S. Senate, completing the ritual of Georgia's return to the Union. Georgia's refusal to ratify the Fourteenth Amendment, which attempted to force a state to give the Negro the right to vote or suffer a reduction in representatives in Congress, brought on the military rule already described. Senators Stephens and Johnson and Georgia's congressmen were refused their seats, and the state became part of the Third Military District under General John Pope. This brought on a clamor of denunciation in Georgia like that which had been heard during the fierce debates before the Civil War. Benjamin H. Hill, who had fiercely opposed secession although voting for it, now fulminated, in mighty oratory and a barrage of newspaper articles, against the military regime. Howell Cobb, who had resigned as secretary of the treasury in President Buchanan's cabinet to come home to lead the fight for secession, now was as bitterly opposed to Reconstruction by threat of force. Robert Toombs came home from Europe to add his voice to the criticism. Charles Jenkins sought to bring suit in the Supreme Court against the army commanders and the War Department. The Court refused to act.

Of Georgia's antebellum leaders only former governor Joseph E. Brown, a pragmatic man, surveyed the situation with cold eyes, unmoved by scarred hopes cherished in the past and now outworn. He urged Georgians to accept the inevitable, to bow docilely under the military yoke and to await with patience the day of deliverance that in time would come. For this he was excoriated. Brown had even gone so far as to welcome General Pope to Atlanta and entertain him at a banquet, which may or may not have helped to persuade Pope not to tie the yoke too tightly at the start. His first job was to register the Negroes to vote—which was accomplished in various ways, some of them illegal, such as registering the same man under different names, and bringing in blacks from South Carolina to be registered in

GEORGIA

A photographer's essay by Bruce Roberts

Photographs in Sequence

Wild grass on old Callaway plantation.
Near the top of Brasstown Bald.
Downtown Atlanta parking garage.
Highway near Clayton.
Church signs, Menlo.
Wednesday night church service, Menlo.
Rural church service, Northwest Georgia.
Farm near Clayton.
Peachtree Center, downtown Atlanta.
Bank building, Atlanta.
Old home near Washington.
Farming near Athens.
Riverfront at Savannah.
Bridge over Savannah River, Savannah.
Fort Pulaski, Savannah.

Georgia. The end result in 1867 was the registration of some 93,000 Negroes, as compared with 95,000 whites. Though the whites had a 2,000 majority in registration in the next election of delegates to a constitutional convention, white conservatives stayed away from the polls, refusing to join their former slaves at the ballot box. Thus out of 166 delegates elected to write a new constitution for Georgia, thirty-seven were Negroes of varying degrees of intelligence and integrity, nine were carpet-baggers equally diverse in character, and only about a dozen were conservative Democrats. The majority of the delegates were once wealthy and conservative Whigs, native-born white men, who like Governor Brown, saw the futility of opposing Republican—meaning Reconstruction—rule, and by their attitude earned for themselves the contemptuous name of scala-wags. Among the Negroes many were moderate, earnest, and intelligent men; one of them, Henry M. Turner, born free in South Carolina, had come to Georgia as a chaplain in a Negro regiment of the Union Army, and remained to become a highly respected bishop of the AME church. Others were of less laud-able character. One A. A. Bradley, elected from Savannah, had served a prison sentence in New York for seduction and had been disbarred from the practice of law in Massachusetts. An-other, Tunis G. Campbell representing McIntosh County, had come south from New Jersey after the war and had set up a so-called black "republic" on St. Catherines Island, where he ruled like a potentate. Carpetbagger delegates, on the whole, were a fairly respectable lot. A number of them were thieves and rascals, but many had come to Georgia before the war, and chose to stay on after Reconstruction was over in the firm belief that here in the South, now that slavery was destroyed, Yankee brains, Yankee industry, and Yankee concepts of democracy could create a new heaven and a new earth. Many were teachers who saw themselves as missionaries to a benighted land. All were pro-Negro in their feelings, and as was to be expected they wrote a constitution which gave the vote and full civil rights to all male citizens, regardless of color, and provided for a system of free education for all children of the state, black or white. And war-battered Atlanta, still rising from the rubble of her de-struction three years earlier, was made the capital of the state, replacing the smaller, more sedate, and far more "Southern" Milledgeville.

On the whole, Georgia's new constitution was more reasonable and more workable than those in other states where blacks and carpetbaggers were in a greater majority. It did, however, possess certain flaws. By permitting the state and local governments to aid the railways and other public projects, it opened the door to the pillaging of the state treasury which was to follow. It also brought on an immediate collision between the military and the conservatives still in office. General Pope demanded of State Treasurer John Jones $40,000 to pay the expenses of the convention. Jones refused to pay without a warrant from the governor, and Governor Jenkins refused to sign such an order, saying that there was no legal authority for this expenditure. About this time General George Meade replaced Pope, and when his demand for the money was also refused, he fired the governor, the treasurer, the comptroller general, and the secretary of state, and replaced them with military officers. In the midst of this turmoil, Governor Jenkins hid the great seal and took off for New York City, carrying $400,000 of the state's money, which he deposited in a New York bank to keep it out of the hands of the military government.

For all its harshness, conservatives in Georgia preferred military rule to a government controlled by civilian outsiders determined to raise the freedman to a position of complete equality, and they urged that the new constitution not be adopted. Their plea went unheeded. The constitution was adopted by a large majority, and Rufus B. Bullock, a Republican who had come to Georgia from New York in 1859, was nominated as the Radical Republican candidate for governor. The conservatives or Democrats did demonstrate a certain strength, however, ending up with a small majority in the House, a fact which disturbed Governor-elect Bullock, This body assembled in Atlanta on July 4, 1868, Bullock was inaugurated, the Fourteenth Amendment was ratified, and before the month was out, General Meade declared military rule at an end. Before the troops could be withdrawn, however, Bullock's government, too, found itself in trouble with the federal Congress. Twenty-nine Negroes were in the House and three in the Senate. Bullock, in an effort to find reason to expel some of the white Democrats who were in both houses of the legislature, asked General Meade to test the eligibility of all members against the requirements of the Fourteenth Amendment—which denied citizenship to former Confederate officials. None were found ineligible, and Meade dropped the matter, feeling, evidently, that he was being used by Bullock in an effort to get control of the legislature. Furthermore, the general felt that the legislative body should be the final judges of their own membership. He did not interfere, therefore, when conservative senators charged that the Negro members of the assembly were illegally seated—the Democrats pointing out that though the state constitution granted the Negro the right to vote, it said nothing about his right to hold office. One, A. A. Bradley, the ex-convict from New York, was expelled for "malicious mouthing," twenty-six others were expelled because of their color, and four were allowed to keep their seats because it could not be determined whether or not they were Negro. Those unseated were replaced by the white candidates whom they had beaten.

The expulsion of the black legislators caused bitter resentment among the Negroes, particularly against their Republican friends who had voted to cast them out. It also alarmed and angered Governor Bullock, who felt his power slipping away. He went to Washington, appeared before the Senate, declared that Georgia had never been reconstructed, and recommended reinstatement of the Negroes and of the legislature as constituted in the election of 1868. Again Georgia congressmen who had been admitted to the national House were unseated, and the newly chosen senators were denied admittance. For the third time, the state went under military rule, which placed Governor Bullock and all state officers under the orders of Union General Alfred H. Terry. A final Reconstruction Act was passed, making it an act of rebellion, which could be stamped out by military force, to exclude anyone duly elected from holding office by reason of "race, color, or previous condition of servitude." [2] The black legislators were reseated, their replacements

2. *Family Encyclopedia of American History* (New York: The Readers Digest Association, 1975), pp. 284–285.

expelled, and twenty-two Conservative Democrats were expelled by Terry's soldier-inquisitors. This gave the Bullock forces a majority in both houses. The Fifteenth Amendment was ratified—specifically barring states from denying the Negro the right to vote. And for good measure the Fourteenth Amendment was ratified again. Once these things were done the state's representatives went back to Washington to take their seats in House and Senate, and on December 5, 1870, after six years of Reconstruction—and intermittent military rule—Georgia was at last restored to the Union, this time to remain as a sovereign state.

It had been a trying time, and there were lean times still to come, but for her comfort, Georgia had produced two men who were neither politicians nor soldiers, but story tellers—men whose warmth and wit and humor helped the dark days pass. Charles H. Smith, under the pen name of Bill Arp, wrote gentle satire, humor blended with philosophy, in letters to the *Constitution,* which, the *Louisville Courier-Journal* said, lifted up the drooping hearts of a whole people, bringing relief and hope to thousands. And in Putnam County, in a paper called the *Countryman,* a young printer named Joel Chandler Harris began writing the essays which brought back nostalgic memories of plantation days.

Some relief, comic, nostalgic, or philosophical, was needed when Georgians found out what was happening in their civil government. While the squabble over Negro representation was going on, Bullock and his Radical Republican cohorts were busy in other fields. Though in Georgia, where there were fewer carpetbaggers, corruption and extravagance in the use of public funds was less flagrant than in some states, the totals here were startling enough. Between 1866 and 1870, costs for civil administration rose from $20,000 to $76,000, printing from $1,000 to $57,000, and advertising proclamations rose from $5,000 in 1855–1860 to $98,000 in 1868–1870. Much of this money went into the pockets of Governor Bullock's friends. Bonds were sold for far less than their worth and the money used for unauthorized purposes, and in two years of operation by the Bullock regime the Western and Atlantic Railroad lost $750,000. One railroad employee, asked how he could acquire a fortune of $30,000 in two years' time on a salary of $2,000 a year, said it was done "by the exercise of the most rigid economy." [3]

The guiding genius behind Governor Bullock's financial operations was a Northern adventurer named Hannibal I. Kimball, "a steam engine in breeches," [4] who became the president of three Georgia railroads. He also sold an opera house which he had under construction in Atlanta to the state as its first capitol building, and built a fine new hotel, which became a favorite meeting place for generations of Georgia politicians.

Much of the financial manipulation in Georgia centered around the railroads. In 1870 the legislature, dismayed by the huge deficits the W&A was running up under the management of Bullock's administration, ordered that the state-owned railroad be rented to private operators for not less than $25,000 a month. Former Governor Joseph E. Brown, as sharp a businessman as he was an astute politician, immediately put together a company to operate the road under his presidency. Among his associates in this venture were Alexander H. Stephens and Benjamin H. Hill. Hill, like Brown, finally had come to a compromise with his own conscience that allowed him to accept Republican rule as being the only alternative to chaos. Stephens soon withdrew after drawing down upon his head the wrath of unreconstructed Robert Toombs, but Hill stayed on.

The passing bell by now was tolling for Republican rule in Georgia. In an election in December 1870, the Democrats seized control of both the House and the Senate—and began an investigation of the Western and Atlantic railroad deal which showed that another group had offered the state a rental of $35,000 a month. These implications were not lost on Governor Bullock. In October of 1871 he secretly wrote out his resignation and silently stole away, back to his old home in Albion, N.Y. He was gone a week before he was missed, and he did not come back again for six years. At about this same time, Mr. Kimball, his financial empire in ruins, joined Mr. Bullock in temporary exile—departing for Chicago.

3. Garrett, *Atlanta and Environs,* 1:832.
4. Garrett, *Atlanta and Environs,* 1:833.

In a special election in December 1871, a new governor, James M. Smith, a Democrat, was elected. The Democrats, led by Robert Toombs, now began to dig into the actions of Mr. Bullock and his cohorts. It was found that Bullock indeed had been guilty of indictable offenses, particularly in connection with issues of state bonds, but when he was brought back to face trial in 1876, Georgia was in a forgiving and forgetful mood, and he was acquitted. The bonds, however, were repudiated by the legislature and were never paid. H. I. Kimball came back in 1874 and challenged anybody to prove that he had done anything wrong in connection with bond issues or anything else. No indictments were brought against him, and soon both he and Bullock were numbered among Atlanta's leading businessmen. "Kimball and Bullock," said Franklin Garrett in his history of Atlanta, "were as careless with the public money as was General Sherman with fire, but they built, where he destroyed." [5]

In August of 1868, the *Atlanta Constitution,* founded two months earlier by a "man of fire and dreams," [6] Col. Carey W. Styles, had printed a premature obituary of the Radical Republican party in Georgia. Four years later, in October of 1872, the general election returned Governor Smith to office for a full term, soundly defeating his Republican opponent. The *Constitution's* lyrical editorial this time was more accurate. Under the title, "Downfall of the Radical Dynasty," the paper exultantly proclaimed:

> Once more we breathe. The reign of law and order begins. Since Governor Jenkins was deposed by military despotism, we have had a long night of Radical rule and Cimmerian darkness. That rule is ended. The darkness is succeeded by light. Thank God Georgia is redeemed. [7]

This "redemption" came about because the North by now was beginning to tire of the complex and wearisome task of Reconstruction. There was a growing tendency to forgive the South, to find some mutual ground both regions could accept, to

5. Garrett, *Atlanta and Environs,* 2:788.
6. Harold H. Martin, *Ralph McGill, Reporter* (Boston: Little, Brown, 1973), p. 40.
7. Garrett, *Atlanta and Environs,* 1:875.

get on with the important task of doing business together. All over the South at this time, states were wresting political power from the hands of Reconstruction governments—their self-styled "Redeemers" including a number of the old landed aristocracy. Many of them in Georgia, like Robert Toombs, Alfred Colquitt, and John B. Gordon, were ex-Confederate officers. Others, like Joseph E. Brown and Charles J. Jenkins, were antebellum governors or high officials. Strongly conservative, distrustful of the black vote and the poor white alike, this class of Bourbon leadership strongly encouraged the growth of railroads and industry of all kinds—particularly mining in the Georgia hills, where under a law passed by the Bullock regime, convict labor was widely used.

Though the history of the Reconstruction period in Georgia is dominated by the stories of financial corruption and political chicanery, in fairness it must be said that in this time was laid the groundwork for the strong and prosperous Georgia that was to be. The state, and particularly its resurgent capital at Atlanta, found the period one of booming economic growth and increasing prosperity. Hardly had Sherman's troops left burning Atlanta when the people began with fierce energy to rebuild their city. By December of 1865, this rebirth was well under way, and Atlanta, home of the railroads, with no "old plantation" tradition to turn its thoughts to a dear, dead past, had the drive of a Western town.

The secret of Atlanta's quick rebirth, in fact, lies in those Northerners who came to Georgia not to victimize or reconstruct, but simply to do business. These agents and drummers scrambling frantically to make a dollar by peddling Yankee manufactures did not confine their efforts to Atlanta. They kept the livery stables busy, renting rigs in which they traveled the muddy country roads, seeking out the little merchants whose stores by now were rising at every crossroads.

Here in the Georgia backcountry the tremendous social changes brought about by war and reconstruction were most poignantly felt, for here, even more than in the cities, a new and workable relationship between white and black had to be evolved—a relationship which not only complied with federal law, but which took into consideration also the economic realities of life in rural Georgia. The first and most important change was in the relationship between the planter and his former slave. The slave had been the white man's responsibility. Regardless of his age or sex or his capacity to do work, he had been fed, clothed, sheltered, and cared for by his master. He was now a free man on his own to provide for himself as best he could. He could offer his labor for a wage or withhold it, as he chose. The one thing that had not changed was the fact that the whole structure of Southern society still depended on his labor, as it had before the war.

Black man and white, each needed the other, and out of this need a new system was worked out, a tenant system which was to change the face of rural Georgia and the lives of rural Georgians, black and white. The slave cabin moved from its cluster near the Big House to become a solitary shanty in the fields, where the former slave could work at his own pace, unsupervised, required only at the end of the year at "settling time" to pay an agreed-upon rent in cash or a share of the crop.

The crossroads store was one manifestation of this change. The old plantation ran its own commissary, out of which the plantation worker was clothed and fed. As the great plantations were broken down into smaller units, hundreds of little rural communities grew into towns and became distribution centers for a wider surrounding area. They brought into the back country a new type of man, unfamiliar with farming but anxious to sell goods to farmers—the new equivalent of the old factoring class who once bought the plantation owner's cotton and supported him with all his needs from a city warehouse. Some of these new tradesmen were Yankee expatriates. More, though, were native Georgians—ex-soldiers, onetime plantation owners unable to make a go of farming without slaves, ex-Army sutlers, and Jewish pack peddlers. All came into the backcountry, settled down, and opened little places of business selling cloth and plows and patent medicines. And around this commercial nucleus grew up little industries, a cotton gin, an oil mill, a fertilizer plant, perhaps a little textile mill. Then a church was built and a doctor moved in, and a lawyer hung out his shingle, and a pharmacist set up shop, and a little town was born. Out of these rural communities rose a new middle class, to back up, and sometimes to challenge, the old Bourbons operating out of Atlanta, Augusta, Macon, Columbus, and Savannah, with their larger interests in banking, railroading, insurance, and the operation of mines. And so, in the two decades just after the war, in rural Georgia the little towns thrived while the little farmer struggled to build a new agricultural economy on the ruins of the old plantation.

The spokesman for all of Georgia in these years, for the capitalist as well as the farmer, was a brilliant young orator and editor, a boy wonder named Henry Grady. Brought to the *Atlanta Constitution* in 1876 by its new owner, Evan P. Howell, from then on until his untimely death in 1889 at age 38, he had held before the eyes of all Southerners his vision of a New South, busy and prospering, though still treasuring the memory of the South that was.

Three days before Christmas in 1886, Grady had made a speech before the New England Society in the city of New York. In that speech, which brought enduring fame to Grady and made him a national figure overnight, he painted a picture of the South that was no more, and the South he and many another Georgian dreamed would come into being. Preceding him on the program were a noted preacher, the Rev. T. DeWitt Talmadge, and General William Tecumseh Sherman himself. Sherman reminisced of his march through Georgia, and, almost as if in apology to Grady, said to him:

> I assure you that we who took part in that war were kindly men. We did not wish to kill . . . I know that I grieved as much as any man when I saw pain and sorrow and affliction among the innocent and distressed, and when I saw burning and desolation. But these were incidents of war and were forced upon us—forced upon us by men influenced by a bad ambition; not by the men who owned these slaves but by politicians who used that as a pretext, and forced you and your fathers and me, and others who sit near me, to take up arms and settle the controversy once and forever.[8]

Grady was the next speaker, his assignment to respond to the toast, ''The New South.'' He began by quoting a famous utter-

8. *Report of the Eighty-First Anniversary Celebration of the New England Society in the City of New York,* Dec. 22, 1886, p. 37.

ance by Benjamin H. Hill in 1866: " 'There was a South of slavery and secession—that South is dead. There is a South of union and freedom—that South, thank God, is living, breathing, growing every hour.' " [9] This, he said, would be his text. He went on to describe the American as a blend of Puritan and Cavalier, adding:

> . . . from the union of these colonist puritans and cavaliers . . . slow perfecting through a century, came he who stands as the first typical American, the first who comprehended within himself all the strength and gentleness, all the majesty and grace of this Republic—Abraham Lincoln. He was the sum of both for in his ardent nature were found the virtues of both, and in the depths of his great soul, the faults of both were lost. [10]

At this unexpected tribute to Lincoln there was loud and continued applause.

He also paid his respects to General Sherman as "one who is considered an able man in our parts, though some people think that he is kind of a careless man about fire"—telling his audience that "from the ashes he left we have raised a brave and beautiful city; that somehow or other we have caught the sunshine in the brick and mortar of our homes and have builded therein not one ignoble prejudice or memory." [11]

Dr. Talmadge had graphically pictured in his speech the marches of triumphal Union armies coming home victorious "reading their glory in a nation's eyes." Grady, in turn, told of another army coming home—"in defeat and not in victory, in pathos, not in splendor, but in glory that equalled yours, and to hearts as loving as ever welcomed heroes home." [12]

The speech was reported in the *New York Tribune,* and in North and South alike the reaction was one of highest praise. Not since Lincoln's Gettysburg Address had a speaker so well expressed the feeling in the hearts of a people and a nation, and in his summation, when Grady asked, "What is New England's answer? Will she permit the prejudice of war to remain in the

9. *New England Society,* p. 39.
10. *New England Society,* p. 41.
11. *New England Society,* p. 44.
12. *New England Society,* pp. 42–43.

hearts of the conquerors, when it has died in the hearts of the conquered?'' The answer from the audience was a thundering ''No, no, no!'' [13]

Echoes of that ''New South'' speech have come down the years, for it marked the ending of one civilization, the birth-cry of another. It represented, too, Grady's mood of literally loving the nation back to peace. In other speeches, he was equally eloquent about the special problems facing the South. First, it must free itself from the thralldom of King Cotton by diversifying its agriculture. Next, it must concentrate its money, time, and thought on the creation of new industry. In his attitude toward the Negro he was bluntly outspoken. His great fear was of the Negro vote, which Grady predicted the Negro would happily sell to the highest bidder, thus foiling all efforts at progress by giving state governments into the hands of venal men. The Negro vote, he stressed, would never be allowed to control in the South, and in time the North must come to understand this.

Grady's words pleased Southerners, for they expressed the Southern view. They mollified the North, which now, under Grover Cleveland and the first Democratic administration since the Civil War, was no longer as fiercely devoted to the Negro's cause as it had been. So the South now turned solidly Democratic, set up the barriers which in effect again disfranchised the Negro. There were many tricks known to Georgia politicians that could accomplish this, no matter what rights were guaranteed to the Negro under the Constitution. Literary tests, the poll tax (which disfranchised the poor white as well as the black), the grandfather clause (which required proof that the voter's ancestor was eligible to vote), and the white primary, each in its own time was used, and each in turn came under attack from the NAACP or others, and was struck down by the Supreme Court. The earliest effort to keep the Negro from the polls and to force his white friends to keep a low profile was pure intimidation, the threat of the Ku Klux Klan. Riders robed in sheets and peaked helmets that hid their faces rode through the Negro sections of the small towns on the night before election, and the mark of their mysterious symbol—KKK—and the sight of the

13. *New England Society,* p. 44.

crosses they burned on the hills at midnight struck terror into the hearts of the superstitious blacks. So the Negro, threatened and thwarted, went back to his plow and his hoe on the farm, and his yardman's and helper's job in the city, making no issue of the fact that he could not vote. And on the surface at least, peace prevailed for more than half a century, until the great civil-rights struggle of the mid-Twentieth century began.

The poor white Georgian could vote and he was more likely to be a member of the Ku Klux Klan than to be intimidated by it. But his economic situation, particularly if he was a farmer, was no better than that of the Negro. For the Georgia farmer, white or black, the New South that Grady had dreamed of remained just that—a dream. The system of land tenure that had replaced the plantation held the tenant in a new kind of bondage—to the landowner, or the storekeeper who "furnished" him and who at gathering time bought his cotton and gave him not cash, but a note marked "paid"—which meant he was now ready to go in debt for another year. The landowner, in his turn, was held in the same servitude—to the small town merchant and banker. And these, too, ended each crop year in debt to Northern merchants and banking houses.

While the rural Georgian, both white and black, sank deeper into debt and despair, the trumpet Grady had sounded calling on Georgia to industrialize was heard and heeded, particularly in brash and bustling Atlanta. A remarkable group of men, most of them native Georgians, some of them Northern born, all of them believers, gave the city new life and vigor. Pioneers and newcomers alike, they founded banks and expanded railroad lines, built textile mills and flour mills, and set street railways running on Atlanta's still muddy streets. They laid out parks and built tall buildings, founded newspapers and developed subdivisions of handsome houses. And there was one among them who built no tall building and set no railroads running, but whose name is still remembered, not only in the city but in all the world. In the time of Atlanta's postwar surge, the young printer in Putnam County, Joel Chandler Harris, was giving to readers North and South the gift of gentle laughter in the Uncle Remus stories, which were to make him and an old black man and a feisty rabbit immortal in the annals of American folklore.

In 1881, in a burst of civic pride Atlanta staged its first exposition, the World's Fair and Great International Cotton Exposition, at which it set forth for all the world to see what it had accomplished in the fields of commerce and industry. This brought more people and more money flowing in, and once the exposition had closed, the huge Exposition Cotton Mill, a factory employing 500 workers, was opened in the main building. From then on until the turn of the century Atlanta's growth was steady—industrialization sharing the city's once pre-eminent importance as a commercial and distribution center. Steam power was now in the ascendancy. A factory could be established anywhere near a railroad that could bring it coal to fire its boilers and haul away its finished product. Thus Atlanta became important as a manufacturing center for farm implements, cottonseed-oil products, construction materials, furniture, glass, pianos, and all kinds of machinery. It was, until the coming of the tractor, the world's largest mule market.

In 1887 it held another huge fair, the Piedmont Exposition, which brought President and Mrs. Cleveland to town to be splendidly entertained at the Gentlemen's Driving Club (now the Piedmont Driving Club) on whose grounds the fair was held, and at the almost new Capital City Club. The theme was closer co-operation between agriculture and industry, but somehow there was overlooked an achievement by an Atlantan which was to do more than any other thing to bring great wealth to Atlanta and make its name a by-word around the world. A year earlier, in 1886, a druggist named John S. Pemberton blended in a secret formula certain flavors to form a syrup he called Coca-Cola—which two Atlanta families, the Candlers and later the Woodruffs, were to make into the most widely advertised and consumed commercial product in the world.

A financial panic in the early 1890s slowed the city's progress temporarily. By 1895, though, it had recovered faith and vigor sufficiently to again boast of its achievements in another exposition—the Cotton States and International Exposition. This one, also held in Piedmont Park, featured the ten cotton states and all their resources, and was designed to promote Georgia's trade with South America. To the dismay of some diehard racists, the Negroes had a building at which they proudly presented their achievements, and Booker T. Washington was a featured speaker.

Though Atlanta's surging industrial growth in the first decades after Reconstruction made headlines nationally, there were other good things happening, in other fields, in other places throughout the state. Georgians had quickly returned to their antebellum drive to expand and improve education, from the common schools to the university level. Gustavus Orr was appointed School Commissioner in 1872 and did such noble work on behalf of the elementary schools that by his death in 1887 he had truly earned the title of father of the common schools in Georgia. Nor was university education static. The School of Agriculture and the Mechanic Arts opened at the university in Athens in 1872, and in the following year the North Georgia Agricultural College branch was opened at Dahlonega, in the old U.S. mint building. In 1885 another branch of the university was founded, the School of Technology in Atlanta, and in 1889, a Normal and Industrial College for Girls was authorized at Milledgeville.

The churches in the late 1800s extended their interest in higher education to schools for women. In 1873 the Baptists established, at Rome, Cherokee Female College, which four years later became Shorter College; in 1878, they established at Gainesville the seminary which was to become Brenau College. In 1889, the Decatur Presbyterian Church started Decatur Female Seminary, which in time was to become Agnes Scott, one of the state's leading colleges for women. The needs of mountain children attracted strong support in the early 1900s. Miss Martha Berry became a legend in Georgia when she started her Berry Schools at Rome, where mountain girls and boys were taught manual skills as well as book learning. Tallulah Falls Industrial School, organized by the Georgia Federation of Women's Clubs, began in 1908, to be followed by Rabun Gap Nacoochee School, founded under Presbyterian auspices in 1920.

In the years just after the war, many institutions for Negroes were started, mainly by church groups in the North. Among the first was Atlanta University, founded by the American Missionary Association in 1865, followed by Baptist-sponsored

Morehouse College in 1867; Clark University, supported by the Methodist-Episcopal Church, in 1870; Spelman College, started by the Misses Sophia A. Packard and Harriett Giles in 1881; Morris Brown, founded by Negro Methodists in 1885; Paine College, established by Southern Methodists in 1883; and Fort Valley Normal and Industrial College, founded in 1896 by the Episcopal Church. The concentration in Atlanta of Atlanta University, Morehouse, and Spelman made the city the largest center for Negro education in the world.

In politics, much was happening to shape the Georgia of the future. A new constitution in 1877 wiped out the old "Republican" document of 1868. a new state flag was created in 1879, and on July 4, 1888, a new state capital, costing just under a million dollars, was opened on a green knoll in Atlanta, replacing the old structure that had begun as Kimball's opera house. In high political office, the old heroes of the Confederacy still held sway. In 1873 General John B. Gordon became U.S. senator; in 1876 Benjamin H. Hill followed him to Washington. In 1882 Alexander H. Stephens reached the peak of his brilliant career in Georgia as he took the governor's chair in a state where mob violence, in the form of lynching, now was beginning to attract national notoriety, and where Georgians themselves were beginning to argue, angrily, a prohibition law. In February 1883, Governor Stephens died, of a cold contracted while attending ceremonies at Savannah celebrating the Sesquicentennial founding of the state.

There were other moments of deep nostalgia. On May 1, 1886, Jefferson Davis and his daughter, Winnie, "the daughter of the Confederacy," came to Atlanta to unveil a monument to Senator Benjamin H. Hill. They received a wild ovation; later that month they were guests in Savannah, where the Chatham Artillery celebrated its centenary by firing the cannon General Washington had sent the battery after his visit there in May of 1791. Three years later, in December of 1889, Jefferson Davis died at New Orleans. His body was brought to Atlanta on its way to burial in Virginia, and was viewed by thousands as it lay in state at the capital. It was a month of sorrow for Georgians of the old South, and the new. Two days before Christmas Henry Grady died at his home in Atlanta of pneumonia contracted on a last speaking trip to Boston, where he had made the second most famous speech of his career. Speaking before the Bay State Club, he had described the funeral of a poor, one-gallus Georgia farmer, buried in a grave cut into solid marble, in the heart of a pine forest beside the best sheep-growing country in the world, and nearby to a deposit of iron. Yet the marble tombstone that was set above him was carved in Vermont, and the pine coffin was from Cincinnati, and the iron nails that held it together and the iron shovel that dug the grave came from Pittsburgh, and the woolen coffin bands were Northern-made. Georgia, said Grady, furnished nothing but the corpse and the hole in the ground. But that was changing, he promised his Northern hearers. Now near that grave was the biggest marble-cutting establishment on earth, and woolen mills, and iron mines and iron furnaces and iron factories. Georgia, he told his Yankee listeners, was going to take a noble revenge by invading the North with iron as the North had invaded Georgia twenty years before. He came from this last trip white-faced and shaking with fever, to die at thirty-eight, and all over Georgia, high and low, rich and poor, white and black, heard the sad news and wept. No Georgian, before or since, had done more to persuade both North and South to put away old hatreds and old fears. He was a racist, as the term is now understood, but he spoke for the realities of his day and his words are still remembered.

7

Grady's Dream, Watson's Vision

ND now there came upon the political scene another
Georgian with a vision, a man who did not share Grady's dream
of an industrialized Georgia. Just as Grady had been primarily
the spokesman for the man of business, Thomas E. Watson became the voice of the little man, black and white, the sharecropper, the tenant, the working man in the mill and the mine, men
who, despite the prosperity around them, were growing more
and more dissatisfied with their own lot. A lean, square-jawed,
redheaded man with intense, hypnotic eyes, Watson burned
with a fierce desire to take political power from the hands of a
Bourbon aristocracy supported by a complacent middle class
and place it with the mass of the people, with the farmer and the
laborer, who would take control of the state's politics and shape
its destiny.

Born on his grandfather's plantation near Thomson, in Columbia County, in 1856, raised under the influence of Robert
Toombs and Alexander H. Stephens, who were frequent guests
in his father's house, Watson grew up in the aftermath of the
Civil War to see his family's once ample holdings in land and
money lost to creditors. To him this was the work of an economic system rigged to favor the capitalist and the industrialist.
His memories of Reconstruction were bitter and vivid. Opposition to Union occupation was particularly violent in the Thomson area, where the blacks made up sixty percent of the population. Here much of the white population was disfranchised, and

133

under the protection of federal rifles the Negroes' votes were openly and shamelessly bought and sold by carpetbaggers and scalawags. Watson was a teenager in those days and the memory never left him of the times when Union cavalry patrolled the roads by day and the white-robed Klansmen came out by night to terrify the Negro who was bold enough to vote. He remembered, too, organ-voiced orators—Howell Cobb, Rance Wright, John B. Gordon, Robert Toombs, and Benjamin H. Hill—roaring from the stump their tributes to the old days and their defiance of the new. Watson began his self-admitted search for fame by earning an early repuation as a fiery orator before local Temperance societies, a choice of vocation inspired perhaps by the fact that his father, after losing the family plantation to his creditors, became addicted to drink. For all his sobriety, though, he was a dancing man, and he could make sweet music on the fiddle. And out of his memories of the square dances, the corn shuckings, the gander pullings, the quilting bees, the barn raisings, the courthouse oratory, he formed his own vision of a new South far different from that of Mr. Grady, with his smoking factory chimneys. Watson's Georgia was the Georgia of simple rural folk, their lives bound to the rhythms of seedtime and harvest and the slow turning of the seasons. As Georgia at Henry Grady's urging would bind herself into ever closer alliance with Northern capitalists, Watson saw the future in a different light. Georgians, he argued, should not ally themselves with Northern money-changers, but with simple farm folk from the Western states. Before he could do much to further this bucolic dream, however, he had to find a form of livelihood more rewarding than his first profession, that of a country schoolteacher. After two years at Mercer, he began to "read law" in the office of Judge W. R. McLaws in Augusta, and in a year had passed the bar examination. He was twenty years old, and was launched at last into that fabled career—triumphant in the beginning, tragic at the end, full of paradoxes all the way—which did lead him on, as he had dreamed, to fame and fortune, and finally to abject failure. But in the course of it all he left a mark on Georgia's psyche the passing years have not erased. His specialty was criminal law, always as attorney for the defendant, and he became so famous for bringing off the accused unpunished that his services were in demand all over Georgia. His work was in country courthouses, before country juries, and the language he spoke was the language they understood, wry humor touched with a trace of bawdiness, changing suddenly into flights of oratory so poetic he could leave his hearers in tears. His strength lay in the fact that he understood and could vividly articulate what the little people, the farmers in particular, seemed only dimly to realize—that in the postwar Georgia, they were getting a minuscule share of the new wealth that was being created. Not only industrial Atlanta but the cotton ports, where the baled cotton was bought and sold, were also booming. In Watson's view, this prosperity was a capitalist prosperity—benefiting only the banker, the broker, the warehouseman, and the shipping magnate. Too little of it trickled down to the people he hoped to speak for, the backcountry farmers, both black and white, who grew the cotton. In the early 1880s, before he had turned so savagely against the Negro, he addressed both races with fire and passion, telling them that they were made to hate each other because in that hatred was based the financial despotism which made beggars of them both.

Those who in Watson's view imposed this despotism were men of great renown in Georgia. For nearly thirty years, from the end of Reconstruction to the turn of the century, Georgia politics had been dominated by a triumvirate who in their persons represented an unbeatable combination of political assets. Joseph E. Brown, John B. Gordon, and Alfred Colquitt were old Confederates. Brown was a mountain man, but the other two were steeped in the myth and legend of the old South Georgia of plantation days. Brown, the fiery secessionist, was the wartime governor. Gordon was a bullet-scarred veteran of many a fierce fight. Colquitt was a planter who had raised a thousand bales of cotton a year before he became a Confederate major general. Yet each was a shrewd, hard-driving businessman deeply involved in the developing and expansion of railroads, factories, and mines. It was they, the Bourbon aristocracy, who in defense against the Negro vote, had brought all white Georgians, rich and poor, rural and urban, together under the banner of one party, the Democrats. and it was they who would bear the brunt when dissident elements would begin to split off into factions within the party.

In 1880, when Senator John B. Gordon resigned to go into the railroad business and Governor Colquitt appointed Joseph E. Brown in his place, Watson and other insurgent Democrats looked upon this as political trickery of the most arrant sort. As a result, in the convention which met to nominate a governor, a long and bitter fight took place against Colquitt's candidacy. Now for the first time outside the courtroom or on a temperance lecture's platform, Tom Watson began to make his mark upon the public mind. A delegate to the convention, his speech against the nomination of Colquitt rang all the changes, from humor to dramatic defiance to lofty metaphor, in a forensic *tour de force* that was widely printed in newspapers throughout the state. From then on until he died, Georgia, and in time, the nation, would remember the scrawny little man with the searing tongue and the flaming eyes and the temper to match.

Despite Watson's opposition, Colquitt was renominated, and in one of the bitterest election contests ever held in Georgia, won re-election. Watson, well aware that his fiery attack on Colquitt had brought him statewide fame, was not discouraged. Two years later, in 1882, he was back, feisty as a gamecock, running for the legislature. He won, and in his first year fought hard for reform. He blasted the convict-lease system, which Governor Colquitt favored and Senators Brown and Gordon found most profitable in the operation of their coal mines in Dade County. He introduced bills which would protect the tenant farmer against loss of his crop for debt. Neither bill passed, and Watson, angry and discouraged, left the legislature before the session ended.

For some six years thereafter he practiced law, made money, bought land, and stayed out of politics. Then, in 1888, he stumped the state, as a presidential elector-at-large, for Grover Cleveland, and again mesmerized his audiences with his oratory. The acclaim he was receiving convinced him he should again seek public office, this time on a national scale. In him a deep rebellion had long been stirring. His sojourn in Atlanta as a legislator had convinced him that Henry Grady had led the

South along a path that made the urban few affluent and left the many who lived on the land impoverished. ''Mr. Grady,'' wrote Watson, ''says that 'plenty rides on the springing harvest.' It rides on Grady's springing imagination.'' [1] He then contrasted Grady's pastoral vision of fat cattle grazing in scented meadows with the realities as he saw them—bony cattle starving on gullied slopes. Watson admitted that the Southern farmer was indolent and sometimes careless, but attributed this to repeated failure and discouragement brought on by banking laws and tariff laws and high taxes in an economic system rigged against him.

In 1890, he ran for Congress, preaching this anticapitalist doctrine, and won. In this race, he had strong help from beyond the boundaries of his own district as he began to sing his new song—the war chant of an agrarian protest movement that was by now nationwide. In the 1870s there had begun to appear in the South individuals calling themselves Patrons of Husbandry, or Grangers. They came out of the West and their purpose was to defend the tenant farmer from those who exploited him by keeping him in perpetual debt to the landowner and his company store. By 1875 there were 18,000 of them in Georgia. They accomplished little, but out of the Grangers grew another, stronger group, an organization of farmers, mainly in the Midwest and Texas, calling themselves the Alliance. In 1887 they held a Southwide meeting in Georgia and spread their rebellious doctrine. Its points: The farmer of the South was being victimized by bankers who would not lend the farmer money, thus thrusting him into the talons of the local merchant with his inflated prices; by Wall Street speculators who gambled on his crop's futures; by railroad owners who overcharged him to haul his products; by the tariff makers, the trusts, and the government itself—even by his own party, the Democrats, now in the hands of the owners of stocks and bonds, banks and factories. Trying to fight his way out of this trap, the Georgia farmer had raised too much cotton, and decade after decade the price had fallen—from twenty cents in the Seventies to seven cents in the Nineties, less than the cost of production.

1. Thomas J. Watson, quoted by C. Vann Woodward, *Tom Watson: Agrarian Rebel* (New York, London: Oxford University Press, 1938), pp. 126–127.

Georgia's farmers listened avidly while the Alliance preached this doctrine and laid out a counterplan under which the farmer would sell his cotton directly to the consumer, thus eliminating the middleman and the Eastern capitalist. The Alliance also preached what Grady had preached to the farmer—that he should raise less cotton and more food crops. The Alliance would increase the money supply by having the government coin silver in unlimited amounts, and notes would be issued on farm products in warehouses around the country, thus doing away with national bank issues. The Alliance would regulate the railroads or have the government take them over. It would abolish the brutal system of leasing convicts to private industries, and would put them to work on the country's miserable roads. It would improve the schools and reduce taxes, and the tariff. In fact, it would revise the whole system of taxation in Georgia. And in doing all these things the Alliance would create around the farmer and his family a new Eden, sprung from the richness of the land.

As these ideas caught fire in Georgia, Tom Watson became their champion, and the old political hierarchy that had controlled the state since the Civil War soon realized that it must bend to the storm or be blown away. In the 1890 campaign Democratic candidates fell over each other getting to the stump to announce their allegiance to the Alliance's ideas. The triumph at the polls was impressive. The president of the State Agricultural Society, W. J. Northen, was nominated for governor. Alliance men were named to 160 out of 219 seats in the legislature, and the Alliance had the support of all ten congressmen elected. Among them was Thomas E. Watson who, as a practicing lawyer, was forbidden formal membership—as were bank cashiers, railroad officials, real estate agents, cotton brokers, or "anybody who buys or sells for gain." [2] But he spoke the Alliance's language, and marched to its drum. Soon, though, it began to appear that the Alliance had taken in too many converts. The dirt farmers, the "woolhat boys" who had started the Alliance in the first place, began to feel that they had been swallowed up by the latecomers to the cause, the "plughat

2. Woodward, *Tom Watson: Agrarian Rebel*, p. 137.

crowd'' from Atlanta. They began to cast about for other leadership, a third flag to follow that was neither Democratic nor Republican. The leader they were looking for had been there all along. Tom Watson, Tenth District representative in Congress, for good or ill was making a name for himself in Washington as a rebel against the party that sent him there. He refused to be bound by any Democratic caucus agreements or any rules and regulations. He became highly unpopular with some of his congressional colleagues from other states by accusing them of being the tools of the lobbyists, and he lectured them sternly for appearing, drunk, on the House floor. But he did one thing for which the lonely farmer on the muddy back roads would ever be grateful to him. He sponsored the bill which created the RFD, the rural free delivery of the U.S. mail.

Around the nation there had by now grown up a third political party, made up in the main of farmers strongly discontented with their lot, calling themselves the People's party, or Populists. They embraced the politico-economic ideas of the old Granger and Alliance men, and to Georgia Alliance men seeking a wool-hat refuge from the Democrats, this third party seemed to be the answer to their prayers. Tom Watson, who could easily have won the Populist nomination for governor, preferred the excitement of Washington to the trials of the statehouse in Atlanta. He chose to run again for Congress—and lost.

Not since Sherman's march had there been so much blood shed in Georgia as in the days preceding this election of 1892. Most Alliance men in Georgia refused to be led out of the Democratic party into a third party, fearing that by their dividing the white vote, the Negro Republicans, with their handful of lily-white cohorts, would seize the balance of power. Arguments flared into fist fights at the polls and fist fights into gang fights. Populist speakers were set upon with rocks and eggs, and on several occasions Watson spoke while friendly farmers protected him with their rifles. The Democrats, howling that the Populist candidates were messengers of anarchy and communism, shouted down Populist speakers and used every trick in the book to assure Watson's defeat—and that of W. L. Peek, the Populist candidate for governor against Northen.

Watson pretended to take it calmly, but his loss of this election left a mark upon him that time could never erase, and shaped his attitude in bitter ways thereafter. He charged, justifiably, that the most arrantly corrupt practices had been used against him, including the buying of Negro votes, sometimes for money, often for a drink of cheap liquor. This, to Watson, was the sin unpardonable on the black man's part. The program of the Populist party had called for a united front between the Negro and the white farmers. To Watson, the cry of white supremacy, of complete and utter separation of the races, was not willed by God, as most Southerners, including Henry Grady, believed. It was an effort to keep poor black and white apart politically so that they could be separately robbed of their earnings. Watson, in his fervor, had spoken out against lynching in a state which had led the world in lynchings; he had pleaded— not for social equality, since this was a matter of individual choice—but for "political equality," arguing that "the accident of color can make no difference in the interests of farmers, croppers, and laborers." [3] He praised Negro accomplishments, and with an evangelist's fervor preached "tolerance, friendly co-operation, justice, and political rights for the Negro." [4]

And now, to Watson's anguish and outrage, instead of supporting the party which offered him the freedom and acceptance he had always sought, the Negro had amiably sold his vote—for a drink, for a dollar—or, out of fear, he did not vote at all.

The goal of the Populists, to establish a third party that could break up the old Solid South, had failed, in Georgia and the nation. But Watson was to keep on fighting. The old giants had gone from the political scene—Toombs, Stephens, Ben Hill, Colquitt, Gordon—done in by death or old age. A new Democratic leadership had arisen—each heading a faction within the party. Clark Howell of the *Constitution* had his strong following, Hoke Smith of the *Journal* had his, and it was on these spokesmen for the Democrats that Watson trained his guns. His task was to win the discontented Southern Democrat over to the Populists, and he outlined to Populist stump speakers how this could be done.

3. Woodward, *Tom Watson: Agrarian Rebel,* p. 221.
4. Woodward, *Tom Watson: Agrarian Rebel,* p. 220–221.

His points were simple—that the Southern and the Western
farmer were brothers sharing a common interest, and their common enemy was the financier, the plutocrat, whether he be
Democrat or Republican, North or South. Lending strength to
Watson's words was the miserable economic situation in which
Georgia, and the South, now found itself. In 1891 and 1892,
cotton had sold at its lowest price in history. The doors of courthouses were placarded with the notices of sheriff's sales, and
the roads were full of displaced tenants, black and white. The
little merchants themselves were going broke as the farmers
they had furnished failed to "pay out." In the mill towns and
the factory slums of the cities, conditions were no better. The
Atlanta Journal reported that at Exposition Cotton Mills, so
proudly hailed by Henry Grady ten years before as the harbinger
of a New South, the mill workers were making thirty-six cents a
day, and "famine and pestilence are making worse ravages than
among the serfs in Russia." The *Journal*'s dreadful picture
went on to tell of "rooms wherein eight and ten members of one
family are stricken down, where pneumonia and fever and
measles are attacking their emaciated bodies; where there is no
sanitation, no help or protection from the city, no medicine, no
food, no fire, no nurses—nothing but torturing hunger and
death." [5] The Panic of 1893 was nationwide. Everywhere
banks were failing, factories closing, mortgages were being
foreclosed, and out-of-work men were leaving the hungry cities
going back to the farms they came from in the hope that there,
at least, they might find something to eat.

Tom Watson was out of office, but far from silent. As editor
of the *The People's Party Paper,* he reported with bitter irony
every plea of the Democrats to the Democratic president, Mr.
Cleveland, to do something. And he took great pleasure in noting that many of the things they pleaded for were Populist Party
planks he had long advocated—free silver, postal savings, a
graduated income tax. Readers who agreed with what he wrote,
the crowds, and the growing power of the Populist party gave
him confidence that in the election of 1894 he would regain his
seat in Congress. He lost, but in an election so rife with corrupt

5. Woodward, *Tom Watson: Agrarian Rebel,* p. 225.

practices at the polls that a special runoff election was held in 1895. This time he won—in nine counties out of eleven. But Augusta—where in one ward Negroes voted against him, 989 to nine—helped pile up the majority that beat him. Again he felt that he had been betrayed by the blacks, whose rights he almost alone had defended. And to his list of enemies he added the Catholics of Augusta, who he felt had led the fight against him.

The next year he was back in the public eye again, this time on the national scene—as vice-presidential nominee on the Populist ticket headed by William Jennings Bryan—who was also the Democratic presidential candidate with a Northern banker, Arthur Sewall, as his running mate. But the seeds of dissolution were already in the Populist party, in Georgia as well as elsewhere. Its main planks, the issues that had breathed life into it in the first place, had already been taken over by the two old parties. Populist leaders, too, for all their idealistic chanting, had proved in recent state elections to be as prone to vote-buying as were their enemies. As Watson had warned would happen, by fusing with the Democrats the Populists had been swallowed up. The crowd-thrilling oratory of the thirty-six-year-old Bryan was not quite enough. Out of a vote of slightly under fourteen million, William McKinley's Republican plurality was a thin 600,000.

To Watson this election of 1896 was a catastrophe, personally as well as for the Populist party. As for himself, he felt that he was ruined both politically and financially, and he was convinced that he was on the verge of losing his mind. With this dark mood upon him, he went into a period of seclusion. In 1898, two years after his defeat as the Populist vice-presidential candidate, Georgia Populists named him as their candidate for governor. Still bitter, he refused. The Spanish-American War had started, and he was irrevocably and violently against it on the ground that wars benefited nobody but the capitalists, the national bankers, the privileged classes, and the politicians. All that "the people" would get out of this war, he thundered, was the fighting and the taxes. He now sought to repair his fortunes by writing—first *The Story of France,* next, a *Life of Napoleon.* Later, for the publishers of *Smart Set* magazine, he edited *Tom Watson's Magazine,* which found its place beside the Bible in many a Georgia farmhouse parlor. Soon he had made enough from his writing to buy cotton land and build his dream house, to which in the plantation tradition he gave the name of Hickory Hill. It was like a Greek temple, with tall white columns, a broad veranda, and a curved carriageway approaching it through tall trees, past a flowing fountain. The possession of such a house seemed to bring about a change in the public attitude toward Watson. How could a rebel, an anarchist, a communistic enemy of the capitalist class surround himself with such a patrician hall? Here obviously was the dwelling of a gentleman in whose breast there beat a great, warm heart. From Colonel, the title of respect the South bestowed upon any practicing lawyer, he became known as the Major, and finally the title that seemed to please him most—The Sage of Hickory Hill.

But Watson was not ready to slip ungrumbling into the status of lean and slippered pantaloon. When in 1904 the surviving Populists asked him to be their presidential candidate, he accepted. He knew he could not win, but he could not resist the idea of heading a national ticket, for win or lose, it would bring him the fame he had always sought. The Populists by now had little organization, in Georgia or elsewhere, nor any clear-cut platform. All they had was the stump-speaking magic of Tom Watson. And he proved over and over again that the old charisma was there. He could make them slap their legs and shout as he described how Republican candidate Teddy Roosevelt could tie his hands behind him and run Democrat Alton Parker out of the ring by merely shining his teeth at him. And he could make even a white-collar, middle-class audience, whose members had never milked a cow or hoed a row of cotton in their lives, weep as he spoke in hushed, cracked tones of the plight of the farmer under the lash of the capitalist.

He stumped the nation from coast to coast, singing his angry song. All to no avail. Roosevelt won by a landslide. Watson's Populist vote was only 117,183. Defeat was bitter, but some of the edge of his disappointment was dulled by the honors which soon came his way. Once Grady had been the feted guest at New York dinners. Now Watson was honored there by hundreds of guests who paid to see and hear him.

Elbert Hubbard delivered an address titled ''Thomas E. Watson of Georgia, a producer of History as well as a producer of Literature and the Foremost Man of America.'' [6] President Roosevelt called Watson ''fearless, disinterested and incorruptible,'' [7] and invited him to the White House.

Watson's writing also kept him the public eye. It was the age of the muckraking magazine, and his icon-shattering *Tom Watson's Magazine* caught on from the start. Theodore Dreiser, Edgar Lee Masters, Edwin Markham, Maxim Gorky, Clarence Darrow, and Judge Samuel A. Seabury all contributed to it. But the fire and flash and impact of it came from Watson's own editorials, in which he gave his talent for invective full rein— sometimes going so far as to threaten mayhem to some startled capitalists who had stirred him to wrath. He called them by name, denounced them as ''shameless unprincipled, lawbreaking robbers,'' [8] and threatened to so rouse the people that they would hang the sinners to the nearest lamppost. Soon there began showing up in his magazine editorials that revealed a changed attitude toward the black man from that which previously had guided him. Once the staunch defender of the Negro's right to vote, he now pledged his support, and the support of Georgia's Populists, to any candidate for governor of Georgia who would find a way to perpetuate white supremacy in Georgia. Already, in nearly every other Southern state the Negro had been formally disfranchised by constitutional amendment, and Watson argued that it must happen in Georgia in the same way, rather than by the working of the white primary. The man to carry out this task, he felt, was Hoke Smith, owner of the *Atlanta Journal* and political foe of Clark Howell, the other leading candidate for governor and owner of the *Constitution*. Both Smith and Watson had been born into families impoverished by the war. Both were essentially self-educated. Each had supported himself by teaching school, each had ''read law'' and practiced law, and both had an overwhelming desire to see their ideas in print—Smith in his newspaper, Watson in his magazine. Each had the same strong views against child labor and the

---

6. Woodward, *Tom Watson: Agrarian Rebel,* p. 363.
7. Woodward, *Tom Watson: Agrarian Rebel,* p. 364.
8. Woodward, *Tom Watson: Agrarian Rebel,* p. 367.

convict leasing system. Each was instinctively against the corporation and for "reform." When Smith ran for governor in 1906 his platform might have been written by Watson himself. It would domesticate all Georgia railroads, and submit them to state courts, and increase their taxes. But the key plank, to Watson, was the one which, as a *Journal* headline claimed, would legally eliminate the Negro from politics without disfranchising any whites. To Clark Howell, this was not necessary; the white primary could effectively disfranchise the Negro. He also took a kinder attitude toward the railroads, holding, like his father before him and Henry Grady, that the railroads were prime developers of the state.

Watson announced publicly that he was going to vote for Smith, and asked every Populist in the state to do the same. Smith won in a landslide. But his victory had a tragic sequel—the most terrible race riot in Atlanta's history. Watson's campaign in support of Smith's efforts to disfranchise the Negro legally and forever had brought into the open all the white man's fear of the black, fears augmented by rumors of a series of assaults by Atlanta Negroes upon white women. Four of these reportedly occurred in a period of days, and the papers fanned the flames with sensational stories. The riot broke out a month to the day after the 1906 election, and raged for four days. It was one of the more shameful episodes of Georgia—and Atlanta—history, and was the bloodiest confrontation on Georgia soil since the Civil War. Drunken mobs of angry white men hunted down Negroes in the streets, dragging them from streetcars, restaurants, barbershops. Ten blacks were killed—and two whites—and more than sixty blacks were wounded.

In his magazine Tom Watson wrote an editorial more widely quoted, in Georgia and the South, than any he had ever written. Its point—that civilization owed nothing whatever to the Negro. This was a little more than his Yankee backers could stand. After a bitter dispute Watson withdrew from the editorship of *Tom Watson's Magazine,* which expired soon thereafter. He quickly started another called *Watson's Jeffersonian Magazine.*

Smith, as a reform governor, did many things highly pleasing to Watson. Railroads and some public utilities were brought under closer supervision by the state, freight rates were reduced, and free passes were forbidden. A constitutional amendment was submitted to the people which Watson joyfully announced would disfranchise 95 percent of the Negroes. A prohibition law was passed, though Watson was by now far less a foe of the demon rum than he had been as a young temperance lecturer.

Watson's regard for Governor Smith did not long endure. When Smith refused to commute the sentence of a Watson supporter condemned to be hanged for murder, Watson changed overnight from a friend and supporter into an implacable personal and political enemy. His first impulse was to find somebody who could beat Smith, if he should choose to run for a second two-year term. His choice was Joseph M. Brown of Marietta, son of the wartime governor and postwar railroad and mining millionaire, Joseph E. Brown. For an old Populist and lover of the common people this was a strange choice. Brown had been an employee or an official of railroads for twenty-four years, a foe of organized labor, who held that unions were enemies of the public welfare. Smith, however, was vulnerable. His reform legislation had outraged many powerful interests. The railroads were angry about restrictions in freight rates and higher taxes; the liquor interests were unhappy with the prohibition law, and the state was in the grip of a financial panic, which Brown's supporters laid at the door of Smith—who they claimed had brought on the depression by his rough handling of the railroads. Watson, too, came out solidly against Smith, not for the reasons Brown was denouncing him—causing the paralysis of business by his denunciation of the corporation—but for just the opposite, for not carrying reform far enough.

Smith lost to Brown by 12,000 votes. He was back again, though, in 1911 with his old campaign against big government and big business and city politicians, and this time his election was assured, for he was the beneficiary of a new method of choosing state officials. The Democratic convention in 1908 had set up a rating system that for more than half a century would insure that the voice of the little counties would drown out the voices of the sin-ridden cities where politicians, hand in glove with the capitalists, so long had ruled the state. Under this "county unit" system of electing a governor, the 8 most populous counties had six unit votes, the 30 next largest, four each, the 121 smallest counties, two votes each. Thus a bare plurality in three small counties could nullify the thousands of votes cast in Fulton, Richmond, Bibb, Chatham, or Muscogee. From then on until 1962, when, in the case of *Gray* vs. *Sanders,* the county unit system was overthrown by the determined legal attack of a young Atlanta attorney named Morris Abram, nearly all the candidates for statewide office in Georgia had to blow Watson's old Populist trumpet, playing on the fears and hopes and hatreds of the rural voter.

Though Watson could play kingmaker in Georgia, there was little chance, he knew, that he ever again could make his influence strongly felt upon the national scene, for nearly all of the old Populists' liberal ideas were now imbedded in the political planks of either the Republicans or the Democrats. He accepted his dying party's nomination as its candidate for the presidency in 1908, but as he received the nomination he frankly admitted he did not know what to do. The Populist party, as a party, was dead. His campaign was a feeble one, nationally, and he pitched it upon the one issue that was ever more and more engrossing him—the doctrine of standing squarely for white supremacy. He made his usual denunciations of capitalistic plunderers, but his showing in the presidential race was miserable. His national vote was less than 30,000, where once he could count on 90,000 from Georgia alone. Licking his wounds, he decided the time had come for him to return to the Democratic party. He would purge it of its weaklings, and take command himself. His return to politics, in a race for Congress against Tom Hardwick, an old friend turned enemy, was undistinguished except for the viciousness with which the candidates defamed each other. Watson called a great rally in Atlanta and an estimated 8,000 people showed up to hear him predict that if something was not done to check the rising tide of discontent in the country, a bloody struggle was inevitable between the rich and poor. But, he thundered, he could tell them what they must do to be saved. They listened closely enough until he got into his all-too-familiar ranting about the Negro vote, charging that it was this bought vote that had deprived him of office in the past. At this, hissing and booing broke out all over the hall—it seemed to observers to be organized—and Watson began to rage almost incoherently. He would trumpet the news of this insult across the state, he shouted, and an outraged people would rally to his defense. He would organize an independent ticket, bolt the primary, and defeat Smith in the general election. He quit the stage abruptly, saying later he had a premonition he would be assassinated. He lost to Hardwick, and his enemy, Hoke Smith, regained the governorship.

For the next ten years, Watson sank deeper and deeper into the dark shadows of racial and religious hatred. Out of his memory of old political battles fought and lost in Augusta, where the Catholic vote was anti-Watson, came a campaign of undiluted hatred against the Pope and all who followed him. At Hickory Hill, he built a $100,000 printing plant and from it each month sent out his diatribes. He began to feel that he was a man inspired by God himself, and his hatred for Catholics took on a pathological taint. Even the sight of a Catholic enraged him. To his delight, Watson noted in 1914 that his campaign against the Catholics was having its effect on Georgia politics. His audience was growing, and they were listening. Old farmers, bent with years of work and with little or nothing to show for it, and discontented urban workers eking out a living on a miserable wage, were happy to feel their pulses throb with a new excitement as Watson struck out against these new, and therefore, evil antagonists. Neither did he forget the old "enemy," the Negro, so long known and feared. Again and again he came back to the Negro in vicious attack. And to their shame and to their ultimate sorrow, Georgians would read these malignant tirades, and nod solemnly in agreement.

It was his campaign against the Jews, however, which made Watson's name a household word—to be praised or vilified or simply deplored in Georgia. His venomous attitude toward the Jewish race finally surfaced in the senate campaign of 1914, when Joseph M. Brown opposed Hoke Smith. Watson, to help his friend Brown, charged that not only was Smith an enemy of white supremacy and a truckler to Rome, he was the mastermind of the forces that sought to free Leo Frank, a Jew, of the charge that he had murdered Mary Phagan, a girl employee of his pencil factory who had come to town on a holiday to draw her past week's pay.

When the fourteen-year-old youngster's body was found, horribly mutilated, in the basement of the pencil factory on the morning of April 27, 1913, the press, as might be expected, went wild, accusing Frank of all manner of sadistic perversions for which they had no supporting evidence. The trial lasted a month, with mobs howling around the courthouse, shouting threats to hang the jury unless the jury voted to hang Frank. Frank, of course, was found guilty and sentenced to die, and the prosecutor, Hugh M. Dorsey, became a popular hero, which would make him a powerful force in politics later on.

Then began the long fight for Frank's life, the appeals to higher courts, financed in the main by Northern Jewish organizations which believed that an innocent man was being railroaded to his death. Time after time, over a period of two years, the date for Frank's execution was put back, and Watson's voice, silent at first, rose to a scream. He began to call for vigilante action, for lynching. Finally, the date for Frank's execution was set. He would die on June 22, 1915. On the twenty-first day of June, Governor John M. Slaton's term would expire. The day before he went out of office, Slaton, in an act of high political courage—acting in large degree on the urging of the trial judge—commuted Frank's sentence. That night an armed mob marched on his house. Firing began, and sixteen of the soldiers guarding the governor were wounded. Watson's reaction was a shriek of rage. Slaton had gone to Hawaii to ride out the storm, and Watson warned that he had better not come back. He now turned his guns on the little Jewish merchants who could be found in every small Georgia town; he urged their Gentile neighbors to boycott them. His tirades caused statewide excitement. Crowds met the trains in Atlanta, Augusta, Savannah, and Columbus, all the way-stations between, grabbing for the latest Watson paper. Finally Watson's violent appeals for action—spelled out in editorials calling for a lynching—were more than certain murderous-minded "patriots" could stand. On the night of August 16, 1915, twenty-five armed men, only two of whom were timorous enough to cover their faces, took Leo Frank from the state penitentiary, transported him by car to Marietta, which had been the hometown of Mary Phagan, and there hanged him.

Whatever gains Georgia had made in the eyes of her sister states as a decent place to live and work and bring up a family had been sorely set back, first by the brutal race riot in 1906, now by this savage outbreak of anti-Semitism, both set off by politicians fanning the flames of racial prejudice.

In California, Governor Slaton called the lynching a consummate outrage, and urged the federal government to prosecute Watson for publishing material calling for violence and riot. The government was wary. It had already lost two rounds in the courts in a case against Watson for publishing obscene matter in his anti-Catholic campaign. It sought to extradite Watson, knowing that he would be invulnerable in Georgia. He answered by saying he would die before he would permit any officer to take him out of Georgia. The charges were dropped.

The next year Hugh Dorsey, still basking in the hero-worship he received as the successful prosecutor of Leo Frank, ran against Nat Harris, who had succeeded Slaton as governor. Despite the fact that Harris had tried to intercede for him with the federal government, Watson denounced Harris as a Slaton man and supported Dorsey. All state races were tainted by the Frank case, and Watson's anti-Jewish candidates won all down the line.

More grim an omen than this, however, came one summer night in 1915 when on the top of Stone Mountain a fiery cross blazed against the sky, lighted there by a revived Ku Klux Klan that would in years to come add to Georgia's reputation as the home of bigotry and violence. There is no evidence that Tom Watson was there among the hooded figures who set the cross on fire, though he had hinted editorially that a new Klan was needed. But no student of the times would question C. Vann Woodward's observation: "If any mortal man may be credited (as no one man may rightly be) with releasing the forces of human malice and ignorance and prejudice which the Klan merely mobilized, that man was Thomas E. Watson." [9]

Watson's next great crusade must have bewildered and confused even his blindest and most unquestioning followers. The war in Europe was blazing. The Germans had invaded Belgium.

9. Woodward, *Tom Watson: Agrarian Rebel,* p. 450.

A hatred of war and all things military was deeply imbedded in his soul, and he took savage issue with President Woodrow Wilson for taking steps to prepare this country, arguing against our arming on the grounds that armaments insure not peace, but war. Americans, he argued, could not be drafted except to defend their own state and country, on her own soil, an old argument first advanced by Joseph E. Brown during the Civil War. As the United States entered the war, Watson, crying that the conflict was a result of ravenous commercialism, renounced it completely—and then for a brief while fell silent. He came back to the battle in full cry—against the wartime powers the president had assumed, the Espionage and Sedition laws, the universal military training and conscription. He set out to organize draft-resisters all over the country, and when he announced that he was going to attack the Conscription Act on Constitutional grounds, and appealed for funds, small checks totaling nearly $100,000 came in.

It was the attack on the Conscription Act that finally did Watson in. It was held to be a violation of the Espionage Act, and in August of 1917, the Post Office Department denied the use of the mails to his *Jeffersonian*.

With his presses stilled, a period of deepest melancholy, made more profound by the death of his daughter, descended upon Watson. He took to drugs and to drink, and on the verge of a nervous breakdown he left Hickory Hill and went to Florida. There a son, John Durham, his last child, died while visiting him. Watson's mind cracked. A Negro servant found him wandering on the beach, repeating over and over phrases from old speeches made long before. Over and over again in his mind he fought the old battles—the great adventure of agrarian revolt, which ceased to become a burning public issue in the year he became its national leader, the other ideals he had fought for, which became strong planks in the platforms of the two great political parties while he, their author, was forgotten.

He was ever a fighter, though. So, as physical and mental health gradually came back, he turned back to politics, running against Carl Vinson for congressman from the Tenth District—and lost. He was old and withered now, and his hair was silver and his eyes sunken. His voice was low and shaking, and there was no longer in him the old fire that set audiences to stomping, shouting, cheering his every angry phrase. Watson, as always when defeated, believed there had been trickery at the polls, and he contested the election in three counties. At the state convention, which would decide the issue, his charges of ballot-box burning were thrown out, and there was a general feeling in political circles that the old warrior at last was through.

But he still fought on. As the war ended, he started publishing a new weekly paper—the *Columbia Sentinel*—in which he returned to his old battles against Wilsonism. He demanded immediate repeal of all wartime legislation that interfered with the people's liberties; he called for amnesty for all political prisoners; called the Versailles Peace Treaty an iniquitous document, which forced the German people into bondage at the point of a bayonet; and described the League of Nations as an unholy alliance which, if joined, would commit the U. S. to bailing out every bankrupt nation and taking part in every future quarrel between countries around the world. He urged the U. S. to get out of Europe and stay out. He saw no reason for American troops to be in Russia as that country suffered in its own agony of revolution, and he bitterly attacked Attorney General Palmer for his Red-baiting campaign in America. It was directed, Watson declared, against working people, as they tried to organize unions, and Palmer used the hated Sedition acts, which were still in force, to break up their meetings. To Watson, this conduct was as arrogant and despicable as that of the czars.

The fact that Georgia was listening to Watson, and many Georgians were agreeing with his isolationist doctrine, was made manifest a year later in the race for the Senate. Hoke Smith, the incumbent, was seeking re-election, opposed by Governor Hugh M. Dorsey, who had the strong support of the Wilson administration nationally and the backing of the powerful Howell faction in Georgia. Now, for the first time, Watson could run on his own, seeking to mollify neither faction but fighting them both. His platform was simple: He opposed the League of Nations and all its works; he was for the immediate repeal of all conscription, compulsory military training, and the Espionage and Sedition acts.

The newly formed American Legion backed Governor Dorsey

for his one-hundred-percent Americanism and paid his entrance fee. It attacked Watson as a slacker, a pro-German disloyal to America who had connections with the Bolsheviks. It heckled Watson at his rallies and tried to break them up. Watson in his turn called on the Klan to protect him from the Legion, which he denounced as being an elite officer corps which hauled innocent young men off to training camps where they subjected them to unspeakable indignities, and then carried them onto the battlefield where they were slaughtered. Watson, as the campaign went on, became almost explosively violent, and the wilder he became, the larger were the crowds turned out to hear him. In the September primary he led the ticket, with 102 out of 159 counties giving him 111,725 popular votes and 247 county unit votes. Dorsey was second, Smith third. In the race for governor, Tom Hardwick, once Watson's friend, later his enemy and now again his friend, won handily.

Watson quickly made his presence felt in Washington. He continued to denounce the League of Nations, fought the enforcement of the Prohibition law by federal officers, opposed paying Colombia for the Panama Canal, and spoke almost by rote against the United States Steel Corporation, the American Legion, Pennsylvania coal mine owners, and any tariff duties whatsoever. Militarism in all its forms remained his unforgivable enemy. A standing army of 25,000 men would be enough, he argued, and all the navy needed were a few ships "for the admirals to sail around in." [10] The advocates of a big army and navy were not afraid of foreign invaders, he said. They were afraid of their own people. It was the capitalists, Watson thundered, naming them, who wanted a huge standing army, so that it might beat down the hungry, jobless working people made dissatisfied and discontented by the insatiable trusts.

Under the pressure of trying to remedy in a few short years the evils which to him had been building up in the three decades since he had last held public office, he became highly belligerent toward his Senate colleagues. He attempted to fight a senator who asked about post office appointments in Georgia to which Watson objected, and he had to be restrained from attack-

10. Woodward, *Tom Watson: Agrarian Rebel,* p. 480.

ing a young army officer who had denied his charges of officer-caste brutality. Along with his fits of rage there also came periods of deepest melancholy, enhanced perhaps by long periods of drinking.

On September 22, 1922, after a bout of illness, he attended the second session of the Sixty-Seventh Congress, speaking shakily to ask that letters he had received from striking miners in Pennsylvania be printed in the Record. It was his last official act. On the night of September 25th, during a severe attack of asthma and bronchitis, he died. At his funeral at Hickory Hill, attended by more than seven thousand people, one floral tribute stood out above the rest. It was a cross made of roses, sent by the Ku Klux Klan. On another wreath, the card read "Eugene Debs."

So passed Tom Watson—a complex and paradoxical figure whose virtues, which were many, and whose faults, which were myriad, were the virtues and the faults of his native Georgia. His statue, fist clenched in oratorical pose, now stands on the statehouse grounds in Atlanta, the echoes of his angry voice may still be heard in its halls, and the seed he planted in the soil of Georgia politics still bears both good and evil fruit.

Though Watson's interest throughout his public career lay mainly in the welfare of the farmer, the worker in the mills of Georgia had begun to assert himself. In 1886, the Knights of Labor had entered a strike that shut down all the textile mills in Augusta—which the mill owners had countered with a lockout. There were other strikes—and in 1891, labor was strong enough in Georgia to ask for and receive a special labor holiday, the first Monday in September. Women began to make their influence felt in these decades around the century's turning, going into business and the professions, and by 1897 they had established the legal right to keep their own wages rather than turning them over to their husbands. Women began to write books, to join the preachers of the state, and Watson, in speaking out for Prohibition. And one of them became nationally recognized. Mrs. Rebecca Latimer Felton, widow of the fiery Independent Democrat William H. Felton, a monument in Georgia politics, became the first woman senator when she was appointed by Governor Hardwick to fill the late Tom Watson's unexpired term. She served one day after taking the oath, and was succeeded by Judge Walter F. George, a far more stable man than Watson, who in a special election began the distinguished career of statesmanship that was to last for more than thirty years.

8

Prelude to the Present

*T*OM WATSON'S picture of the Georgia farmer as being poor, hungry, and ill-clad had been a gross exaggeration, at least during and just after World War I. After a dismal drop in the early days of the war, England began to buy cotton again, and the price soared to forty cents. The backcountry farmer was to be seen driving to church on Sunday, not in a buggy or wagon as in the past, but in a new automobile—a Dart or Moon or Star, a Maxwell, a Saxon, a Chevrolet, known as a "Shivvy," or, as was more likely, a "Tin Lizzie" made by Mr. Ford. Instead of overalls he wore a neat black suit, set off by a candy-striped silk shirt, a high, stiff collar like that worn by town folk, and his tie might be fastened with a diamond stick-pin, or one fashioned from a gold nugget. Nor had Grady's, and Watson's, plea that the farmer diversify his crops gone unheeded. Since 1908 the strong and effective College of Agriculture at Athens had been sending out trained experts, county agents going out to teach Georgia farmers the value of new crops and new ways. It had also established in each Congressional district a special agricultural and mechanical school. Peach and apple orchards began to blossom from Fort Valley into the northern counties. Vast pecan groves soon covered the gray lands of South Georgia, and tobacco fields took over where once only slim pines had stood. Corn, watermelons, and peanuts became highly valuable cash crops. Under the guiding genius of Dr. Charles H. Herty, working in his new forest laboratory at Statesboro, the once great naval-stores industry had begun to revive, and a vast new paper industry was envisioned, based on the fast growing Georgia slash pine. Cotton was still king, but courtiers of almost equal wealth now surrounded the throne.

As the state turned away from its old allegiance to cotton, it turned also from other customs inherited from its plantation past. The convict leasing system, adopted in the late 1860s because the state could not afford to expand and maintain a vast prison system, provided another way of keeping men in bondage, and the serfdom now applied to white as well as black. In 1879 Joseph E. Brown, John B. Gordon, and W. D. Grant, who proved to be as adroit in business as in politics, had made a highly profitable deal with the state. Under its terms, which were to last for twenty years, the companies were to pay the state half a million dollars, in twenty annual installments, for the services of the able-bodied convicts. The men hired were put to work digging coal, farming, lumbering, making bricks, and building railroads. Whipping was permitted, and the men worked in "shacks"—shackles made up of iron rings fastened around each ankle and connected by a chain. The chain was long enough for the prisoner to walk with short steps, but he could not take a running stride. County grand juries were supposed to make periodic inspection of working conditions but, despite this supposed supervision, there were widespread rumors of savage cruelties. Some of these were true, and as a result there was strong protest against the system as being a relic of medieval barbarism. It was 1897, though, before the protests brought about change, and these did not go far. The new rules provided that the old, the young, and the sick should be kept at a prison farm, under the supervision of a prison commission. Short-termers would be divided into "chain gangs" and assigned to various counties as road builders, but a long-termer could still be leased to the individual who bid highest for his labor—$100 a year was the going rate paid the state. It was well into the twentieth century, in 1908, before this system of leasing convicts to private corporations was finally abolished. For the prisoner, the change was no great blessing. The county chain-gang guards proved to be as cruel in their treatment of the convicts as had the whip-toting gang bosses of the private lessors. The men lived in steel, mule-drawn cages set up wherever a nearby river could provide water, and were transported in these movable cells to wherever road work was needed. Heads shaved, dressed in striped clothes of coarse black-and-white cotton, they worked in chains by day and slept in the clothes they worked in, chained to their bunks, by night. Soon the Georgia chain gang became as infamous an institution in the national mind as had been slavery itself. It was not until 1943, when the introduction of machinery into road building had long since made convict labor obsolete, that the last Georgia chain gang was closed. This meant that the prison camps only moved indoors, to crowded cells in county jails. Today, more than thirty years later, the state is still seeking a humane and financially feasible way of housing and rehabilitating its prisoners.

Another ancient problem which has plagued Georgia since its earliest days still exists, though gradually it is diminishing. Georgia was founded as a colony from which strong spirits were barred, but this restriction did not long survive the early colonials' protests, and the state soon turned legally "wet." By the mid-1880s, though, the Prohibition forces led by the preachers were in full cry, and by 1919, when national Prohibition went into effect, Georgia already had voted itself dry. A citizen could not manufacture, sell, or even possess liquor. Many, though, who voted dry still suffered a great thirst. Thus there was created another peculiar Georgia institution, the moonshiner. Hiding the smoke of his illicit still in the deep coves of the hills, he would send his potent white lightning to market in fast cars driven at blinding speed by reckless mountain boys—many of whom went on to become famous stock-car racers. Moonshining was a form of private enterprise that endured in Georgia long after the repeal of national Prohibition in 1933, for under local option many counties still remain dry.

The glow of prosperity which the Georgia farmer felt in the silk-shirt days during and after World War I did not long survive, for soon there was to come an invasion that was to prove an economic catastrophe more damaging than Sherman's march. Around the turn of the century a little snouted insect called the Mexican boll weevil started moving north and east through

Texas, Louisiana, Mississippi, and Alabama, thrusting its pro-
boscis into the cotton "square" and laying its eggs there where
the larvae fed on the forming boll. By 1915 it had made its way
into Georgia, and by 1923 it had reduced the Georgia cotton
crop to 588,000 bales—about a third of what had been produced
in 1919. The trials of those first days of boll-weevil infestation
are still green in the memories of those who lived through them.
First, the farmer and his sons went stooping and crawling down
the cotton rows, picking off the punctured squares for burning,
and catching the mature weevils and crushing them between
their thumbnails. By 1921 the state was providing the farmer
with a poisonous powder, calcium arsenate. The farmer would
go to bed at sunset, get up at moonrise and go to the fields,
where he would dust the dew-wet cotton plants with the poison.
Later, the poison was mixed with molasses and daubed onto the
cotton square with a swab—a messy, sticky job. Billions of
bees, hundreds of cattle, and some children died when they
found the sweet poison pleasing to the taste.

The damage done by the boll weevil in Georgia brought disaster not only to the farmer, but to the small-town merchant
and banker who had backed him. Banks failed, mortgages were
foreclosed, and men whose families had lived on their own land
since Revolutionary days found themselves having to load up
the wagon and move. The younger ones went north, where the
economy was surging upward. The older ones moved to the
towns to go to work in the little textile mills or overall plants, or
take whatever odd jobs of painting or carpentry they could find.

Ralph McGill, in his farm articles for the *Atlanta Constitution*
in the early Thirties, gives the most poignant picture of those
times in which 60,000 farms were abandoned, leaving three and
a half million acres of cotton land to grow up in sedge and
pines. He wrote of the lonely chimneys in the abandoned fields,
the old houses falling in, and he took his readers into these
empty houses and let them hear the ghostly voices speaking
there, telling the story of hope abandoned, of a dream that had
died.

Nobody starved during the boll weevil times, for there was
always land available somewhere on which a man could plant a
garden. But the moving of the people in search of work left an

enduring mark on the face of Georgia and the South. They left behind them not only empty cabins in the fields, but dying communities supported only by little cotton mills, their worn machinery capable of making only the roughest duck or drill, and paying wages so low a man could hardly feed and clothe his family on what he earned.

Thus, for nearly a decade before the market crash of 1929 ushered in the Great Depression, Georgia had known her own depression. The stage had been set for political, social, and economic confrontation between capital and labor, between the have and have-not Georgians. The textile unions would come in to organize the textile mills, and bitter strikes would follow, and the strikes would be put down by the National Guard, called out by a union-baiting governor, Eugene Talmadge, who pitched his appeal to the working man but whose heart was with the mill owners. Georgia no longer could boast of being ''The Empire State of the South.'' Low wages in industry, the inroads of the boll weevil, and the out-migration of her people had its effect not only on the farmer, but on the small-town businessman and manufacturer. Georgia had fallen far back of neighboring North Carolina and Tennessee in population, industrial growth, and the value of her manufactures. By 1933 these indexes were only half what they had been in 1929. Her roads were the most miserable in the South, and the tourist from the North, Florida-bound, felt as he entered Georgia that he was setting out on a journey on which he might be buried in the mud and never heard from again. Her public education was in an equally deplorable state. By nearly every measurement of excellence, Georgia's schools ranked at the bottom of the forty-eight states.

But always throughout our history, when all ways seemed dark, Georgians somehow managed to carry on. Though governors' races remained as bitterly fought as ever, and charges of lying, cheating, vote buying, and general fraud and corruption were bandied about as they had been since Reconstruction days, the state did succeed in electing a series of governors who earnestly, and as most believed, honestly, tried to pull the state out of debt, and to reorganize and streamline its duplicating and often ineffective bureaus and agencies.

Thomas W. Hardwick was the first of these, coming into office in 1921, when the boll weevil attack was at its height. Hardwick, in the U.S. Senate during the war, had made many enemies because of his anti-Wilson, antiwar stand, and in Georgia a vindictive legislature, backed by a hostile press, paid little attention to his program calling for streamlining the state government and economizing wherever possible. His successor, Attorney General Clifford Walker, came in for two terms, and had somewhat better luck. During his term industry, supported by tax exemptions, for the first time in Georgia's history produced manufactured goods worth more than the products of Georgia's agriculture. In 1925 the gasoline tax was increased, and the proceeds used to start bringing Georgia's highways out of the mud. A bill to reconstruct the State Highway Department, a notorious source of political boodling, was passed, and an issue of scrip was authorized to pay the back pensions of Confederate veterans.

None of these things seemed sufficient to a Jackson County physician, cotton manufacturer, miller, banker, and farmer owning land in seven counties. Dr. L. G. Hardman of Commerce felt that the state had been run long enough by lawyer-politicians. It was time a businessman took over the reins. In 1926 he was elected governor. For all his honesty and earnestness, though, he could get little legislation past a stubborn and suspicious legislature, despite the fact that the studies he initiated to find ways to make the government simpler, more efficient and more economical, laid the foundation for the wide reorganization Governor Richard Brevard Russell, Jr., brought about later.

Son of the state supreme court justice, Dick Russell went into the governor's office in 1931 at the age of thirty-three, the youngest governor in Georgia's history. The cold winds of depression were blowing now, not alone in Georgia and the boll-weevil South, but everywhere. To meet the challenge of this uncertain financial future, Russell argued that a far simpler government had to be more economically run. Miraculously, his legislature agreed, and under Russell's sweeping reorganization plan more than one hundred boards, bureaus, and commissions were cut back to eighteen. A board of regents consisting of a dozen members took over the guidance of a single streamlined university system, replacing the boards of trustees of twenty-six separate educational institutions. Many weak schools were abolished, and those remaining were strengthened both in finances and curriculum. The lure of Washington became too strong for Russell in his last year as governor, and on the death of Senator William J. Harris he ran for and was elected to the Senate, defeating the dean of the Georgia delegation, House Speaker Charles Crisp, who had been in Congress for more than twenty years. Thus Russell in 1933 moved up to join Walter F. George, and the two Georgians for a quarter-century thereafter, until George's retirement in 1956, made up what was perhaps the most distinguished pair of lawmakers sent to the Senate by any state. Russell's field was the Senate Armed Services Committee and the Appropriations Committee, George's, the Finance Committee and the Foreign Relations Committee, and either, if they had lived elsewhere than in the South, could have been strong contenders for the presidency.

As Russell moved on to Washington, there came upon the Georgia gubernatorial scene a new face, grim-jawed and glaring, a new voice, harsh and strident, but preaching an old philosophy familiar since Tom Watson's day—the superiority of the little man, the common man, over anything big or out of the familiar mold, whether big government or big business. But he put his message in such a way that, though the little man would whoop and shout and flock to the polls to vote for him, the big men who headed corporations understood it too. They would look at each other and wink and smile, and finance him. "Ol' Gene," they reassured each other, "has a great respect for property." [1]

Eugene Talmadge was born in 1885, grandson, on his mother's side, of Eugene R. Roberts, a hot-tempered lawyer with the reputation of being the meanest man in Jasper County, a reputation Eugene Talmadge was to cherish for himself—as being "mean as hell" in politics. A sickly baby stricken early with jaundice, he came into a farming family wealthy enough to buy books, and to start their children to school early, and to see them on through college. He wore the brogans and the overalls

---

1. Harold H. Martin, Unpublished Interview, 1941.

of a farm boy, and he occasionally went to the fields with a mule and a plow, but it was at his own volition, not the daily dawn-to-dark routine of a typical farmer's son. He also worked at his father's gin, but at record-keeping, not the hard labor of shoveling seed or pushing around heavy bales of ginned cotton.

His youthful heroes were two—Napoleon, with whom he seemed to feel some special kinship, and from whose biography he could quote long passages without error—and Tom Watson. Watson, the old Populist, was Talmadge's ideal of a politician, particularly as a speaker, and wherever Watson spoke, young Talmadge was there, listening avidly, filing away in his mind Watson's forensic tricks. Talmadge, like his father before him, went to the university, where he acquitted himself well as a debater and football manager, and his scholarship was high enough to earn him a Phi Beta Kappa key. An impeccable dresser and a member of the Sigma Nu fraternity, he looked and acted like what he later so effectively pretended to be, a drawling, one-gallussed, tobacco-chewing good ole boy from the forks of the creek. Like his hero Watson, he first tried school teaching, which he found that he disliked as much as he had disliked plowing a mule, and again like Watson, he turned to law, graduating from the university in 1907 and going with a firm in Atlanta. Nor did he like the humdrum routine of the law office much better than he liked the schoolteacher's equally dreary round. He did enjoy the drama of politics, though, and found himself hanging around the statehouse talking with the farmer-legislators. Soon, though, at the urging of his father, Tom Talmadge, and his father's friend, Representative William Peterson from Montgomery County, young Talmadge moved from Atlanta, a hotbed of sin, to Ailey, Georgia, a town which the Peterson family owned. There he hung out his shingle as a lawyer, and found room and board at the home of Mr. Peterson's sister Carrie, with whom was living Mr. Peterson's widowed daughter-in-law, Mattie Thurmond Peterson, known as Mitt. Immediately, the two young people fell in love, courted briefly, and then were married. There was no fanfare about it. They just got married, and with her son John, aged six, they moved down the road to Mount Vernon, where Talmadge had set up his law practice. It was not a highly successful practice.

The only cases he got to try were the very poor, who could not pay, or had to pay in meal or meat or firewood. He even tried to sell mules for a while, and this didn't work either. So he moved once more—to McRae, twenty-three miles away where Mrs. Talmadge owned a large farm left to her by her deceased first husband. He found himself no more welcome in McRae, a courthouse town, than he had been in Mount Vernon. The so-called ''courthouse gang'' was suspicious of this abrasive, blunt-spoken stranger, and the members saw to it that he got little legal work. He found himself spending more and more time playing checkers with the loafers at the courthouse. With his law practice getting nowhere, he for the first time seriously tried farming. He went to the fields with his plow mule and another plowman he had hired, and broke the land and planted it, and before planting season was over, he knew that this was something he did not want to do the rest of his life. He was ready to listen, therefore, when a young legislator and fertilizer sales-man named Tom Linder came to him one day while he was plowing and told him the time had come for some young man with a farm background to take on the old agriculture commis-sioner, J. J. Brown. There was feeling among the farmers, Lin-der said, that the commissioner was letting the fertilizer com-panies sell fertilizer with too much rocks and dirt in it. And there were one hundred farmer-legislators in the capitol who had delegated him, Linder, to find somebody who could dethrone the powerful Brown, whose organization, based on a statewide network of more than one hundred so-called ''fertilizer inspec-tors,'' was the strongest in Georgia.[2]

Talmadge at last had found what he wanted to do, and what he could do best, and what he would do until the day he died—run for office. What he had learned from watching and listening to Tom Watson he had learned well, and he brought to the hus-tings all of Watson's old tricks—of humor, drama, angry dia-tribe, and forensic hyperbole, though delivered in a more folksy, down-to-earth language than the more erudite Watson had affected. His speaking manner on the stump was, in a

2. William Anderson, *The Wild Man from Sugar Creek* (Baton Rouge: Louisiana State University Press, 1975), pp. 34–35.

sense, a put on, for Phi Beta Kappa Talmadge could speak the language of the college seminar as easily as the language of the cotton field. Nor did his thinking have the depth and scope or understanding of Watson's. But the Georgia farmer needed a champion. In these hard days, when everybody but him, seemingly, was enjoying the fruits of the new indus-trialization—telephones and tractors and radios and indoor plumbing and lights and water piped into the house—there was nobody to say that he too should have these things, or to name those who were holding them back from him. Except Mr. Tal-madge. He was the farmer's friend. He was standing between the farmer and his enemies. And those enemies were, of course, Mr. Brown and his fertilizer inspectors.

He had found the formula that would win for him throughout the rest of his career. The county unit system, loaded in favor of the rural voter, gave him 362 unit votes to 52 for Brown. Twice more, Talmadge ran for commissioner of agriculture, and both times he won. He took over the *Market Bulletin,* and made it the voice of his political philosophy. He wiped out Brown's state organization and built up his own, loaded with his friends and relatives. Echoing Watson's old rabble-rousing arguments, he blamed Wall Street and its bankers for all the South's prob-lems, and began to list all the nation's financial institutions as the enemies of the farmer. As a result, Ol' Gene began to take on the image of a bucolic Robin Hood, taking from the rich cap-italist to give to the poor farmer.

Talmadge came into 1932, an election year, feeling that he was ready for higher things—the governorship, or a Senate seat—but not knowing exactly which way to make his move. He knew that for all his bawl-and-jump evangelism on the stump he would not be able to beat the good, gray Senator George for the Senate. Georgians could tolerate all manner of erratic conduct in their governors, but they wanted their senators to be men of calmness and dignity. Nor did he feel quite sure that he could unseat young Governor Russell, for Russell him-self, for all his progressive ideas, had shown that he, too, had the common touch. This left the possibility of running against Senator William J. Harris, who was ill and reportedly might not run again. But it was a long jump, in Georgia politics, from commissioner of agriculture to the U.S. Senate. While Talmadge was pondering, fate made the decision. Harris died toward the end of his term. Governor Russell immediately jumped into the Senate race. And Talmadge, urged on by his old checker-playing, tobacco-chewing, rabbit-hunting, cotton-farming friends, entered the race for governor.

He soon demonstrated that he knew how to pick an issue that would catch the eye and warm the heart of the impoverished Georgia farmer. The complex economic forces that had brought on the Great Depression might be too abstruse for many men to understand. But anybody could understand a $3 automobile tag. This issue, plus a promise of good roads, plus the showmanship—the motorcade arriving late, the planted cheerleaders in the crowd urging him on to assail his enemies ("Tell 'em about old Ralph McGill, Gene."), the Tree-Climbing Haggards from Danielsville, and Fiddling John Carson with his wild screeching fiddle—elected him over a field of nine.

The so-called "little man," the farmer and the country-born city dweller with deep ties to the farm, had always been the basic voting strength in Georgia in point of numbers. Never, though, had they used that strength. Before the Civil War the power lay with the planters, after the war with the Bourbon dynasty of new industrialists, the politician turned manufacturer, miner, and railroad builder. Now, at last, the country-bred felt they had a leader of their own. He soon let them know that on the stump or in the governor's mansion, he was still one of them. He ordered that chicken coops be put in the back yard at the mansion, and for a while, a cow grazed on the lawn.

Talmadge was soon to prove that he was, indeed, as mean as he once had boasted that he was—treating with high-handed arrogance anybody who crossed him. He had run on the promise of a three-dollar tag, of lower freight and utility rates, and lower taxes, and on a pledge to reorganize the highway department. His program got off to a bad start, for the legislators, many of whom had a deep-down dislike for and distrust of Talmadge, would not go along with him. This brought on a conflict which ended with Talmadge, acting on a law passed in 1821, suspending all state taxes until the legislature would meet again two years hence—and by executive fiat he dropped the auto tax to

$3. He began his battle with the highway department by order-ing the chairman to cut his budget by lowering salaries and fir-ing a number of engineers. The chairman refused, so Talmadge fired him, put his own man in the office, and called out the Na-tional Guard to take over the departmental offices and patrol the capitol grounds—the first time since Reconstruction that the statehouse had come under bayonet rule. He moved next against the Public Service Commission, charging that its members were tools of the public utilities whose stock was owned out of Georgia, and that they conspired to keep utility rates high. Sit-ting as judge and jury, Talmadge found them guilty. He cut the property tax from five mills to four—and went on to attack headon the Department of Agriculture, ordering the firing of thirty-three employees.

He ran again in 1934, going into a second term so explosive it made the first one seem serene. When the legislature failed to pass an appropriations bill for 1936–1937, he took over finan-cial control of the state, bypassing the state auditor, the comp-troller general, and the state treasurer. By executive order he declared the appropriations bill covering the past two years still in force and ordered the state comptroller and treasurer to make the payments. Each refused and was fired. The comptroller gen-eral went quietly, but State Treasurer George B. Hamilton re-mained at his desk until Talmadge's Guardsmen arrived. The electors of the state were startled the next morning to see in the paper a picture of Mr. Hamilton, a neat, professional man wear-ing glasses, being borne bodily from his office by two husky Guardsmen. There followed a great squabble between the gov-ernor and the banks which were state repositories, who refused to honor checks signed by J. B. Daniel, the new treasurer named by Talmadge. The courts, faced by the indomitable gov-ernor, finally solved the problem by ruling that Mr. Daniel was in fact the treasurer and could act as such. The state's agencies slowly began to function again.

Hardly had Talmadge gone into his second term than prob-lems not of his own making began to crop up. Around the na-tion labor was growing restless under the grinding impact of the depression. Talmadge in his campaign speeches had promised that he would never use troops to break up a strike. Nobody, he claimed, was a closer friend to labor than he was. He showed them his hands, lean and muscular, and the color of his skin, tanned by the sun, to prove it. He boasted that a labor organization had given him the red suspenders that became his trademark. This warmth did not long survive. In September of 1934 textile unions moved into Georgia and set up their picket lines outside the cotton mills. Fights broke out, and curses and rocks were hurled as company strikebreakers tangled with union recruiters at the mill gates. By the first week in September fifty-nine mills throughout Georgia had closed, and letters were pouring in to Talmadge, from strikers wanting his support for their wage-hour demands, from men shut out from their jobs who wanted to go back to work. Of more impact on Talmadge were the calls he was getting from the mill owners, his quiet financial contributors, calling on him to turn out the Guard. Four thousand militiamen were called out, armed with rifles, bayonets, and tear gas. At least two strikers were killed, and thousands were arrested and interned in barbed-wire pens. Talmadge's handling of the textile strikes did nothing to diminish the farmer's faith in him, but there was nothing he could say thereafter to bring back labor's trust in him, or its votes.

As Talmadge fiercely thrashed about, striking out at those he considered his political enemies in his own state, he soon put on his list of those to be destroyed all the representatives of the New Deal in Georgia, and particularly the guiding genius of the Welfare State, Franklin Delano Roosevelt himself. Talmadge at first had expressed great admiration for Mr. Roosevelt and had voted for him in 1932, and for some two years thereafter he had continued to support the president, if not all of his New Deal measures. Soon, though, Talmadge had begun to feel that he had been betrayed. Roosevelt was no conservative, as he had thought. He was a socialist, and maybe even worse, a Marxist. He began openly to express his fears and angers. The picture of their folk hero, Talmadge, turning upon their father-image, FDR, left Georgia's farmers puzzled but not too greatly concerned. Talmadge still fascinated them, but it was Roosevelt and his New Deal bureaucrats that were handing out the jobs, and helping the farmer save his farm from the mortgage banker, and working out ways to control crops so that he could get a decent price for what he grew. And it was not Mr. Talmadge but Mr. Roosevelt who was assuring the working man of the right to organize, and guaranteeing him a minimum wage, and setting up unemployment insurance for him and a pension for his old age.

Georgians, farmer and working man alike, permitted Talmadge to denounce Roosevelt and all his works as virulently as he pleased. But following their own self-interest, they continued to vote for Roosevelt and his New Deal, and they took special pride that he had chosen Warm Springs, in the heart of Georgia, for his Little White House and second home. The merchants, bankers, and manufacturers in the small towns as well as the cities did not share this view, of course.

Two Georgia politicians who were well aware of the strong pro-New Deal feeling in grass-roots Georgia were Speaker of the House Eurith D. Rivers and the wise old pol, Roy Harris. They pushed through the legislature many New Deal-inspired measures—bills providing for a sales tax, old-age pensions, free textbooks, a seven-month school term. They also pressed for slum clearance and a child-labor amendment. And as fast as these measures came to his desk, Talmadge vetoed them. As a result not a single piece of New Deal legislation passed. Despite this, federal road funds began at last to flow into Georgia. In one evening, in a smoky hotel room in Atlanta, Talmadge and his road contractors got together and on a map laid out new roads and divided among the road builders the nine million dollars now available.

Now Talmadge again began to dream of higher things—this time the presidency itself. He would run as a "true" Democrat, on a platform which opposed Negroes, the New Deal, and Communism. Invitations were sent out to seventeen Southern and border states to a grass-roots convention to be held in Macon. Thirty-five hundred delegates came, sat facing a huge Confederate flag, read literature attacking Roosevelt for appointing Negroes to high office and Mrs. Roosevelt for consorting with them. Talmadge was introduced as the presidential candidate of something called the Constitutional Jeffersonian Democratic ticket. Talmadge, not wild-eyed and rumpled now, but sedate and neatly pressed, as befitted a presidential candidate, refused to take off his coat. His speech was formal and contained no fireworks. He was for a tax cut, local self-government, tariff reform, and an end to federal bureaucracy. As in the past, men in overalls rushed to bear him from the platform on their shoulders, but afterward, nothing happened. The convention adjourned with no platform worth presenting, and no plans for the future. It was plain to Talmadge now that though his people might want him for governor, nobody wanted him in the White House. In that case, he would take another tack. He would run against Dick Russell for the Senate.

The campaign that followed was one of the bitterest ever fought in a state renowned for the malignant savagery of its faction-ridden one-party politics. Russell himself remembered it as a campaign which "tore the state to pieces. It had brothers stop speaking to brothers, and partners dissolving partnerships." [3]

E. D. Rivers ran for governor on a straight New Deal platform, approving all that had been done in Georgia. He ignored Talmadge's hand-picked candidate for governor, Charles Redwine, and concentrated on Talmadge. He would bounce across the platform with a rifle in one hand—reminiscent of Talmadge's calling out the Guard to put down the textile strikes—and a book in the other, his pledge that all the children of Georgia should have free schoolbooks. He won handily over Redwine, who was brutally caricatured in *Constitution* cartoons as a little bald-headed gnome chirping "Me Too" to everything Talmadge suggested.

It was a close race between Russell and Talmadge, and the issue was in doubt until Senator George came down to bestow his blessing upon his junior colleague. Speaking in a South Georgia tobacco warehouse, he told his rural hearers that he could not see how a Georgia farmer could doubt that Roosevelt had been the greatest friend of Southern agriculture to hold the presidential office since the War Between the States. Not only farmers, but every Georgian, he said, had good reason to remain loyal to President Roosevelt and the New Deal.

This plus the fact that Talmadge's antilabor policies had cost him thousands of votes turned the tide for Dick Russell. At his speaking engagements thereafter, the farmers began taking off

3. Anderson, *Wild Man from Sugar Creek,* p. 157.

their red suspenders, badge of their Talmadge loyalty, and toss-
ing them at Russell's feet, and he buried Talmadge under one of
the biggest landslides in Georgia history. Talmadge, always as
gracious in defeat as he was arrogant in victory, wrote a long
congratulatory telegram to Russell.

Historians who are just beginning to try to give meaning to
the events of those days, purport to see in them the stronger stir-
rings of great social, economic, and political changes that had
long been rumbling and boiling beneath the surface. To many
the important thing was that more than 100,000 Georgians
would still vote for Eugene Talmadge even though he fiercely
opposed the federal measures that were putting bread on their
tables, a roof over their heads, and clothes on their backs. He
stood for things that deep down were more important to them
than food or shelter—for a pioneer pride in their own strength,
for a pioneer distrust of big government, even one bringing
largesse. And above all, he stood for white supremacy.

The racial theme was not greatly stressed in this race, except
in Talmadge's protest against Roosevelt's appointment of blacks
to high office—but Dick Russell was quick to recognize it for
what it was to become, a dangerous and inflammatory issue. In
the future, he said, any politician who had run out of reasonable
arguments on other issues, could revive his flagging campaign
simply by waving his arms and shouting the warning cry of
"Nigger!" Russell's words were prophetic. It was a cry that
would be uttered with increasing venom in Georgia in the years
ahead.

With Rivers in the governor's chair Georgians could now
share fully in the New Deal philosophy and the largesse which
Talmadge by his vetoes had denied them—old-age pensions,
homestead tax exemptions, health services, an intangibles tax
which fell mainly on the well-to-do, and a seven-month school
term with free text books and higher pay for the teachers. All
these things the legislature passed, and Mr. Rivers happily
signed into law. As a result a grateful electorate in 1938 swept
him into office for a second term. They soon had cause to regret
this, for in Rivers's second term, the bills his friendly legislature had passed so joyfully now began to come due, and not
enough taxes were coming in to pay them. The intangible tax

was a help, but a sales tax and a chain-store tax had failed to pass. Beer and wine had been legalized but an effort to legalize liquor so that it could be taxed failed of passage twice. Then, however, in desperation counties were allowed to vote whether they should be dry or wet. As other governors had done before him, Rivers and the legislature sold the Western and Atlantic Railroad rentals for two years ahead, collecting more than two million dollars in advance. Still there was only three-quarters enough money to pay for all the services offered, and Rivers decided to tap the highway fund, which was heavy with gasoline taxes. The chairman of the highway board refused to pay over the money, and Rivers, repeating an act he had harshly criticized Talmadge for performing, fired him, called out the state troops, and declared martial law around the highway building. The fighting ended in federal court with Rivers under arrest for contempt. He finally purged himself of contempt and got the money, but as he left office at the end of his second term the state was $22,000,000 in debt.

In the 1938 Senate election in Georgia, Roosevelt, by an incredible political blunder, did himself more harm with the electorate than Talmadge had managed to do with his most vitriolic attacks. In Washington Senator George, expressing the views of his wealthier and more conservative supporters in Georgia, had been less than enthusiastic over some New Deal measures, and when he took a stand against a Roosevelt bill, there were about forty senators who would follow his lead. This made it very difficult for Mr. Roosevelt, and he resolved to purge Senator George, bestowing his blessing instead on Lawrence Camp, the U. S. District Attorney, a man of great dignity and little political charisma. Another candidate was lawyer William G. McRae. And the fourth man in the field, supremely confident that he would beat the three of them, was Eugene Talmadge, coming out this time, not on the anti-New Deal platform that had beaten him before, but on an oldtime Populist platform, offering free land for the landless, whose needs he said would stimulate a great upsurge in the manufacture of farming tools. Backing Mr. Talmadge was a new campaign manager, a young man already beginning to show great skill at politics, his twenty-five-year-old son, Herman.

President Roosevelt himself came to Georgia for a speech at Barnesville, in which he would administer the coup-de-grace to Senator George, brush off Talmadge and McRae, and canonize Mr. Camp. The big event was to take place in Barnesville, Georgia, near Warm Springs, the president's Georgia residence, and the occasion was the opening of a small Rural Electrification network serving some 350 families. Sensing excitement, several thousand persons crowded into the little town. Mr. Roosevelt began by telling them that he had never known what real poverty was like until he had started driving out into the surrounding countryside from his home at Warm Springs. The total lack of electricity particularly amazed him. Other Southern states, he indicated, shared in this misery—which made the South the "nation's number-one economic problem." These economic ills could be cured, he said, if he only could have the support of Southern senators and congressmen. This led him to the direct confrontation with Mr. George, and the statement that "my friend the senator cannot possibly be classified as belonging to the liberal school." [4] If he were voting in Georgia in the September primaries, he said, he most assuredly would cast his vote for Lawrence Camp. He brushed off Talmadge with the observation that his election would contribute little to practical government.

Senator George, sitting nearby, listened impassively, his face set as Mr. Roosevelt in effect read him out of the party. As the president finished, he rose and said quietly, "Mr. President, I accept your challenge." "God bless you, Walter," the president responded. "May we always be friends." [5]

Georgians may have liked what Mr. Roosevelt was trying to do to make their lives richer and happier. They did *not* like his telling them whom they should vote for. They gave Roosevelt's candidate, Camp, fewer than 80,000 votes to 141,000 for Senator George and 103,000 for Talmadge.

Twice in four years Talmadge had been beaten for the Senate, but he was by no means through as a politician. He set out immediately laying the groundwork for his campaign for the gov-

4. Anderson, *Wild Man from Sugar Creek,* p. 178.
5. Overheard by the author at the scene, Barnesville, Ga., August 11, 1938.

ernorship, when Ed Rivers would leave the office two years
hence. For two years he worked behind the scenes, mending his
fences with county politicians whom he had previously ignored,
and talking to any PTA or civic club which would ask him to
speak. His former friend Hugh Howell, now his bitter enemy,
tried to label him a friend of the rich, rather than of the sweating, tobacco-chewing wool-hat boys who came by the capitol
with him to pay his qualifying fee. Candidate Abit Nix saw in
him an incipient Hitler. Nothing prevailed. One thing more than
any other seemed to convince Georgians that Talmadge again
was the man they wanted in the governor's chair. With war
clouds darkening the world, he promised to bury the hatchet
with Roosevelt, and pledged that Georgia would do all in its
power to support the war effort. He won by 179,882 popular
votes and an overwhelming 320 unit votes out of 410.

Once in office, though, with war drawing nearer, Talmadge
seemed to change his mind. He reverted to a Tom Watson-type
isolationist stance, complaining that Roosevelt was leading the
country headlong into a war that was essentially none of its
business. Foreign aid to him was an unacceptable drain on the
economy—and furthermore it took money from the hungry
farmer's pocket. He preached strength at home as the best war
preventive, and had kind words to say about the Japanese war
machine, then active in China. When accused of being at heart a
military dictator, he supposedly replied that anybody who ever
amounted to anything had a little of the dictator in him.

Talmadge's ability to ride down all opposition was dramat-
ically demonstrated again in 1942. In this, his third term as governor, a constitutional amendment had increased the governor's
term to four years, but he would be ineligible to run again immediately thereafter. He was determined to make the race for
the four-year term, but first he needed a sure-fire issue. He
found it ready at hand, the old anti-Negro cry that Georgia politicians had used to alarm the electorate since the days of the
Freedmen's Bureau. It was a variation on this theme he em-
ployed when, to the surprise of all, he took action against certain faculty members at the university and in state schools,
whom he accused of a dark plot to admit Negroes to their all-
white institutions. He also moved against the regents who did

not share his fears—action that in time was to cost the university system its standing among accredited institutions of higher learning.

Throughout the first four decades of the century, the lot of the Negro citizen in Georgia had changed but little from what it had been in the 1880s. He could not vote, many trades were barred to him, and he could not sit by a white person on public transportation or eat with him in a restaurant. Schools were rigidly segregated from grammar school to college, and it was accepted as a fact of life that the schools the state provided for the black students were totally inferior, in plant, curriculum, and teaching staff, to the white schools. In the late 1930s, though, as New Deal concepts began to permeate to some degree the old thinking of the South, certain steps had been taken to remedy this situation, at least on the university level. The regents had hired a distinguished Iowa educator, Dr. Walter Cocking, to make a study of the higher education available to blacks in Georgia. He found that black schools were miserable, and recommended that the state spend more money on them. He also suggested that white facilities be made available to blacks for use on a separate and segregated basis. Another study by Cocking's staff recommended that a school for training teachers, both white and black, be built near Athens. Another educator, Dr. Marvin S. Pittman, president of the Georgia State Teachers' College at Statesboro, was also suspected by some of his faculty of being too liberal in his views regarding white and black students sitting down in classrooms together. To Talmadge, this was straight-out race-mixing, and he would have no part of it. In May of 1942 at a Board of Regents meeting, he sought to remove both Cocking and Pittman, pledging that he would "remove any person in the university system advocating Communism or racial equality." [6] The regents, taken aback, agreed, which so outraged the president of the university, Dr. Harmon W. Caldwell, that he resigned, and the meeting broke up in chaos. It resumed again some weeks later in the governor's office, where Dr. S. V. Sanford, chancellor of the university sys-

6. Minutes of the Board of Regents, 1941, pp. 213–216, quoted in Anderson, *Wild Man from Sugar Creek*, p. 197.

tem, and Dr. Caldwell both denied absolutely that they had ever had the slightest thought of letting whites and blacks share the same classroom in any Georgia school. Reassured, the regents reversed themselves and voted 8–7 to reinstate Dr. Cocking. This action in turn so enraged Mr. Talmadge that he demanded the resignation of two regents, Clark Howell, Jr., editor of the *Constitution,* and Lucian Goodrich, and appointed two who shared his own views. His next hearing of the charges against Dr. Pittman he turned into a circus. It was held in the chambers of the General Assembly—with Cocking required to be present to hear ''new evidence'' against him. This stressed the fact that the Rosenwald Foundation had financed his studies of black colleges, a charge that was reminiscent of Tom Watson's poisonous anti-Semitism in that it stressed the spending of Jewish money for the benefit of Negroes. For Cocking and Pittman both, it was a brutal experience, with Talmadge glaring at them from the floor and his supporters booing and jeering them from the galleries. After it was all over, the captive board voted 10 to 5 to fire Cocking and Pittman.

The result was disastrous. Throughout the nation, various accrediting agencies made investigations of their own, came to the conclusion that the Georgia educational system had been ''the victim of unprecedented and unjustifiable political interference.'' [7] The Southern Association of Colleges and Secondary Schools withdrew its accreditation from all ten state institutions serving white students. This meant that their credits would no longer be acceptable in other schools. Professional educational associations, such as the American Bar Association, American Medical Association and Phi Beta Kappa, took similar action. A wave of rage and shame swept the state. Students burned Talmadge in effigy and parents flooded the governor's office with protests. For the first time almost the entire state press was against him, and many of his oldest and staunchest friends turned upon him in anger.

One man who knew well the meaning, in political terms, of this outpouring of criticism was the brilliant, breezy young attorney general, Ellis Arnall. He had been a supporter of Tal-

7. Anderson, *Wild Man from Sugar Creek,* p. 201.

madge in the past, but he had ambitions of his own to be governor of Georgia. Now he had his issue. It was not segregation, it was "academic freedom." Of one thing Arnall, a university graduate, was sure; the old school had a special place in the hearts of Georgians. Anybody who did it a disservice, even a Talmadge, was in trouble.

In this race for the governorship Mother Nature herself seemed to conspire against Mr. Talmadge. A cloudburst drowned out his kickoff fish fry, to be held at Moultrie with fiddle music and all the claque which had followed him in the past. On the way, Talmadge asked his driver to stop at a farmhouse where he could use the outdoor privy, and there a black widow spider bit him on a particularly sensitive spot. Groaning in pain, he went on to Moultrie, but when he got up to speak the heavens opened, drenching him and sending his audience running to their cars for shelter. Soaked to the skin, and still in anguish from the spider bite, he gave up and left the platform. Later, he blamed the spider and the rainy day for the fact that Ellis Arnall beat him, 174,000 popular votes to 128,000. The county unit vote was equally heavy, 261 to 149. The Arnall victory did not mean that Georgians were ready to accept a mixing of the races in the schools. They knew that Arnall was just as strong a segregationist as was Talmadge, for he took pains to tell them so before passing quickly on to his real theme—the freedom of the schools from political influence. It did mean that Georgians were not as quick to panic at the old anti-Negro cry.

Happily for Georgia, the date for disaccrediting Georgia schools had been set far enough ahead that it came during the first days of Governor Arnall's administration, so they did not have to suffer for long the embarrassment of being cast out. The legislature moved quickly to repair the damage done by Governor Talmadge. They passed a law removing the governor from the Board of Regents and set the regents' term of office at seven years—thus making it almost impossible for a governor to stack the board with his friends, as Mr. Talmadge had done.

Once the disaster to the schools had been averted, Mr. Arnall turned his attention to the penal system. Governor after governor had been charged, openly or furtively, with corruption in the selling of pardons. Arnall sought to cease these ancient evils by setting up a Pardons and Parole Board, which denied him the power of showing executive clemency. There was much house-cleaning needed, too, to protect those who were able to receive neither pardon nor parole—men who labored on the roads in leg-irons, slept in iron cages, and were punished by confinement in sweat boxes. To eliminate these evils, Arnall set up a Board of Corrections with a director at its head who was responsible for seeing to it that Georgia convicts were humanely treated. Under Governor Talmadge, federal funds had been obtained to build a new prison facility at Reidsville and the ancient structure at Milledgeville was emptied. And now Arnall—mindful of the shameful national publicity that Georgia's prison system had received in a movie called "I am a Fugitive from a Georgia Chain Gang," which was based on a book by Robert E. Burns, an escapee—took another giant step toward reform. Shackles and chains were banned, on county farms as well as state prisons. Whipping was forbidden, and stripes were abandoned except as punishment for breaking the rules. Soon the state was earning high praise from the same Northern magazines and newspapers that had been so strongly critical before. Other actions instigated by Arnall marked him as one of the most progressive governors in Georgia history—and one who was able to bring out the best in its people. The elimination of the poll tax brought Georgia further acclaim, and his fight to lower Southern freight rates by eliminating the differential—a battle he had begun as attorney general and continued as governor—attracted national recognition.

Georgia went into World War II with almost reckless zest, thousands volunteering as the armies began massing for battle in Europe, Japan, and the Pacific. More than 320,000 served, and 6,754 were killed or listed as missing in action. Noting that the draft age was eighteen, and remembering the debt he owed to the young students who had helped elect him, Arnall came up with the slogan that a man old enough to fight was old enough to vote. So, in the new state constitution, an update of the old constitution of 1877, which by now had been amended 300 times, the voting age was set at eighteen instead of twenty-one. With the war on, the state's spending for roads and other construction projects was limited, and Arnall was able to pay off the $36,000,000 deficit he had inherited from the Talmadge administration. For decades Georgia, struggling to get out of the mud, had been spending twice as much on roads as on schools. By Arnall's second year in office this was reversed—schools getting just over $20 million, the highway system just under $11 million. Georgia in 1945 was paying more for education out of each tax dollar than any other state in the Union.

Certain ancient evils were corrected by the new constitution. Remembering Reconstruction and the bond scandals of the Bullock administration, it provided that "the bonded debt of the state shall never be increased except to repel invasion, suppress insurrection, or defend the state in time of war." [8] It forbade deficit spending by the state or its municipalities, and it nullified all exemptions from taxation that had been granted in corporate charters. This was costly to certain railroads which for a century had enjoyed a tax-free ride. The constitution also eliminated all reference to the white primary, which was under attack in the Supreme Court, and to make government employees less subject to the whim of a governor it sought to replace the old spoils system by a process under which state employees would be selected and promoted on a basis of merit.

Good things were happening, too, beyond the statehouse. Cotton was still a big money crop, bringing in more than $100 million in 1943, but Georgia was now ranked fifth among the cotton-growing states. It had come up, however, as the leading producer of pecans, peanuts, pimiento peppers, watermelons, sweet potatoes, and velvet beans—reflecting a growing interest in diversification stimulated by Cason J. Callaway, whose experiments near Pine Mountain proved that Georgia's old eroded fields could, under proper treatment, become richly productive again. Manufactures increased to $700 million, doubling the value of agricultural products, and the state's mines in the mid-Forties were producing clay and metals worth $21 million.

Georgia in the years after World War II pushed with such success for industry and commerce that throughout the Fifties and into the booming Sixties, it managed to keep up a wartime pace in business and manufacturing. One impetus came from

8. Coulter, *Georgia,* p. 454.

the Georgia Ports Authority, created in 1945, which turned Savannah, that sleepy, somewhat frayed and tousled old city, into one of the busiest ports on the eastern seaboard, moving more than five million tons of cargo a year through four deep-water terminals handling fifty-three ships at once. A new pride in its past history and concern for its present appearance came with its new-found prosperity. An organization calling itself the Savannah Historic Foundation, Inc., bought up, remodeled, and restored and put back into useful service dozens of business houses and residences that had been standing on the ancient squares since colonial times.

Other cities—Columbus, Atlanta, and finally Macon—followed Savannah in restoration projects as the state as a whole shared in a business renaissance that would have made Henry Grady glow with pride. Throughout the Fifties, regional development districts were set up in many areas where surveys could be made of land, water, and population resources which might attract industry. Studies were also made of community lacks, in schools, housing, hospitals, and transportation facilities. Federal grants were obtained for these things, as Georgians joined happily in the national sport of "milking the Feds." In the Seventies, Governor Jimmy Carter created a computerized data bank that provided economic profiles of sixty Georgia communities that were seeking plant sites and these were made available to industries seeking locations in the South.

These and other measures were reflected in a rise of per-capita income in Georgia from $340 in 1940 to $3,909 in 1972, well below the national level of $4,492 but a thousand-percent increase for Georgia. Georgia's status was still that of a supplier of raw materials and labor, the most valuable exports being forest and quarry products, but the pattern was slowly changing. The little towns were becoming centers of light industry, making a variety of products other than the state's traditional textiles. And under the impetus of the Ports Authority, Brunswick and Savannah again became important shipping ports for shrimp, lumber, and naval stores.

All of these things meant that Georgia was moving ahead economically into a new day. In other areas, though, the picture was less bright. Georgians had changed little in their attitude toward the Negro. They had deserted Talmadge and gone with Ellis Arnall when Talmadge seemed determined to wreck the university, for the voteless black man was then more a bogey-man than a real threat. But when in March of 1946 a federal court in New Orleans declared illegal the Georgia white primary which had disfranchised the Negro, suddenly the whole picture changed. The Negro was no longer at the back door with his hat in his hand. He would soon be walking up to the polls with a ballot in his hand. And once he could vote freely and without fear, who could tell what might happen? Talmadge knew what these portents meant. They meant that the political gods were smiling on him. Again they had put into his hands the old bludgeon, the white Georgian's fear of the black, and he was quick to raise the issue as he went into the race for governor against businessman James V. Carmichael, heir to Ellis Arnall's support, and a revived and again hopeful Ed Rivers.

For all the efforts by Talmadge and Rivers to put some fire into it, the campaign was a bore. Georgians' tastes in politics were growing more sophisticated. The radio carried the speeches—and now nearly every house in Georgia, no matter how far in the backwoods, had a radio. The old colorful tree-climbing, fiddle-playing characters were gone and the pre-speech music squealed and screeched from a tinny loudspeaker. Food was scarce after the war, and the big barbecues and fish fries were no longer held.

When finally the votes were counted, James V. Carmichael had won the votes of 313,389 Georgians; Talmadge trailed by more than 15,000—at 297,245. Rivers was far back, with 69,489. But Eugene Talmadge was elected, for the fourth time, governor of Georgia. His county unit vote was 242, to 146 for Carmichael and 22 for Rivers. The general election which followed confirmed the primary victory.

It was the last hurrah for Ol' Gene Talmadge, the Ishmael of Georgia politics. Before he could be inaugurated, he was dead. Talmadge's death threw Georgia into a state of political confusion which will bemuse students of the electoral process for years. The possibility of his passing had not been unanticipated by those closest to him. An old law was dug up which said that in case a winning candidate in the general election should die before being sworn in, the person getting the second largest number of votes would be inaugurated in his stead. This word was quietly passed around and Herman Talmadge got 675 write-in votes. The Carmichael people also got the word, but their write-in for him was only 669.

So, Herman was the new governor. Or was he? For the first time in its history, Georgia had a lieutenant-governor, elected under the revised constitution of 1945. Melvin E. Thompson, a schoolteacher, an earnest, honest, but not very forceful man, had won that post. The General Assembly was not persuaded that on the death of a governor before inauguration, the lieutenant-governor should be sworn in. The assembly met and declared Herman Talmadge the next governor, by virtue of his write-in vote. Not convinced that the legislature had this power, Governor Arnall refused to yield to young Talmadge. Talmadge, showing some of his father's old arrogance, took forcible possession of the office and the mansion, and for sixty-seven days was the de facto governor. Neither he nor Arnall, who set up office in the rotunda of the capitol, could effectively carry on the state's business, for Secretary of State Ben Fortson, not knowing who was the legal chief executive, refused to affix the Great Seal of Georgia to papers signed by either. He sat upon it by day, and took it to bed with him by night. It was the third time in the state's history the Great Seal had been hidden. Finally the state supreme court ended the ludicrous muddle by ruling that Melvin E. Thompson, the duly elected lieutenant-governor, should succeed to the governorship.

In a special election the following year, 1948, Herman Talmadge won it on his own—using his father's old scare tactics in a typical "white supremacy" campaign. He did, however, push through a three percent sales tax, and cut property taxes, using the increased income to fund the newly chartered Minimum Foundation Program for Education, under which state schools would offer equal opportunities and services to *all* Georgians, black or white. This was not pure altruism on the part of Georgia and her elected representatives. Attacks on the segregation of the schools in cases before the Supreme Court caused great concern in Georgia, and a definite effort at last was being made to bring the Negro schools up to par so that the state might take refuge in the old "separate but equal" doctrine, of which in the past only the "separate" requirement had been observed. Now handsome new schools for black children began to replace the old-field shacks of the past. But by other criteria by which a school might be judged—quality of teaching, libraries, support for bands and drama groups—nearly all the old inequalities still remained.

9

And Finally,
It Was Monday

$\mathcal{G}$OING into the Fifties, the legal and political attacks on segregation and its obvious inequalities began to increase. In 1948 President Truman proposed a far-reaching civil-rights program. Lynching was specifically outlawed, a statute which was of special interest to Georgians, because Georgia for generations had shared with Mississippi the sombre distinction of being the lynching capital of the world. This peculiar form of murder seemed to be based as much on economic as on sociological factors. As falling cotton prices beat more and more little farm owners down to the status of tenant and sharecropper, on the same economic level with the Negro, the white man had struck out against the black in a blind rage at some real or fancied wrong. These acts of murder could be tied statistically to the price of cotton; as the price of cotton dropped, lynching rose.

Truman's civil-rights package required the elimination of separate seating for whites and blacks on interstate trains and buses and also proposed a Fair Employment Practices Commission, to provide equality of job opportunity to the Negro. Georgians were strongly opposed, and knowing their feelings, Herman Talmadge in his two campaigns for governor, in 1948 and 1950, ran on the platform that no FEPC would be allowed to function in Georgia and that he would preserve segregation at all costs in the schools, in the parks and playgrounds, theaters and restaurants—wherever it existed. The crucial issue, of course, was the segregation of the schools, not only in Georgia but in sixteen other states. Once the Supreme Court should decide that such separation was unconstitutional, the whole complex pattern of segregation in Georgia and the South would be destroyed.

For years, as Georgians angrily or nervously watched the attack on their ancient institutions, Ralph McGill, as editor of the *Atlanta Constitution,* tried to lead them on a path they could accept. He opposed a federal antilynching law and a Fair Employment Practices Act on the grounds that the states themselves should provide the Negro this protection. But in his column he savagely attacked the Klan and the Columbians, and the nameless "murdering morons" [1] who made up the lynch mobs, and he decried the White Citizens' Councils who gave an air of respectability to the fight against any dilution of white supremacy. On the school issue, he did not argue for integration at first, knowing if he did he would lose his audience. But he did crusade strongly for fairness—for the separate-but-equal school system which the Supreme Court in 1896 had ruled legal. But, he asked, could Georgia's poor rural counties afford an adequate dual system when they could hardly afford two poor ones? Some of the richer counties could, and did, upgrade their black schools. In most, though, nothing was done, and this was of great concern to McGill. "Someday," he warned in his column in the *Constitution,* "it's going to be Monday" [2]—the day when the Supreme Court handed down its decisions—predicting that when that day did come, it would end segregation by color in the public schools.

And finally that Monday came, the day nearly all white Georgians had dreaded. In May of 1954 the Supreme Court ruled that separate schools were inherently unequal, and directed that "with all deliberate speed" segregation must be brought to an end.

That fall, Marvin Griffin succeeded Herman Talmadge as governor, promising flatly in his slow south-Georgia drawl that

1. Martin, *Ralph McGill, Reporter,* p. 150.
2. Martin, *Ralph McGill, Reporter,* p. 132.

come hell or high water there would be no mixing of the races in Georgia's schools. And for the next five years, while Georgians waited and watched as school segregation barriers were struck down in Florida, Arkansas, Tennessee, Texas, and Louisiana, Georgia's children, white and black, went to separate schools. Griffin's first gambit was to secure a constitutional amendment which gave the governor and the legislature the power to abolish the public schools and create a system of private schools, and Little Rock, following Georgia's example, drew up a plan to lease her public schools to "private" operators. The Supreme Court ruled that this was a subterfuge, an evasive scheme that could not be permitted to nullify the Court's ruling.

Georgia did all she could to prevent, or at least postpone, any mixing anywhere, in schools or out. Governor Griffin, without success, tried to force the regents of the university system to prohibit any state school from playing against a nonsegregated sports team, or before a nonsegregated audience. The parks director announced that he would lease nine state parks to private citizens. (In Atlanta in 1955, the public golf courses had been opened to Negroes, but not the pools and playgrounds.) When a group of black ministers in 1957 tried to break Atlanta's bus seating plan that required Negroes to sit in the back, they were arrested.

Still no formal move had been made against the schools themselves. Finally, in December of 1958, suits were filed to enforce desegregation of the Atlanta city buses, the restaurant at the airport—and the city's schools. A year later, the Atlanta Board of Education drew up its desegregation plan, submitted it to a federal judge, and it was accepted.

It was, in a way, a tribute to the leadership of Ralph McGill. Ever since the Supreme Court had handed down the schools decision, he had urged his fellow Georgians to accept it, whatever their personal views might be, for it was now the law of the land and there was only one way it could be resisted—by secession and the use of armed force. The South, he suggested, had tried that once before, and it had not worked out so well. Finally, to his surprise, he got support from an unexpected quarter. In January of 1959, Herman Talmadge, who in 1955 had succeeded the ailing Walter George as U.S. senator, and to whom all Georgians defiant of the school decision now turned for leadership, said publicly that the Supreme Court decision on the schools was an accomplished fact and would remain so until reversed by the Court itself or nullified by Congress and the people. This did not mean that Talmadge was any less the enemy of the desegregation ruling. The next year—in one of the most amazing oratorical demonstrations ever seen in a chamber famous for its forensic displays, he spoke for six hours against the Court's civil-rights decisions.

The year after the school decision, candidate Ernest Vandiver in his campaign for lieutenant-governor had sworn that he would go to jail before bowing to this edict from the courts. Four years later, in 1960, when he succeeded Marvin Griffin as governor, he had declared that not a single Negro would be permitted to enter a Georgia school. There would be no integration, token or otherwise. Nor was there—until January of 1961. Then two intelligent and courageous young Negroes, Charlayne Hunter and Hamilton Holmes, showed up at the University of Georgia with a court order, requesting admission. A great furor followed. Lawyers in fast automobiles, representing both the students and the state, raced over the highways from Athens to the Federal District Court one hundred miles away in Macon, seeking a stay of the court's order, and racing another hundred miles from there to the Appellate Court in Atlanta. While this old-time movie chase was going on, there was one night of violence on the Georgia campus, when a thousand students rioted outside Miss Hunter's dormitory. By now the word was sweeping over the state. Phones began to ring in the governor's office and in the legislature, and telegrams by the hundreds began pouring in. Vandiver had made the alternatives clear. The students would have to be admitted—or the university would have to close. The tone of the calls and the telegrams was one of resignation, but the message was equally clear. The people of Georgia did not like what was happening. But of one thing they were certain. The university must not be closed. If this had been some little country school, the attitude might have been different. But this was the university, with its special place in the hearts of all Georgians.

Vandiver got the message. He ruefully but firmly announced that he would not defy the law, and the Negro students were formally admitted. At the statehouse, where out of 600 letters received, only 12 wanted the schools closed, the General Assembly began abolishing all the laws so carefully put together over the years, which the state's "constitutional experts" had promised would maintain segregation of the races forever. That summer three black students were accepted at the Georgia Institute of Technology without protest. And in the fall, in the Atlanta public school system, ten black students entered white high schools. With a calm old mayor named William B. Hartsfield and a veteran police chief, Herbert Jenkins, keeping an eye on a tense and troubled city, the day went off quietly. There was no violence.

Here was a beginning, a token, truly, but walls had been breached that never could be built up again. In years to come there would be conflict over busing and pupil placement, and teacher assignments and pay scales. But the action of the governor and the Georgia legislature and the Atlanta school board marked a turning point not only for Georgia but for all the Deep South. The ancient pattern of total defiance was ended.

To a great degree the quiet acceptance of desegregation in Atlanta was the result of a document called the Sibley Report. In 1960, a distinguished Atlanta lawyer, John A. Sibley, had been named by the legislature to head a committee that would travel about the state, going into every congressional district to assay the sentiment of the people. The evidence was conclusive—the people were universally against the action of the Supreme Court in ordering the integration of the schools, but they recognized that the alternative—closing the schools—would be disastrous, a tragedy unthinkable.

The integration of the schools was followed by the breaking down of other barriers. The next year, in 1962, after boycotts, demonstrations and sit-ins had wracked Atlanta, and black students had been arrested in Albany, court actions and an ICC ruling ordered the abolition of all segregated travel facilities in Georgia. The separate waiting rooms, toilets, drinking fountains, and ticket lines at bus and rail terminals were opened to all. In Savannah, Augusta, Macon, and Columbus the city bus lines and lunch counters were desegregated, and in Atlanta in 1963, under a bold new mayor named Ivan Allen, Jr., who had defeated a fiery segregationist named Lester Maddox, all ordinances requiring segregation, on the buses, in the libraries, parks, playgrounds, restaurants and theaters, were withdrawn.

The race issue, of course, was not dead. In 1962, Marvin Griffin, seeking the governorship again, based his race against Carl Sanders on Sanders's tie-in with Ivan Allen and his "Atlanta crowd" who Griffin claimed had brought shame to Georgia by leading in the move to wipe out segregation. Georgians, though, were not disturbed by these charges. Sanders, though instinctively a segregationist, came over as a new breed of Georgia politician, projecting the image of a progressive in business, of honesty in the handling of the state's funds, and his attitude toward race was moderate. Though not for integration, he was for "equal opportunity." He won by a wide margin. He too, like Arnall, gave the state one of the most progressive administrations in its history, spending during his term $176 million on education, $30 million more than all the money that had been spent in the university system since 1933. He set up prison reforms, a regional mental health program, and developed a commission on science and technology to bring Georgia into the Space Age.

With Sanders in the governor's chair and Ivan Allen, Jr. in the mayor's office, Georgia—and Atlanta—moved ahead on all fronts. It was far from easy, though, particularly for the young mayor. Though instinctively a man of good will, an able politician, and like his father before him a natural civic leader, Allen was nonetheless inexperienced in administering a great city wracked with tensions between elements of a mixed population of black and white, rich and poor. His first efforts to improve Atlanta's lot in all areas suffered from a still lurking fear of the Negro, deeply imbedded in the psyche of the white. He proposed an $80 million bond issue to improve schools, streets, and sewers, to develop a civic center and rapid transit. Part of it was a plan to turn Piedmont Park into the most beautiful city park in the country. This would cost nine million dollars, and Allen already had four million of it pledged, anonymously, from his friend Robert W. Woodruff of the Coca-Cola Company. But somehow, in the public mind, this contemplated park became part of a purported plan for the Negro to invade the still all-white north side, and on this false assumption the entire bond issue was defeated. The Piedmont Park plan never was carried out, but not long afterward, again with Woodruff's anonymous help, a beautiful thirteen-million-dollar Memorial Arts Center was built, in memory of 106 Atlantans killed in a plane crash at Orly Airfield in Paris in June of 1962. No one seemed to worry about whether this magnificent facility would draw blacks as well as whites, and the public, stunned by the tragedy, was generous in its gifts. Nor was there concern about who was to sit where when Ivan Allen pushed through one of his other projects, a huge eighteen-million-dollar stadium which brought big-league sports to Atlanta.

When Allen took office in 1962, there had been token integration in the schools, on the buses, and in the parks. When he left office, there had been complete desegregation of all public facilities in Atlanta, a Negro was serving as vice mayor, and there were black police officers on the force (earlier a black policeman could not arrest a white person). Black and white children were studying side by side in most schools, and busing was being considered to bring about integration of the others. Black brides were pictured in the society section of the newspapers, and in a state where Governor Marvin Griffin had once sought to prevent Georgia teams from competing with other teams which had Negroes in their lineups, Hank Aaron, a black home-run hitter who was to break Babe Ruth's record, was the hero cheered most loudly at Atlanta's new stadium. And all around the city there was evidence that Atlanta, for all its black-white tension, was one of the most progressive, most prosperous big cities in the nation. Its new hotels, business offices, and apartments towered against the sky, its new manufacturing plants sprawling on the outskirts, creating more than 20,000 new jobs a year. Truly it seemed as the Sixties rolled on that Mayor William B. Hartsfield was right when he said that Atlanta was "a city too busy to hate." [3]

3. Irwin Ross, "Mayor Hartsfield Uses the Light Touch," *Readers Digest* (April 28, 1958), pp. 203–207.

But there were old fears still latent in Atlanta as well as in small-town Georgia. While tall buildings rose downtown, white residents moved by thousands from the city, now growing toward a black residential majority, to the still all-white suburbs. And there was still in the heart of the rural Georgian a deep distrust of the black man, a reluctance to give any ground in the field of civil rights that would dilute white supremacy—political, social, and economic. In 1961, Ivan Allen, with the help of the black vote, had defeated segregationist Lester Maddox in the race for mayor. Five years later, in 1966, to the amazement of most Georgians and the dismay of many, segregationist Maddox succeeded moderate Carl Sanders as governor of Georgia. He was not elected by all the people, but by the legislature at the end of one of the most bizarre campaigns known to Georgia politics. In the five-man primary the Maddox campaign had been straight out of the Tom Watson-Eugene Talmadge book—a fervent appeal to the prejudices and suspicions of the rural voter. But where Watson and Talmadge had only talked against the Negro, Maddox had acted. He was for absolute segregation, in the schools and churches and all places of public accommodation, and when Negroes had tried to eat at his fried-chicken restaurant, he had driven them out at pistol point with his son brandishing an ax handle. When the law closed in and he was told he would have to serve Negroes or quit business, he chose to close the doors of his prospering restaurant, thus making himself a folk hero to thousands of Georgians. He attacked his principal opponent, Ellis Arnall, who from 1943 to 1947 had given Georgia one of its most progressive and effective administrations in modern history. To Maddox, Arnall was a tool of the big-city interests, the rich folks in Atlanta, who were beginning to give the Negro far too free a rein, and this charge, which had no effect when Marvin Griffin attacked Carl Sanders, worked for Maddox against Arnall. In the primary, Arnall got the black vote and the more affluent whites, which gave him a plurality over Maddox and three others, including an ambitious young ex-naval officer-turned peanut grower-turned politician whose name was Jimmy Carter. But the primary race went into a runoff, and to the vast surprise of those who had refused to take Maddox seriously, he won, taking over fifty-four percent of the popular vote. (There were dark rumors that a number of Maddox votes came from Republicans who felt that Maddox would be an easier man to beat than Arnall.)

The Republicans went into the general election feeling confident. Thousands of newcomers from the North had come in, Republicans by birth or instinct, men and women having no memory of the old plantation. Thousands of young native Georgians, their minds attuned to business and manufacturing rather than to farming, were showing strong leanings toward the Republican party. They, with thousands more breakaway Democrats, had put Georgia in the Goldwater column in 1964—the first time since Reconstruction that the state had voted Republican. Their reasoning was the same as that of four other Southern states—Louisiana, Mississippi, Alabama, and South Carolina—which, along with Goldwater's home state, were the only ones who voted for him. Goldwater had voted against the Civil Rights Act of that year—a piece of legislation passed by the Johnson administration as devastating in its effect on white Southern mores as the school decision had been ten years earlier.

Now in Georgia the Republicans were shooting for the governorship. Their candidate was Howard "Bo" Callaway—handsome, cleancut, rich from family textile mills. Profoundly a conservative and as much a segregationist as Lester Maddox, he had gone up to Congress in the 1954 election, where he set a record for conservative voting that would have made Goldwater himself look profligate.

Faced with the choice of voting for Democrat Maddox or Republican Callaway, Georgia's more liberal-minded citizens were faced with a dilemma. They could stay away from the polls; or they could cast a write-in vote for Ellis Arnall—despite the fact that in the liberal view he represented a long-dead past. The write-in vote was chosen. It accounted for seven percent of the votes, and as a result no candidate had a majority—though Callaway finished with a slight plurality in the popular vote. The Democratic Georgia legislature did not long debate the issue. They chose Maddox the Democrat as governor of Georgia.

To many a Georgian, notably to most liberals and progressives, and to all blacks, it was incredible that this little man, a pistol-brandishing, ax-handle-waving, fried-chicken cook who found in the Bible justification for all his efforts to keep the black man in his place, would be chosen to govern a state that seemingly had left far behind his brand of white-supremacy politics. But to political analysts, the reasoning of the legislature was clear. Maddox was flung into the office by the backlash of white reaction to the Watts riots, the Selma and the Albany demonstrations, and the far-reaching Civil Rights Act of 1965, which Lyndon Johnson looked upon as one of the supreme achievements of his administration. And above all, perhaps, it was Georgia's answer to the growing threat of another Georgian, the charismatic Reverend Martin Luther King, Jr., and his supposedly nonviolent, but ever more militant, Southern Christian Leadership Council.

Maddox as governor did relatively little—there was nothing he could do, really—to reverse the rising tide of integration or repeal civil-rights laws already on the books. He toned down his old diatribes against the black as an inferior race, and, under pressure from black groups, quietly started hiring black clerks and secretaries in small state jobs. His latent fear of the black, though, was often obvious. In the hot summer of 1967, when blacks were rioting in the North, Maddox seemed terrified by the prospects that Georgia might be next on the list after Detroit and Newark and Cleveland. When in June of 1967 rioting did break out in Atlanta's Dixie Hills section, Maddox called Mayor Allen and offered him the service of the state police and National Guard. Allen thanked him politely but declined. In August, when demonstrators against the War in Vietnam planned a weekend march and rally, Maddox deployed tanks and troops to National Guard armories all over the state. The march went off peacefully.

His behavior on the occasion of Martin Luther King's funeral did much to reveal his deepest fears and angers. He could not, of course, be expected to go to the funeral of the man whom he hated and had endlessly vilified, nor did he send a representative of the government, though two state officers, the attorney general and the commissioner of labor, did attend. He also insisted that the capitol building be open for business on the day of the funeral, and was angered when the City Hall nearby, and many business houses downtown, closed and hung mourning ribbons on their doors. He was particularly enraged when Secretary of State Ben Fortson ordered the state and national flags in the capitol grounds to be flown at half staff, and he called Fortson at home and told him to rescind the order. Fortson refused.

In sharp contrast to Maddox's attitudes and actions was the way Mayor Ivan Allen had handled the city's planning for the funeral march. Allen did not hate King—he had instead a profound respect for his qualities of leadership. It was Allen, in fact, who with the quiet support of Robert Woodruff and Paul Austin of the Coca-Cola Company, had insured the success of the biracial dinner the city gave for King on his winning the Nobel Prize for peace in 1964. To Allen, King was "a big man, a great man," [4] who had shown the highest courage in marching with the people of his Southern Christian Leadership Conference in the face of police dogs and clubs and guns in the tragic but still triumphant marches in Montgomery, Birmingham, and Selma, Alabama, and Albany, Georgia, and finally in the city of Memphis, where he was to die.

Allen himself had much of that same high courage. Early in his administration, a white Atlanta policeman had shot a black car thief, and Stokely Carmichael had sparked a riot in a fetid Atlanta slum called Summerhill. Into a glowering, shouting, half-drunken mob the gray-headed Allen had walked unflinching, his face as gray as his hair—along with his driver, George Royal, and a young uniformed policeman named Morris Redding. They were spat upon and cursed, and fists were raised and clenched and shaken in their faces. When Allen asked them to go to the stadium and name some leaders who could come to City Hall to talk with him about their grievances, Carmichael's SNCC leaders began screaming that this was a plot to herd them into the stadium to be penned up and shot. Allen climbed up on the top of a car and tried to talk to the crowd there in the streets, but bricks began to fly, and black hands seized the car and began to rock it violently, and Allen plunged headlong off the

4. Ivan Allen, Jr., *Mayor: Notes on the Sixties* (New York: Simon and Schuster, 1971), p. 99.

car-top into the arms of Morris Redding and George Royal. By now the crowd was out of control, and Allen, as a last resort, called for the police to use their tear gas, which was done, and the crowd began to break up. Allen himself was grabbed by his police chief, Herbert Jenkins, who shoved him, choking and coughing, into the chief's car and hauled him back to City Hall.

Allen went back to Summerhill that night. All was quiet, and he stood on the street corner with the press and the police, and the few people who came warily out. A newsman asked him if there was any way that such an uprising could have been prevented.

"Yes," said Allen. "If we had started a hundred years ago making the necessary corrections, and had the wisdom in America then not to let these slums become the places they are . . ." [5]

Allen was at home, watching television with his wife, Louise, on the night of April 4, 1968, when the news flashed on the screen that Martin Luther King, Jr., the man who since the Nobel dinner had become his friend and quiet confidant, had been shot in Memphis, where he had gone to support a sanitation workers' strike. Immediately there flashed into his mind a memory of that night two years earlier when the shooting of an unknown black car thief had set off the fierce rioting in Summerhill. How much wilder, bloodier, more far-reaching might the black reaction be when they learned that King, their charismatic leader, had been shot!

He gave orders to the airport that a plane be held, and left immediately with Mrs. Allen for the King home, far across town in the black neighborhood of Vine City. There he greeted Coretta King, and then escorted her by police car to the airport. And it was there he learned that Dr. King was dead, and it was he who gave her, officially, this sad news. They drove back to the King house in the dark, in the rain, and Allen gave orders that the house and the family be protected from intrusion as long as necessary. While he was there, President Johnson called to talk with Mrs. King, and Allen went back to his office at City Hall, to learn that all over the country riots were breaking out.

5. Allen, *Mayor*, p. 192.

To keep the same thing from happening in Atlanta would be Allen's job, and one of the most difficult he had ever faced. Talks with two men whom he respected gave him strength to face it. He called Washington and spoke to the president. Johnson was cool and calm. He told Allen that he was receiving frantic calls for troops from mayors all over the country—and he had committed a lot of troops already. He would do what was necessary to help Allen, but he hoped Atlanta and Georgia could keep things under control with their own forces, the city and county police and National Guard. Allen assured him he was taking all necessary steps. He was calling every policeman in Atlanta to duty, and would run two twelve-hour shifts. Just as Allen was leaving to go home he got another call from Washington. It was his friend and unofficial advisor, Robert W. Woodruff, who with former governor Carl Sanders had been with the president that evening.

"Ivan," said Woodruff, "the minute they bring King's body back tomorrow—between then and the time of the funeral— Atlanta, Georgia, is going to be the center of the universe." He paused and then went on, "I want you to do whatever is right and necessary, and whatever the city can't pay for will be taken care of. Just do it right." [6]

Dr. King's body was brought back to Atlanta on Friday afternoon. Allen, with his vice mayor, Sam Massell, went with Mrs. King to the airport, and with her accompanied the body to the funeral home. The night passed quietly in Atlanta, though there had been rioting all day in Washington and many of the Eastern cities. On Saturday night, with his police chief Herbert Jenkins, Allen toured the city, getting out of the police car and walking the streets and talking to people. One thing he discovered was heartwarming. Atlanta homes, white and black, were being opened to the thousands of visitors who were pouring in. Atlanta churches would take them in and feed them.

From Saturday afternoon to Monday the body of Martin Luther King, Jr., lay in state in Sisters Chapel of Spelman College, while an endless line of mourners filed past the open

6. Allen, *Mayor,* p. 205.

casket for one last look at their leader. On Monday afternoon the long march to the church began—the little Ebenezer Baptist Church where King's father was the pastor, and his mother played the hymns. Behind the mule-drawn wagon carrying King's remains moved a crowd of nearly two hundred thousand, singing the old song "We Shall Overcome." The dark tide flowed past the state capitol, and a reporter broke away to find out what was going on inside. Governor Maddox was secluded in his office protected by a hundred troopers—and in the outer office his aides peeped through the blinds. Outside, the river of humanity flowed on under the hot April sun, paying its last tribute to the black leader who would go down in history as one of Georgia's great men, a man who in all his actions so disruptive to Southern mores, had been motivated, not by anger, not by hatred, but by the gentle teachings of Jesus, Thoreau, and Mahatma Gandhi.

Ivan Allen did not run for mayor again in 1969, announcing frankly that he wanted to be free to speak his mind on Atlanta's problems without being accused of pandering to the Negro vote. He then told Atlanta's whites in blunt terms that they were still depriving the Negro of his economic rights and opportunities—and that no plague would fall upon them if on occasion they had some social contact with a Negro.

His vice mayor, Sam Massell, was elected over Rodney Cook, a Republican who had the support of the white conservatives, and Dr. Howard Tate, who proved unable to command the entire black vote in Atlanta. It was an election in which the voting pattern of two decades was shattered. The Negro vote, in silent support of the middle- and upper-class whites living on the north side, had controlled Atlanta's mayoral races since the early Fifties. This combination was now replaced by a coalition of blacks combined with labor and liberals, instead of with the old conservative white power structure. The result was the election of a Jewish mayor, and Maynard Jackson, a huge and personable black man, as his vice mayor.

Governor Maddox by law could not succeed himself in 1970, a fact that so upset him he sought to run his wife instead. This proved impractical so he ran for lieutenant-governor and won, still fanatic on the subject of white supremacy, still appealing to Georgia's "little man" in the old Populist voice of Tom Watson and Eugene Talmadge.

By startling contrast, the man Georgians chose for their governor was the earnest young peanut farmer from Plains, in Georgia's black belt, whom Maddox had beaten in 1966. State Senator Jimmy Carter, a moderate in his views on race, a progressive in his attitudes toward Georgia's business future, was no ranting demagogue of the old breed, but a man cut more nearly in the mode of Richard Russell, Ellis Arnall, and Carl Sanders. In racial matters, in fact, he was bolder and more outspoken than they—affirming at his inauguration in 1971 that "the time for racial discrimination is over." [7]

His four years as governor were marked by the most far-reaching reorganization of the state government since the administration of Richard B. Russell forty years before. State agencies, boards, and commissions were reduced from 300 to 22. An Adequate Education Law was passed, and progress was made in vocational education and special training for the handicapped and gifted. A Heritage Trust was set up to preserve valuable natural and cultural resources, and programs were developed to help the alcoholic and the drug addict in state hospitals, rather than by simply jailing them. A new system of zero budgeting required each department head to justify his entire expenditures, rather than merely the increase over the previous budget. Property tax reforms were set in motion, and industrial development showed tremendous strides—so much so that the expanding economy allowed expenses to grow without a tax increase. (The boom of the Sixties was slowing down, but the grim recession of the mid-Seventies had not yet begun.) Georgia's overseas trade was being vigorously pushed in line with Atlanta's drive to become an "international city," with the prospect in view of free ports at Atlanta and Savannah. Judicial reform was instigated, and an attack on Georgia's overcrowded

7. Carter's Inaugural Address to Georgia Legislature, Jan. 12, 1971 (Addresses of James Earl Carter, 1971, 1975, compiled by Frank Daniel for Georgia Department of Archives and History, Carrol Hart, Director. Privately printed under direction of Secretary of State Ben W. Fortson, Jr. and distributed by Georgia Department of Archives and History, Atlanta, Ga.), p. 78.

and inadequate prison system was begun. And in line with the thinking of the new day, blacks and women in increasing numbers were brought into positions of authority and responsibility in state government. At the end of his term, in January of 1975, the "bottom line" was impressive. Carter left the state with a budget surplus of more than $50 million. It was a record received with such general approbation, both state and national, that he began to dream the impossible dream. Late in 1974, he announced that he would be a candidate for the presidency in 1976—a goal not reached by a Southern-born politician since Zachary Taylor in 1848.

George Busbee, the man who had followed Carter as governor of Georgia, was an ideal successor. Carter was a visionary, an idealist, an innovator, and his reorganization of state government needed time and tinkering before its components could work smoothly. Busbee was the tinkerer, the nuts-and-bolts man who could cause the gears to mesh and the wheels to run smoothly—though the onset of recession made his task extremely difficult. The man Busbee beat was Lester Maddox, the lieutenant-governor. Still assuring the voters that his every thought, word, and deed had the blessing of the Lord, Maddox ran a hard campaign. And in all fairness, in many ways he had made a good governor. He had taken a particular interest in the reform of the prison system, closing down many county work camps when he found them unhealthy and unsanitary fire hazards. In the appointment of judges to high state courts he turned for advice to the state and local bar associations, and the appointments he made under their guidance were excellent. He chose Peyton Hawes, a competent man of unquestioned probity, as his advisor on fiscal matters, and he named William Burson, a far-out liberal, director of the state welfare program. Under Burson, poor counties whose white commissioners had turned down state help because most of it would go to black families, began to share in the food stamp and other programs for the poor.

But the image former governor Maddox still had in his local habitat was of the rabid racist walking a black minister out of his restaurant at pistol point, or of the political clown, riding a bicycle backwards across the mansion lawn. In a time when black people and white could ride the same buses, sit in the same theaters, play in the same parks, use the same restrooms, and eat in the same restaurants without the heavens falling, candidate Maddox's attitudes no longer seemed relevant. He was beaten in the primary and retired to open his restaurant again, one in Underground Atlanta and another in Sandy Springs. But he held onto his role as Bible-guided oracle in all matters dealing with politics, and when the American Independent party in 1976 was casting about for a presidential candidate, their choice was Maddox. His main target was not the Republican, Mr. Ford, but Jimmy Carter, whom he denounced as a Socialist.

Thus Georgia went into the primary contests of 1976 with two native sons seeking the Democratic nomination. And it quickly became clear that the mood of Georgia and the South and the nation was not the old, bitter, racist attitudes of which Lester Maddox was still the symbol. As Jimmy Carter began talking of his vision of America, confused as his rhetoric sometimes seemed to be, the people listened and believed. State after state rallied to him, and he won the Democratic nomination handily. He went into the campaign against the Republican nominee, President Ford, with what seemed to be a comfortable lead in the polls. This, however, dissipated rapidly over the next few months as a series of soporific debates between Carter and the incumbent president presented Carter as a decent enough fellow but no charismatic leader. As a result, he went into the November election neck and neck with Mr. Ford, holding a lead so thin the pollsters said it could not be accurately measured. The popular vote showed how right they were. Out of 78,570,000 votes cast, 40,156,000 were for Carter, 38,413,000 for Ford. This thin margin was reflected in the electoral vote, the closest since 1916. Carter carried twenty-three states with 297 votes, Ford, twenty-seven states with 241. To finish even this far in front he had had to accomplish something of a political miracle. He had drawn labor to his support, and the bosses of the faction-ridden national Democratic party, and in the inner cities of key states they had turned out the votes for him which countered the votes that the affluent suburbs, both North and South, were casting for Mr. Ford. He also won over most of the independent vote. Though roughly a million of them went for

Senator Eugene McCarthy, most of the undecided and apathetic, the angry poor and put-down who felt themselves to be the victims of political, social, or economic injustice, seemed to sense that Carter would be their friend. Also, miracle of miracles for a man from the Deep South, he won the black vote almost en masse, with the help of two black Georgians, Rep. Andrew Young and Martin Luther King, Sr., "Daddy" King, whose prayer of benediction ended the Madison Square Garden convention, told the black world unmistakably that Carter was their man. He won a heavy Catholic vote, despite some bishops' reservations about his views on abortion, and despite the doubts still held by many Southerners as to his views on economics, and on race relations, he brought together again all the states, except Virginia, of the once Solidly Democratic South.

All this had a deeper meaning, of course, than one man's victory over another by reason of his personality, or of one national party's victory over another on the basis of transient issues. It meant that for the first time since before the Civil War the South was again a full and accepted partner in the Union of states; it meant that an amazing change in national attitudes had taken place.

It meant, too, that Georgia as a whole was soon to sense a lifting of the spirit, a psychic rebirth toward which her people had been struggling for a hundred years. With a Georgian in the White House, receiving the homage of all the world's leaders, with a Georgia judge as attorney general, having oversight over all federal law, with a Georgia congressman—and a black one at that—roaming the world as ambassador to the United Nations; with Plains, Georgia, taking on the cachet of a bucolic Hyde Park or Hyannisport, and St. Simons—Sea Island destined to become a Little-White-House-by-the-Sea—it was inevitable that Georgians should begin to walk a little taller, to look on life with a burgeoning sense of well-being.

In her proud new role as the home state of a president, Georgia now could move with greater confidence into a challenging future. Her economy was no longer based on a one-horse farmer working a one-horse farm, but on a diversified agriculture and a thriving, multifaceted industry whose manufactured products were worth more than the product of her fields.

But her people were still faced with complex problems, as they had always been—problems of taxes, problems of schools, problems of welfare and its fair distribution. One great burden, though, was growing a little lighter with the changing times. With black legislators sitting unchallenged in the General Assembly, with black bureaucrats serving in state agencies, with blacks holding city offices throughout Georgia, and with a black mayor seated in Atlanta's city hall, the ancient problem of how black and white Georgians could learn to live and work together in relative harmony seemed to be moving slowly, though sometimes painfully, to a solution.

There were still great difficulties and angry confrontations. Though considered by rural Georgia to be the fountainhead of liberalism in racial matters, Atlanta particularly had her troubles adjusting to a black voting majority. Her black mayor, Maynard Jackson, in his insistence on joint ventures between black and white architects and contractors handling city jobs, sometimes seemed as racist in his inner being as was Lester Maddox. His police department under a black superintendent had its full quota of scandal. And other black officials proved to be as dishonest and immoral, as prone to malfeasance, as some of their white predecessors had been.

As if determined to prove true that sociological cliché, that integration is that brief interval between the arrival of the first black and the departure of the last white, droves of Atlanta's white citizens throughout the mid-1970s continued moving their residences and their businesses to the still all-white suburbs. But citizens vote where they live, and Atlanta's black leaders were puzzled as to how to recapture them, and their lost taxes, without diluting their own black voting power. No longer could a relatively small group of conservative black leaders—Martin Luther King, Sr., William Holmes Borders, Rufus Clement, Jesse Hill, A. H. Walden, Benjamin Mays—work with the white power structure to handle black-white issues on the old "not too much, not too fast" schedule of William B. Hartsfield's and Ivan Allen's day. In the final analysis, the fate of the city, and of Georgia, hung on how responsibly the new breed of black politicians would handle themselves in office. And this, as 1977 wore on, was a mixed picture. One could not help observing, however, the incredible changes which had taken place in Georgia in the past decade, the whites accepting without open rancor, the blacks sharing without overt gloating, associations in daily life and work and play that once would have been unthinkable.

The election of Jimmy Carter leads to the hope that Georgians at last have reached that time which Lillian Smith predicted would come—when the Negro could find a way to live a good life with white people, and each white, in turn, could find a way to live a good life with himself, free of the ancient pain and burden of keeping the Negro "in his place." This change in attitude of the Southerner toward the black, of the nation toward the Southerner, which Carter sensed and acted on in his drive to the presidency, could make possible the realization of a dream as old as the state itself, the desire to come up to the level of the rest of the nation in all those things that make life better, in education, in health services, in aid to the helpless old and young, in prison reform, in the lifting of the spirit that comes from economic independence. These good things could not be had as long as the Negro was held back, a drag and a burden, instead of a free and fully productive citizen. If that day has finally come when Georgians of all races can combine their myriad talents on a basis of equal opportunity for all—then the future indeed will bring that rewarding life for which Georgians, white and black, have for the past two hundred years been striving.

Suggestions for Further Reading

Among the chroniclers of our heritage to whom I am most indebted, and whose works I can recommend with enthusiasm to others, the following stand out: Dr. Kenneth Coleman of the University of Georgia, whose succinct *Georgia History in Outline* (Athens: University of Georgia Press, 1960) served as a chronological guide to the high peaks of Georgia's progress down the years; Amanda Johnson, whose massive *Georgia as Colony and State* (1938; reprinted by William Bailey Williford, Atlanta: Cherokee Publishing Co., 1970) filled in with fascinating detail the valleys between these peaks; Dr. E. Merton Coulter, whose classic, *Georgia, A Short History,* first published in 1933 and in revised and expanded edition (Chapel Hill: University of North Carolina Press, 1960) remains a fundamental source for all those seeking knowledge and understanding of Georgia's past. Others were Charles C. Jones, Jr.'s *The History of Georgia* (Boston: Houghton Mifflin, 1883), the Reverend William Bacon Stevens's scholarly *A History of Georgia* (1847; reprinted Savannah: Beehive Press, 1972), and Robert Preston Brooks's *History of Georgia* (Boston, New York, 1913).

There proved to be rich resources, too, in books and manuscripts covering special periods, special places, and special people. The State Archives, for example, through the Georgia Commission for the National Bicentennial, provided a handsome presentation of historical documents. *Georgia Heritage: Colonial Records 1730–1790* (published 1975) and a reissue of its earlier *Famous Georgians,* corrected, expanded and illustrated, and edited by Kenneth Coleman and Jackie Erney. Major Hugh McCall, Georgia's first historian, was eight years old when the Revolution began, and his two-volume history, published originally in Savannah in 1811 and 1816, is now reprinted in one volume (Atlanta: Cherokee Publishing Company, 1969). Based mainly on McCall's own memory, which scholars charge was sometimes faulty, it is nevertheless a vivid and still valuable account of the struggle for freedom, covering a span of years from 1732 to 1784. Rich in color as

well as fact is the warmly human story of the hard work, the heart-
aches, the failures and successes of Oglethorpe's colonists. Started by
Sarah B. Gober-Temple, finished after her death by Kenneth Coleman,
it gives fascinating insight into the lives of Georgians from the first
concept of the colony to the end of the Trusteeship in 1754: *Georgia
Journeys* (Athens: University of Georgia Press, 1961). Another book
of special focus is William Harden's *A History of Savannah and South
Georgia* (1913; reprinted Atlanta: Cherokee Publishing Co., 1969).

For an understanding of Georgia in Indian days, two Georgians'
books were most helpful: Henry Malone's *Cherokees of the Old South*
(Athens: University of Georgia Press, 1956) and Alex Bealer's *Only
the Names Remain* (Boston: Little, Brown & Company, 1972). Oliver
LaFarge's *Pictorial History of the American Indian* (New York:
Crown Publishers, 1956) was also a source of understanding of the Indian, who was neither the "Noble Red Man" nor a savage, but sometimes a blending of the two.

Any casual student of Georgia's history today is much indebted to
Mills Lane, whose Beehive Press at Savannah has brought back to
library shelves valuable works long almost forgotten. The story of
Georgia's promise is told in *The Most Delightful Country of the Universe,* documents from earliest times, edited by Trevor Reese (Savannah: Beehive Press, 1972), and the sad reality of its troubled early
days is described in *The Clamorous Malcontents,* also edited by Trevor Reese (Savannah: Beehive Press, 1973). Lane's own book *The
People's Georgia, An Illustrated Social History* (Savannah: Beehive
Press, 1975) was particularly helpful.

The picture of Georgia in its unspoiled natural state, unmarred either by political malcontents at Savannah or rowdy and riotous frontiersmen is told by William Bartram in his *Travels* (1792; facsimile ed.,
Savannah: Beehive Press, 1973). The famous naturalist traveled
through the South forty years after Savannah's founding and published
his report in London in 1792.

For the years between the end of the Revolution and the firing on
Fort Sumter, two books give insight into different aspects of Georgia
life and development. Adiel Sherwood's *Gazetteer of Georgia* is a
fact-jammed compendium of Georgia's resources and the founding of
its up-country counties, towns, and villages. First published in
Charleston in 1827 and revised in 1860, it has been reprinted (Atlanta:
Cherokee Publishing Company, 1970). Unfactual, but absorbing for

its portrayal of early Georgians at their sometimes rowdy play was Augustus Baldwin Longstreet's *Georgia Scenes* (New York: Harper and Bros., 1856).

Two other books give a vivid picture of the black man before emancipation set him free. *Slave Life in Georgia,* by John Brown, a fugitive slave, was first published in London in 1855. As edited by F. N. Boney of the university it has been reissued (Savannah: Beehive Press, 1972). A collection of interviews with former slaves compiled by the Federal Writers' Project in the Thirties but never published, has been edited by Ronald Killian and Charles Walker: *Slavery Time When I was Chillun Down on Marster's Plantation* (Savannah: Beehive Press, 1973).

For the period of the Civil War in Georgia the books were many, and so were manuscripts both published and unpublished. The most fascinating memoir, though, was that of William Tecumseh Sherman. Edited by Mills Lane, and titled by him *War is Hell* (Savannah: Beehive Press, 1974), it was mainly derived from Sherman's letters to his wife. Another extremely helpful book covering this period was Franklin Garrett's story of the Atlanta Campaign in his monumental *Atlanta and Environs* (New York: Lewis Historical Publishing Co., 1954; reprinted, Athens: University of Georgia Press, 1969).

For the Reconstruction period, Mildred Thompson's *Reconstruction in Georgia,* a standard since it was first published in 1915 (reprinted, Savannah: Beehive Press, 1974), gives a carefully balanced account of a highly controversial period. Later studies of the period have added further insights—notably Alan Conway's *Reconstruction in Georgia* (Minneapolis: University of Minnesota Press, 1966), James G. Randall and David Donald's *The Civil War and Reconstruction* (Lexington, Mass.: Heath, 1969), and Francis B. Simkins and Charles P. Roland's *A History of the South* (New York: Knopf, 1972). For the classic Southern view of Reconstruction as an almost unmitigated evil, Dr. Coulter's *Short History* is the authoritative source.

For an understanding of Georgia in the years after Reconstruction, three books, dealing with two men, were of tremendous value: *The New South,* a collection of the writing and speeches of Henry W. Grady (Savannah: Beehive Press, 1971) tells in Grady's own words the dreams and goals of the Georgia of the 1880s, and Raymond B. Nixon's biography, *Henry W. Grady, Spokesman of the New South* (New York: Knopf, 1943) gives understanding of Grady's charismatic personality. C. Vann Woodward's *Tom Watson, Agrarian Rebel* (New York, London: Oxford University Press, 1938; reprinted in paperback, Oxford University Press, 1970) gives a clear understanding of the great Populist revolt of the 1890s, and the ideas of its leader in Georgia, Thomas E. Watson.

For an understanding of the forces—political, sociological, economic, and otherwise—at work in modern Georgia, I am deeply indebted to Nunan V. Bartley's *From Thurmond to Wallace: Political Tendencies in Georgia 1948–1968* (Baltimore: Johns Hopkins Press, 1970); to Bruce Galphin's *The Riddle of Lester Maddox* (Atlanta: Camelot Press, 1968); to Pat Watters and Reese Cleghorn's *Climbing Jacob's Ladder: The Arrival of Negroes in Southern Politics* (New York: Harcourt, Brace and World, Inc., 1967). For the impact of civil-rights legislation in a great urban area, Ivan Allen's *Mayor: Notes on the Sixties* (New York: Simon and Schuster, 1971) was of great value. Particularly helpful, too, were the references to Georgia's changing pattern of race relationships in Charles P. Roland's *The Improbable Era, the South Since World War II* (Lexington; University of Kentucky Press, 1975) and in Pat Watters's *The South and the Nation* (New York: Pantheon Books, 1969). For a true and poignant picture of the white and black Georgia farmers, trying to survive boll weevil and depression side by side, a fine source is Jane Maguire's *On Shares: Ed Brown's Story* (New York: W. W. Norton, 1976).

Two other books, far apart in points of view and in the nature of the men they described, seemed to emphasize the dichotomy in the thoughts and feelings of the modern Georgian. William Anderson's racily written story of Eugene Talmadge's political career, *The Wild Man From Sugar Creek* (Baton Rouge: Louisiana State University Press, 1975) pictures the firebrand political descendant of Tom Watson in action; Coretta Scott King's tender memoir, *My Life with Martin Luther King* (New York: Holt, Rinehart and Winston, 1970) portrays a gentler Georgian.

Index

Alabama, 65, 74, 76, 90
Albany, 193–194
Allen, Ivan, Jr., 189–197
Alliance, Farmers', 137–139
Altamaha River, 3, 8, 26
Andersonville prison, 101, 113
Appomattox, 98, 110
Arnall, Ellis, 176–178, 181–182, 191–192
Arp, Bill, 120
Athens, 68, 80, 94
Atlanta: founding of, 79–80; as rail center, 95, 101; Cyclorama in, 100, 104; and Civil War, 101, 103–107; as capital, 117–118, 131; growth of, 121, 123, 128–130, 190; education in, 131, 188; and race riots, 145, 195–197; and desegregation, 186, 188, 190; black leaders in, 202–203
Atlanta Constitution, 122, 125, 140–141, 185
Atlanta Journal, 140, 144–145
Augusta: as a fort town, 26, 77; and Indians, 36; and Revolution, 47, 50, 54, 56; as capital, 61–62, 64; and railroads, 80–81; and Civil War, 93–95

Baldwin, Abraham, 63, 67–68
Baptists, 68, 69, 92
Beaufort (N.C.), 14, 42
Berry, Martha, 130
Black Codes, 33–34, 114–115
Bloody Marsh, Battle of, 29–30
Boll-weevil infestation, 158–159
Boundary disputes, 9, 26–27, 59–60
Bragg, Braxton, 100–101, 110–111
Brenau College, 130
Brown, John, 88–89
Brown, Joseph E.: as Confederate leader, 87, 88, 90–91, 93–97; and Sherman, 107–108; during Reconstruction, 116–117, 123; as businessman, 121, 135–136, 157

Brown, Thomas, 50, 56–57
Bulloch, Archibald, 41, 43, 47, 51
Bullock, Rufus B., 118–122

Caldwell, Harmon (educator), 175–176
Callaway, Howard ("Bo"), 192
Camp, Lawrence, 172–173
Carmichael, James V., 181–182
Carmichael, Stokely, 194
Carpetbaggers, 115, 117, 120, 134
Carter, Jimmy, 180, 191, 198–203
Catholics, 68–69, 142, 148, 201
Causton, Thomas, 19, 20–23
Chain gangs, 157–158, 178
Charleston (S.C.), 7, 13, 55–56
Chattahoochee River, 3, 67, 74, 103–104
Cherokees. *See* Indians
Chickamauga, Battle of, 101
Civil rights, 184–185, 191–193
Civil War: events leading to, 86–95; military service in, 95–96; effects of blockade, 97–98; military engagements, 98–105; defeat in, 102–109, 111
Clarke, Elijah, 54, 56, 58, 65
Cobb, Howell: and compromise, 85–86, 88; as Confederate leader, 89, 91, 96–98; after Civil War, 110, 116
Coca-Cola Company, 129, 189–190, 194
Cocking, Walter (educator), 175–176
Colquitt, Alfred H., 98, 123, 135–136
Columbus, 79, 95, 110, 180
Compromise of 1850, 85
Confederate government, 91–97, 108, 110
Conscription Act: of 1862, 96; of 1917, 151
Constitution (U.S.), Convention of 1787, 63; Eleventh Amendment, 64; Fourteenth Amendment, 114, 116, 118–119, 120; Fifteenth Amendment, 120
Continental Congress, 37, 42–45, 50–52
Convict-leasing system, 136, 138, 145, 157

208

Cotton: beginnings of, 20, 31; cotton gin, 71; mills, 78–79, 94; during Civil War, 97; and boll-weevil, 158–159. *See also* Textile industry
Council of Safety, 42–44, 46
Cox, William, 16–17
Crawford, William H., 66, 84, 86
Creek (Indians). *See* Indians
Cumberland Island, 6–7, 26, 27

Dahlonega, 75, 93
Dalton, 101, 102, 103
Darien, 26, 79, 99
Davis, Jefferson, 91, 95–97, 108, 110–111, 131
Decatur, 81, 104, 107
Declaration of Independence, 37, 45
Democrats. *See* Political parties
Depression, Great, 160–161
De Soto, Hernando, 4–5
Dooley, John, 50, 54
Douglas, Stephen A., 86, 88
Duels, 31, 51–52, 53, 65, 67

Earth mounds, 3–4
Ebenezer (Place of Hope), 18, 25, 31, 53
Elbert, Samuel, 44, 46, 53, 54, 67
Emory University, 70
Episcopalians, 69
Ether, discovery of, 68

Fair Employment Practices Commission, 184–185
Felton, Rebecca Latimer, 154
Fitzwalter, James, 20, 23
Florida, 7, 50–51, 52–53, 74, 90
Forrest, Nathan (general), 100
Forsyth, John, 75, 84
Fort King George, 8, 9, 26
Fort McAllister, 99, 108
Fort Monroe, 111
Fort Pulaski, 91–92, 99
Fort Sumter, 92–93
Frank, Leo, 148–149
Franklin College, 68
Frederica, 26–27
Freedmen's Bureau, 114–115
Frémont, John C., 87
French and Indian War, 35–36
Fugitive Slave Act, 85
Fur trade, 31, 38, 77

George III, 6, 10, 36, 45–46
George, Walter F., 155, 162, 170–173
Georgia: prehistoric, 3–4; exploration of, 4–5; missionaries in, 6–8; Oglethorpe's plan, 8–11; first settlement, 13–18. *See also* Cotton; Georgians; Jews; Land ownership; Negroes; Political parties; Tenant system
—agriculture: and settlers, 18–20, 30–31, 38–39; cattle raising, 31, 38, 46, 137; and slaves, 39, 90; diversification in, 127, 137, 156–157, 179; rural towns, 124–125, 128; depression, 159–160; and Watson, 134, 136, 137; and Talmadge, 164–165
—culture: in Savannah, 17, 39–40; in Athens, 68; in Augusta, 78; restoration projects, 180; Heritage Trust, 198
—economic growth: pre-Revolution, 23, 33, 37–40, 44; post-Revolution, 71, 77–82, 84, 92; war production, 94–98; after Civil War, 123–125, 129; depression, 141, 158–160; after World War I, 156–157, 171; after World War II, 179–181, 184; in 1970s, 198 199, 201
—education: right to, 59, 67–68; universities and colleges, 60, 68, 130–131, 160–162; church-affiliated schools, 69–70, 130; elementary schools, 70; and Gustavus Orr, 130; for women, 130; segregation in, 175, 182–183, 185–186; disaccreditation, 176–177; Supreme Court decision, 185–186; integration, 187–188
—government: under trustees' grant, 9–31; as colony, 31–48; during Revolution, 51–52, 54; self-rule, 31, 57–63, 144; constitutions, 64, 117–118, 131, 178, 182; counties formed, 64–66, 75; frontier justice, 65, 67; Georgia Platform, 86; and secession, 87–91; military rule, 114–120; corruption in, 120, 122–123, 165; Farmers' Revolt, 137–139; county-unit system, 146–147, 153, 165, 181; and Bourbon aristocracy, 123, 125, 135–136; and Watson, 136–140, 153–154; convict labor, 157–158; reform in, 160–162, 176–179; and Talmadges, 166–171, 174–177, 181–183; and New Deal, 168–175; and Civil Rights, 184–200; and Carter, 180, 198–199

—population: early settlers, 9–18; before
Revolution, 38; after Revolution, 61, 73,
76–78; plagues' effect on, 78; English,
8–9, 12–14; Germans, 17–18, 38, 69;
Huguenots, 6–7, 10; Jewish, 17; Moravians, 10, 18, 20; New England Puritans
from Va. and S.C., 37, 38, 40, 42, 69;
Salzburgers, 10, 17–18, 24–25, 31, 37;
Scotch-Irish, 38; Scots, 18, 26, 29, 38
—social change: plantation era, 39–40;
after Revolution, 61–62, 65; after Civil
War, 115, 124–125, 127; after civil
rights program, 185–189, 201–203
Georgia Institute of Technology, 188
Georgians: urge for freedom, 9–10, 31, 37,
40, 59; and religious freedom, 9–10,
17–18, 59, 67; wealthy class, 39, 61;
middle class, 124–125; poor whites, 61,
90, 127, 133; rural Georgians, 128, 166,
169; "lint heads," 78; Georgians at war,
54–57, 98–99, 178; Georgians in peace,
160, 171, 173, 181, 202
Gettysburg, Battle of, 98–99
Gordon, John B.: as Confederate officer,
98, 110, 123, 134, 135; as senator, 131,
136; as businessman, 157
Grady, Henry, 125–128, 131–133, 136–
137
Grant, Ulysses S., 101, 102, 110, 112
Great Locomotive Chase, 99–100
Greene, Nathanael, 56, 58, 71
Griffin, Marvin, 95, 185–189, 191
Gwinnett, Button, 45, 47, 51

Habersham, Joseph, 40–42, 44
Hall, Lyman (minister), 37, 42, 45, 51, 67
Hardman, L. G. (governor), 161
Hardwick, Thomas W., 34–35, 147,
160–161
Harpers Ferry (Va.), 88
Harris, Joel Chandler, 120, 128
Harris, William J., 165–166
Hill, Benjamin H.: as prewar leader, 87,
89–90; as Confederate leader, 96–97,
110, 116; mentioned, 121, 126, 131, 134
Hood, John B., 103–106
Houstoun, John, 41, 45
Howe, Robert, 46, 52–53
Howell, Clark, 140, 144–145, 176

Immigrants. *See* Georgia
Independence and freedom, 10, 37, 40, 59

Indians: first inhabitants, 3–5; and missionaries, 6–7, 20–21; and settlers, 8,
14–16, 35; treaties with, 9, 28, 35, 36,
38, 63; trade with, 26, 35, 38, 77; and
slaves, 33; and land, 36, 38, 59–60, 63,
67, 73; uprising of, 73; migration, 74–76
Industry: pre-Revolution, 22, 30–31,
38–39, 44; after Revolution, 71, 78–79;
during Civil War, 94–97; after Civil
War, 111, 123–125, 128–130; after
World War I, 156–157; after World War
II, 179–180

Jackson, Andrew, 73, 84, 86
Jackson, James: in Revolution, 47, 56, 58;
and duels, 52, 67; and constitution, 64;
as senator, 66–67; and politics, 84, 87
Jackson, Maynard, 197, 202
Jenkins, Charles J., 86, 116, 118, 123
Jenkins, Herbert, 195, 196
Jenkins' Ear, War of, 28
Jews, 17, 148–150
Johnson, Andrew, 110, 112–116
Johnson, Herschel V., 88, 89, 116
Johnson, Lyndon B., 192–193, 195–196
Johnston, Joseph E., 101–103, 110
Jones, Noble, 19, 23, 31, 40–41
Jones, Noble Wymberley, 40–42

Kennesaw, 99–100, 102, 104
Kimball, Hannibal I., 121–122
King, Martin Luther, Jr., 193–197
King, Martin Luther, Sr., 201
Knights of Labor, 154
Ku Klux Klan, 127, 134, 150, 153, 185

Labor: slave, 22–23, 34, 39, 58, 71; con-
vict, 123, 157–158; unions, 146, 154,
160, 167–168, 200
Land ownership: inheritance laws, 23–24;
grants, 31–32, 60–61, 75; speculation,
65–67. *See also* Indians; Tenant system
Lee, Charles, 50, 52
Lee, Henry ("Light Horse Harry"), 56
Lee, Robert E., 88, 98, 101, 110, 112
Liberty Boys, 40, 43, 50, 56
Lincoln, Abraham, 88, 103, 108–109,
112–113
Lincoln, Benjamin, 52, 55, 63
Lincolnton, 36, 38
Longstreet, James L., 98
Lookout Mountain, 101
Lumber industry, 31, 38, 39

Lumpkin, Wilson, 75, 80, 84, 89
Lutherans, 69
Lynching, 140, 149, 150, 184, 185

McGill, Ralph, 159, 185–186
McIntosh, Lachlan, 44, 47, 51, 55
Macon: mounds near, 3; Georgia Teachers College, 70; and industry, 79, 80, 94–95; in Civil War, 108, 110; restoration in, 180
McPherson, James B., 103–105
Maddox, Lester, 189, 191–194, 197–200
Manassas, Battle of, 95
Martin, John, 57, 59
Massell, Sam, 196–198
Methodists, 22, 68–69, 70, 92
Mexican War, 82–84
Milledge, John, 42, 67–68
Milledgeville, 76–77, 86, 95, 107, 108
Mines and mining, 31, 179
Missionary Ridge, 101
Mississippi, 65, 74, 76, 90
Missouri Compromise, 76
Montgomery, Sir Robert, 8, 11
Moonshining, 158
Morehouse College, 131
Musgrove, Mary, 14–15, 35

Naval stores, 38–39, 157, 180
Negroes: free men, 62, 72–73; civil rights of, 114–115, 127–128; in Reconstruction, 113–117; and voting, 62, 115–117, 119, 127, 144–146, 175, 181; leaders, 117, 202–203; schools for, 130–131, 175, 187–188; attitudes toward, 34, 39, 72, 88, 114, 180–181, 191–193, 203; job opportunities, 184; admission to white schools, 187–188; and Carter, 201
New Deal philosophy, 168–171
Nullification doctrine, 84–85
Nunis, Samuel (physician), 17

Ogeechee River, 25, 36, 56, 99
Oglethorpe, James Edward: and trustees, 8–9, 10; as leader, 13, 18; with Indians, 14–16, 28; with Spanish, 18, 25–30; return to England, 30
Oglethorpe University, 69–70

Panic of 1893, 129, 141
Paper industry, 157
Patriots, 40–58
Pine Mountain, 103, 179

Pittman, Marvin S. (educator), 175
Plantations, 31, 71–73, 114, 124
Political parties: Loyalists (Tories) and Patriots (Whigs), 40–58; 82, 87; Troupers and Clarke's faction, 84–86; Democrats, 85, 87, 89, 117–119, 121–122, 127, 136, 140; Republicans, 87, 88, 89, 119, 121–139, 192–193; Know-Nothings, 87; Radical Republicans, 112–115, 118, 120, 122; Negro Republicans, 117, 139; Populists, 139–144; Constitutional Jeffersonian Democratic ticket, 169–170
Presbyterians, 69
Prison system: punishment, 25, 65, 157–158; reforms, 76–77, 177–178, 189, 199
Prohibition laws, 146, 158–159

Race relationships, 33–34, 123–124, 202
Race riots, 145
Racial issues, 148–150, 171, 189, 198
Railroads. *See* Transportation
Reconstruction, 112–132
Religious life: freedom for, 9–10, 17–18, 59, 67; squabbles in, 21–22, 92; evangelists, 68–69; Church of England established, 69; church schools, 69–70, 130
Republicans. *See* Political parties
Revolutionary War: pre-Revolution conflicts, 33–37, 40–45; preparation for, 45–46; military action, 47, 49–53; guerilla warfare, 49, 54–56; turning point, 56–57; recovery from, 58–59
Reynolds, John, 33–34
Rhett, Robert Barnwell, 86, 89
Rice Boats, Battle of, 47, 56
Rice growing, 31, 38–39, 47, 76
Richmond Academy, 68, 78
Rivers, Eruith D., 169–172
Roosevelt, Franklin D., 168–173
Russell, Richard Brefard, Jr., 161–162, 170–171, 198

St. Augustine (Fla.), 6, 9, 26, 45, 49–52
St. Catherine's Island, 6, 35, 117
St. Johns River, 6, 26
St. Simons Island, 7, 8, 26, 29
Sanders, Carl, 189, 191, 196
Sanford, S. W. (educator), 175–176
Savannah: founding of, 3, 13, 34–35; social and cultural life in, 17, 19, 39–40, 68; in

Savannah (*continued*)
  Revolution, 51, 53–60; in Civil War, 106–108, 131; restoration in, 180–181
Savannah River, 3, 13, 99
Scalawags, 115, 134
Secession, 85–86, 87–93, 113, 116
Segregation. *See* Civil Rights; Georgia
Selma (Ala.), demonstrations, 193–194
Settlers. *See* Georgia
Sherman, William T., 101–109, 112, 125–126
Sibley Report, 188
Slaton, John M. (governor), 149–150
Slavery: introduction of, 22–25; slave labor, 22–23, 34, 39, 58, 71; Black Code, 33–34, fear of blacks, 34, 39, 72, 88, 114; after Revolution, 58; slave trade, 71–72; and compromise, 85–86; and Secession, 92; end of, 111
Smith, Hoke, 140, 144–146, 148
Soto, Hernando de, 4–5
South Carolina, 9–10, 25, 30, 42, 90
Southern Baptist Convention, 92
Southern Christian Leadership Council, 193, 194
Spanish: explorers, 4, 5, 8–9; claims to land, 7, 36, 73–74; missionaries, 6–8; Oglethorpe and, 18, 25–30, 52, 63
Spanish-American War, 142
Spelman College, 131, 196–197
State sovereignty issue, 63–64
States' rights, 85, 89
Stephens, Alexander H.: as secessionist, 85–86, 89–91; during War, 96–97, 108; after War, 110, 113, 116, 121, 131
Stephens, William, 27–28
Stone Mountain, 150
Streight, A. D. (colonel), 100

Talmadge, Eugene: early life of, 162–166; as governor, 173–174, 177, 181; and labor, 167–168, 170; and Roosevelt, 168–173; as isolationist, 174; and racial issues, 171–177, 181
Talmadge, Herman, 172, 182, 184–187
Tariff laws, 62, 84
Taxation; Stamp Act, 36–37, 41, 43; poll tax, 62, 64; and Watson, 138, 141, 145; and Talmadge, 171–172; reforms in, 198
Telfair brothers, 41–42, 46, 62
Tenant system, 124, 127–128
Terry, Alfred H., 119–120
Textile industry, 94, 141, 160, 167–168.
  See also Cotton

Tobacco growing, 31, 38, 76, 77–78, 156
Toombs, Robert: as secessionist, 85, 87, 89; during War, 91, 96–98, 110; after War, 116, 121–123, 133, 134
Transportation: by water, 76, 79, 80–81, 180; by roads, 76, 79–80, 94, 138, 157–158, 160–161, 169, 178–179; by railroad, 76, 79, 80–82, 94, 109, 121, 145–146
Troup, George (governor), 74, 84

Unions. *See* Labor
United Brethren, 18
United States Supreme Court: state sovereignty, 63–64; Yazoo Frauds, 67; desegregation, 185–186
University of Georgia. *See* Georgia

Vandiver, Ernest, 187–188

Walker, W. H. T., 93, 103
Walton, George, 43–45, 52–53
Warm Springs, 169, 173
War of 1812, 73, 76, 94
War of Jenkins' Ear, 28
Washington, Booker T., 130
Washington, George, 50, 52, 63
Washington (town), 38, 60, 61, 110
Watson, Thomas E.: background of, 134–135; as orator, 136–137; as congressman, 137–139; and Populists, 139–147; as racist, 148–150; as isolationist, 151–152; as senator, 153–154; influence on Talmadge, 162–164, 174, 176
Wayne, "Mad Anthony," 56
Wesley, John (minister), 20–22
Western and Atlantic Railroad, 81, 99, 120–121, 172
Wheeler, "Fighting Joe," 104–105, 107
Whitefield, George (minister), 22, 24–25
White primary, 144–145, 174, 181
White supremacy doctrine, 144, 147, 171, 174, 182, 185, 191
Whitney, Eli, 71
Woodruff, Robert W., 129, 189–190, 194, 196
World War I, 150–151
World War II, 178–179
Wright, Ransom (general), 98
Wright, Sir James, 35–38, 40–45, 46, 54–55, 58

Yazoo Fraud, 65–67